"Everyone knows that the shorter one's explanation, the more distortion ofte multivolume studies of theology and biblical studies continue to be penned. But, there will always be a place for the visual, the succinct, the summary. Charts remain valuable tools not only for those stated reasons but also because various views legitimately (or sometimes not so legitimately) held can be juxtaposed in close proximity, enabling the student to prepare his mental categories, which in turn help him sort through the perspectives of more extensive literature.

"To my knowledge, Thomas P. Johnston's *Charts for a Theology of Evangelism* constitutes one of the very few such summations available in this critical arena of study. These charts not only examine and contrast methodologies but also delve into theologies of evangelism. Concepts such as sin, anthropology, and the atonement are developed in their relationship to evangelism.

"As you read these chartings of positions, drink deeply from the wells that Dr. Johnston has sampled for years. You will find them enlightening, encouraging, sometimes irritating, but always engaging. The author's prayer, along with mine, is that those who read will be stirred to a renewed proclamation of the gospel, which alone can save the eternal souls of 6.5 billion people around the globe."

Paige Patterson
President, Southwestern Baptist Theological Seminary

"This volume of charts provides an extraordinarily detailed analysis of elements involved in a large number of outlooks on evangelism, its nature, effects, methods, and biblical validation.

"It will greatly assist a researcher in cornering what is common in one's favored theory and the views of others, as well as where significant differences emerge. It will permit one to broaden one's view by including compatible elements not heretofore sufficiently acknowledged and to be more keenly aware of factors incompatible with what one understands as biblical revelation. This type of self-examination is extremely important for the individual Christian in evangelism, and supremely so for evangelistic/missionary organizations that must be alert to know what may be included and what must be avoided in their efforts.

"The author manifests a very detailed knowledge of the Scriptures that are invoked in support of any approach, and also of literature, historical and contemporary, that relates to various options. He appears to have managed to shun any *a priori* prejudice in order to present a fair analysis of what each view considered involves.

"I only regret the use of the words 'reconciliation model' as characteristic of a theory of the atonement in which 'penal substitution' is downplayed. Reconciliation is effectually achieved by the work of Christ; it is the unquestionable result of the atonement, not merely the emphasis of the theory in view."

Roger Nicole
Visiting Professor of Theology Emeritus, Reformed Theological Seminary

"Dr. Johnston summarizes in these compact charts insights encompassing the whole spectrum of evangelism. What a tremendous resource for students!"

Robert E. Coleman
Distinguished Professor of Evangelism and Discipleship, Gordon-Conwell Theological Seminary

"Tom Johnston has done an incredible work in *Charts for a Theology of Evangelism*. I found myself unable to put the book down. This tool is indispensable to the person who is serious about understanding the Great Commission."

Thom S. Rainer
President and CEO, LifeWay Christian Resources

"Rarely have we ever seen any work as complete and as theologically sensitive as *Charts for a Theology of Evangelism* by Dr. Thomas P. Johnston. I know from personal experience that this work has been in the making for several decades now, since I saw its beginnings when Dr. Johnston was my student many years ago. In addition to being a comprehensive academic work, every principle described here has been tested in the life and practice of this writer. I cannot recommend too highly these charts for equipping God's men and women around the world, and thereby enabling them to be fully involved members of the body of Christ and as our Lord has wanted us to minister to the honor and glory of His magnificent name."

Walter C. Kaiser Jr.
Former President, Gordon-Conwell Theological Seminary

"You hold in your hands one of the most useful books ever published in the field of evangelism. Tom Johnston's *Charts for a Theology of Evangelism* is a valiant effort designed to help the reader grasp the breadth and depth of evangelistic theory and practice over the centuries.

"This book covers all the bases. In fact, an entire course on the theology of evangelism could be designed around the charts alone.

"With unqualified enthusiasm, I commend this text to all who love evangelism and wish to become more effective in sharing the gospel with others."

R. Alan Streett
Chairman and Professor of Evangelism, The Criswell College

"Tom Johnston has produced a very helpful book that condenses virtually everything academic one could wish to know about evangelism. Overall philosophy, presentation styles, theology, history, organizations, conferences, tracts, pamphlets—if it has happened in evangelism, it is noted and synthesized into a rational presentation somewhere in this book. As a student Tom demonstrated a relentless search for all the relevant sources, and his papers were models of thorough research; he has continued in that style of scholarship in this book. He also writes out of a passion for truth as the most vital component of evangelistic method and content. This book will have a long life as a companion for those who seek the most biblically defensible and strategically feasible way of setting forth words of life and justification to a world that is dead and condemned."

Thomas J. Nettles
Professor of Historical Theology, The Southern Baptist Theological Seminary

"God has given Tom Johnston to the church for an in-depth look at evangelism. He is out knocking on doors and winning the lost to Christ with his students every week. Yet he is a teacher who has clear, deep insight in the Word of God concerning evangelism.

"I have learned more about biblical evangelism from Tom in the past five years than I have learned in all my life as a vocational evangelist. His book of *Charts for a Theology of Evangelism* will open your eyes to the main purpose of the church and Christianity like nothing else in print. In every section you will see your own work as a pastor, evangelist, or layman. You will see tendencies throughout history and a current look at evangelism today.

"The chart that lays out the verbs of the Great Commission includes the Greek words that will have the same impact on your life if you study them. *Charts for a Theology of Evangelism* needs to be on the desk of every evangelist, teacher, and Bible student."

Keith Fordham
Evangelist

CHARTS FOR A THEOLOGY OF EVANGELISM

CHARTS FOR A THEOLOGY OF EVANGELISM

Thomas P. Johnston

Nashville, Tennessee

978-0-8054-4371-4

Published by B&H Publishing Group
Nashville, Tennessee

Dewey Decimal Classification: 269.2
Subject Heading: EVANGELISTIC WORK \ WITNESSING

1 2 3 4 5 6 7 8 9 10 11 12 • 15 14 13 12 11 10 09 08 07
VP

I dedicate this book to my father, Arthur P. Johnston,

for his insight into a theology of missions and evangelism,

and to my wife, Raschelle, and my three children, Katie, Jon, and Josh,

for putting up with a husband and father who sometimes seems married to a computer!

Contents

Section 4—Methodologies of Evangelism

Section 5—Evangelism, Apologetics, and Culture

Section 6—Linking Theology and Practice

Section 7—The Old Testament and Evangelism

CONTENTS

Section 8—Ecclesiology

Section 9—Evangelism and Cooperation

Foreword

To "do the work of an evangelist" is a clear and definite admonition of Holy Scripture. While it was first given from Paul to Timothy, its implications for the church of today are clear. Evangelism, or sharing the saving gospel message of Christ with a lost world, is not only a wonderful assignment; it is the responsibility of all children of God. After all, Ephesians 4 makes it obvious that a large part of the evangelist's assignment is to equip all of the people of God to do the work of the ministry, which in the context of the evangelist's calling is to teach others to share effectively the good news of Jesus Christ.

This set of charts produced by Dr. Thomas Johnston will put a new and dynamic resource into the hands of God-called servants of the Lord. It will go a long way toward making the task of equipping laborers for the harvest a joy and blessing, which that always should be. Any student of this urgent and vital task will find this resource to be a jewel of a tool. To peruse the charts is to open a treasure trove of thought and research that God will bless in the lives of those who study them.

Dr. Johnston has taught evangelism at Midwestern Baptist Theological Seminary (MBTS) since the fall of 2001. He is an able communicator and equipper of students. His classes are marked by passion, insight, and enthusiasm for the work of the gospel. But Dr. Johnston is more than just an adept teacher—he is also a doer of the Word. Ever faithful to the call of God on his life as an ambassador of Christ, Dr. Johnston shares and leads others to share the gospel. The Midwestern Evangelism Teams, organized and chiefly led by Dr. Johnston, are living testimony to his diligence as a teacher/equipper. Five or six times each week, students from MBTS share the gospel door-to-door as well as on the streets of Kansas City. Consequently, hundreds of souls have been led into the kingdom. Dr. Johnston clearly embodies the principle that evangelism is more caught than taught. But in his ministry, it is not one or the other. Evangelism is not just caught from or just taught by Dr. Johnston. It is both caught *and* taught with excellence.

These charts will introduce you to Dr. Tom Johnston the researcher and thinker. I commend them to you. More than that, however, I commend to you Dr. Tom Johnston, the disciple, disciple-maker, and faithful ambassador of Christ.

R. Philip Roberts
President
Midwestern Baptist Theological Seminary
Kansas City, Missouri

1. The Urgencies That Drive Evangelism

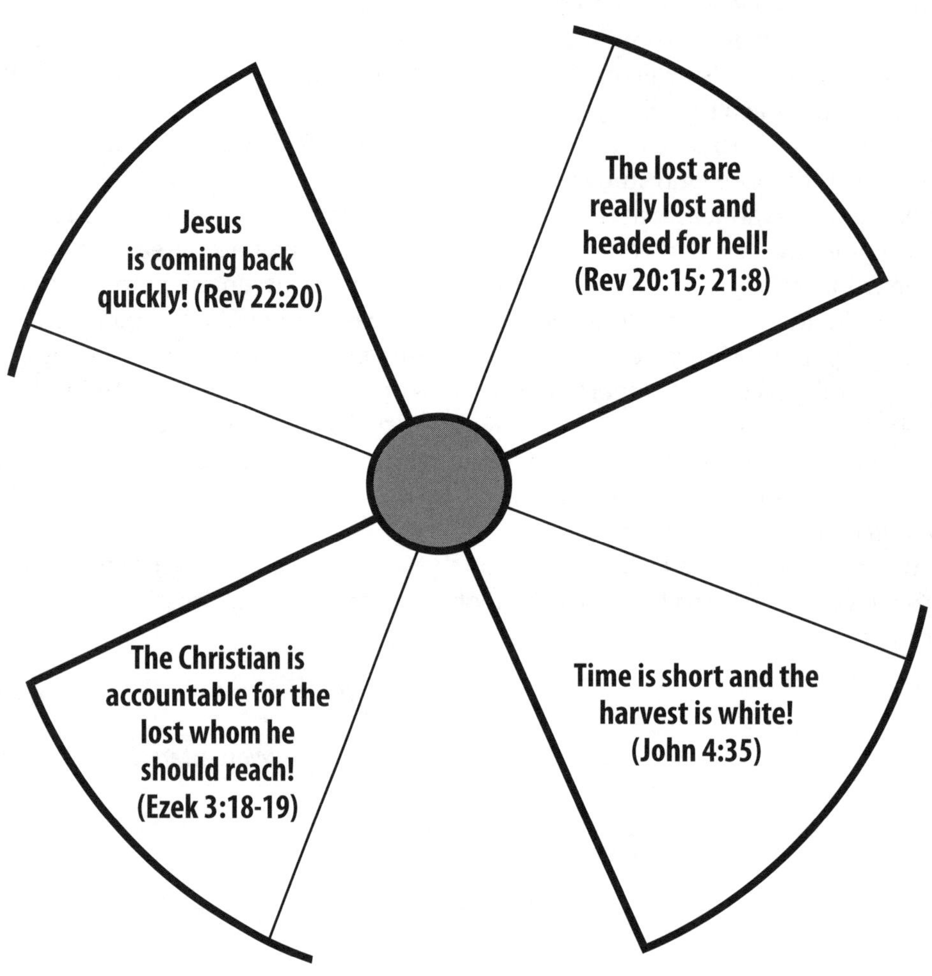

When all is said and done, these urgencies, which are emminently biblical, are the driving force behind any evangelistic thrust. With these urgencies, evangelism becomes expectant and intentional, persecution becomes palatable, and no sacrifice is too great for the work of the gospel. Without these urgencies, evangelism becomes superfluous and passé, persecution is avoided, and sacrifice, if at all, becomes humanitarian in nature.

2. The Great Commission's Common Ground

Christians are often divided over their view of the Great Commission. One may be reminded of the Corinthian church when considering views of the Great Commission: "'I am of Paul,' and 'I of Apollos,' and 'I of Cephas,' and 'I of Christ.'" However, as Paul wrote: "Christ is not divided" (1 Cor 1:13). In the same way, neither are the Great Commission passages in contradiction or contradistinction to one another. If the Holy Scriptures came to us from the one mind of the Holy Spirit (2 Pet 1:21), then it must follow that the meaning or semantic range of all five Great Commission passages intersect. And it is, in fact, at the point of evangelism, the proclamation of the gospel, that they do intersect!

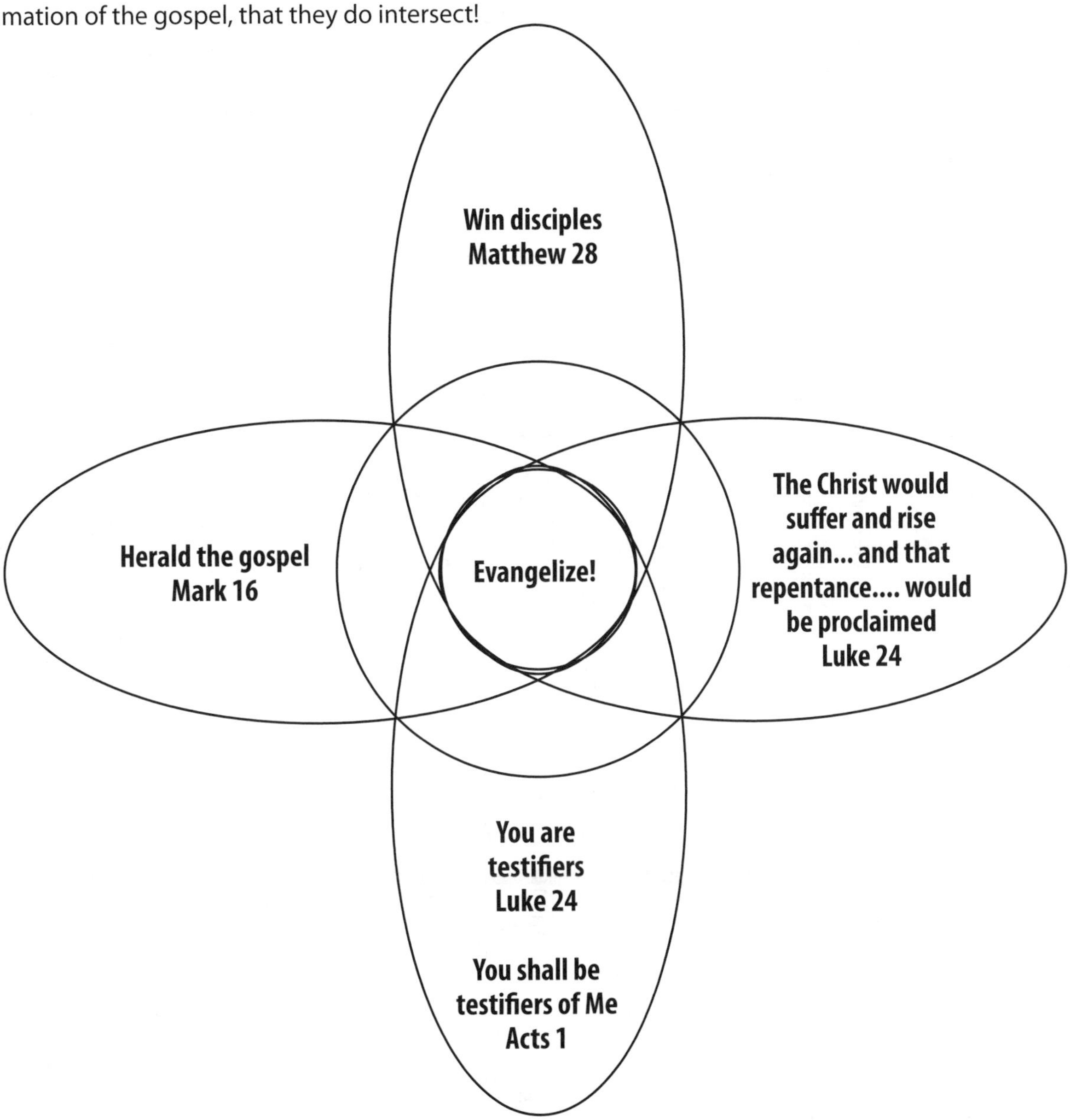

To this graphic may also be added the sometimes-debated Great Commission passage in John, John 20:21: "As the Father has sent Me, so send I you." Note in this regard that one of the reasons for the sending of Jesus was to evangelize (Luke 4:42-44; Mark 1:38), as well as "to seek and to save the lost" (Luke 19:10; Matt 18:11). The itinerant preaching ministry of Jesus and of His disciples is a central theme carried from the Gospel of Luke and into the book of Acts. Also, the use of "win disciples" for Matthew 28:19's *mathēteuō* follows the NIV's precedent in its translation of Acts 14:21, "They preached the good news in that city and won a large number of disciples. Then they returned to Lystra, Iconium and Antioch."

3. A Linear View of the Five Great Commission Passages

The Great Commission has been a volatile subject for many years. Two quotes exemplify historic responses to this debate. In 1914, Scarborough wrote, "It is not wise to say that *soul winning* is the main thing or that *soul building* is the main thing. They are Siamese twins of God's gospel, going hand in hand, and they ought to keep up with each other. . . . And this leads me to say that the main thing in the Kingdom of God is the evangelistic spirit, the martial note and conquest tread" (L. R. Scarborough, *Recruits for World Conquest,* 58). In 1942, Andrew Blackwood wrote, "In writing about soul winning and nurture one can get lost in the fog, or else start a fight. But why should Christians quarrel? There is no desire to exalt the winning of souls at the expense of their nurture in the Lord. In the light of the New Testament the two ways of working are equally essential to

EMPHASIS	BIBLICAL TERMS	SCRIPTURE	RELATED SCRIPTURE
Missionary Effort	Going; go; send	Matt 28:19; Mark 16:15; John 20:21	Isa 6:8-9; Jer 1:7; Acts 5:20; 8:26, 29
Geographic Extent	"All the world . . . to all creation"	Mark 16:15	Matt 24:14
	"To all the nations, beginning from Jerusalem"	Luke 24:47	Gen 12:3; Isa 56:7; Mark 13:10; Acts 13:31; 1 Cor 9:22
	(1) Jerusalem, (2) Judea, (3) Samaria, (4) uttermost parts of the earth	Acts 1:8	Luke 9:60; Rom 9:17; 15:20; 2 Cor 10:16
Missionary Method	Preach; proclaim (*kērussō*)	Mark 16:15; Luke 24:47	Pss 96:2-3; 105:1-2; Isa 43:20-21; Matt 10:7; Luke 9:60; 2 Tim 2:2; 1 Pet 2:9
	Be a witness; bear witness (*eimi . . . martus; martureō*)	Luke 24:48; Acts 1:8	Mark 1:44; 5:19; Luke 8:39; John 15:27; Acts 8:25; 22:15
	Win disciples (*mathēteuō*)	Matt 28:19	Acts 14:21
Missionary Message	"Thus it is written"	Luke 24:46	Death: Lev 17:11; Isa 53:1-12; Resurrection: Ps 16:10; Jon 1:17
	"The Christ would suffer and rise again from the dead the third day"	Mark 16:15; Luke 24:46	1 Cor 15:1-8
	"Repentance for forgiveness of sins . . . in His name"	Luke 24:47; John 20:23	Acts 2:38; 3:19-21; 20:21

3. A Linear View of the Five Great Commission Passages (continued)

the growth and very existence of the Church" (Andrew W. Blackwood, *Evangelism in the Home Church,* 11–12). The issues seem to be deeper than authors express. At stake is the essence of the Great Commission. Concern and clarity drive me to put to paper the following chart. It should be noted that discipleship is a fluid term, and that *mathēteuō* in Matthew 28:19 is more directly related to "winning disciples" (winning souls, Acts 14:21; 1 Cor 9:19-22), than it is to "discipleship," the peripatetic process of training individuals, which has grown to include the fields of moral and cognitive development, educational methods and processes, communities of learning, and mentoring.

Response to the Message	Win disciples	Matt 28:19	Acts 14:21; 1 Cor 9:18-22
	Repentance; belief	Mark 16:16; Luke 24:47	Acts 13:48
	Disbelief	Mark 16:16	Acts 14:2
Necessary Nurture	Baptism	Matt 28:19; Mark 16:16	Acts 8:12, 36, 38; 9:18; 10:47-48; 16:15, 33; 18:8
	Teaching to obey	Matt 28:19-20	Col 2:6-7
Missionary Example	Christ	John 20:21	1 Cor 11:1
Necessary Power	Holy Spirit	Acts 24:49; John 20:22; Acts 1:8	Zech 4:6
Promised Presence	"And lo, I am with you always"	Matt 28:20	Acts 18:9-10
Sure Fulfillment	Prophetically stated	Luke 24:47; Acts 1:8	Rev 5:9-10
Finish Line	The end of the age	Matt 28:20	Matt 24:14

4. Verbs for Great Commission Methodology

Consider the missional emphasis of these summary statements on ministry.

Matthew 28:19-20	Going *(poreuomai)*	Win Disciples *(mathēteuō)*	Baptizing *(baptizō)*	Teaching to Observe *(didaskō + tēreō)*
Matt 9:35	Went about *(periagō)*	Teaching *(didaskō)* Preaching *(kērussō)* Healing *(therapeuō)*		
Matt 11:1	Departed *(metabainō)*	Teaching *(didaskō)* Preaching *(kērussō)*		
Mark 5:19-20	Go *(upagō)* Went away *(aperchomai)*	Report *(apaggellō)* Began to proclaim *(arcō + kērussō)*		
Mark 6:12-13	Went out *(exerchomai)*	Preached *(kērussō + metanoeō)* Casting out *(ekballō)* Anointing *(aleiphō)* Healing *(therapeuō)*		
Mark 16:15	Go *(poreuomai)*	Preach *(kērussō)*		
Luke 8:1	Traveled about *(diodeuō)*	Preaching *(kērussō)* Evangelizing *(euaggelizō)*		
Luke 9:6	Departed *(exercomai)* Went *(dierchomai)*	Evangelizing *(euaggelizō)* Healing *(therapeuō)*		
Acts 5:20-21	Go *(poreuomai)* Went in *(eiserchomai)*	Speak *(laleō)* Teach *(didaskō)*		
Acts 5:42	Not cease *(ouk pauō)*	Teach *(didaskō)* Evangelizing *(euaggelizō)*		
Acts 8:4	Scattered *(diaspeipō)* Went about *(dierchomai)*	Evangelizing *(euaggelizō)*		
Acts 8:5	Went down *(katerchomai)*	Preached *(kērussō)*		
Acts 8:12		Evangelized *(euaggelizō)*	Baptized *(baptizō)*	
Acts 8:25	Started back *(hupostrephō)*	Evangelizing *(euaggelizō)*		Solemnly testified *(diamarturomai)* Spoken *(laleō)*
Acts 8:26-39	Get up *(anistēmi)* Go *(poreuomai)* Got up *(anistēmi)* Went *(poreuomai)* Go up *(proserchomai)* Join *(kollaomai)* Ran up *(prostrechō)* Heard *(akouō)*	Said *(legō)* Evangelized *(euaggelizō)*	Baptized *(baptizō)* Baptized *(baptizō)*	No longer saw [him] *(ouk oraō)*

4. Verbs for Great Commission Methodology (continued)

Matthew 28:19-20	Going *(poreuomai)*	Win Disciples *(mathēteuō)*	Baptizing *(baptizō)*	Teaching to Observe *(didaskō + tēreō)*
Acts 8:40	Was found *(heuriskō)* Passed through *(dierchomai)*	Kept evangelizing (euaggelizō)		
Acts 14:6-7	Fled *(katapheugō)*	Evangelized *(euaggelizō)*		
Acts 14:20-22	Departed *(exercomai)*	Evangelized *(euaggelizō)* Won Disciples *(mathēteuō)*		Returned *(upostrephō)* Strengthening *(epistētrizō)* Encouraging *(parakaleō)*
Acts 17:2-3	Went in *(eisercomai)*	Reasoned *(dialegomai)* Opening *(dianoigō)* Setting forth *(paratithēmi)* Proclaiming *(kataggellō)*		
Acts 18:9	Do not fear *(mē phobeomai)*	Speak *(laleō)* Do not be silent *(mē siōpaō)*		
Acts 19:8-9	Entered *(eisercomai)*	Bold speech *(parrēsiazomai)* Reasoning *(dialegomai)* Persuading *(peithō)*		Reasoning *(dialegomai)*
Acts 20:18, 20, 31	Set foot *(paraginomai)*	Not shrink + declaring *(ouden upostellō + anaggellō)* Teaching (*didaskō*)		Not cease + admonish *(ouk pauō + noutheteō)*
Acts 28:30-31	Welcoming *(apodechomai)* + [All who] came in *(eisporeuomai)*	Preaching *(kērussō)* Teaching *(didaskō)*		
Rom 15:20		Make it my ambition *(philotimeomai)* + to evangelize *(euaggelizō)*		
1 Cor 1:17	Send *(apostellō)*	To evangelize *(euaggelizō)*	Not to baptize *(baptizō)*	
1 Cor 9:6		Evangelize *(euaggelizō)* [Do not] evangelize *(euaggelizō)*		
1 Cor 15:1-2		Evangelized *(euaggelizō)* Evangelized *(euaggelizō)*		Make known *(gnōrizō)* Received *(paralambanō)* Stand *(istēmi)* Saved *(sōzō)* Hold fast *(katechō)*

5. Twelve Approaches to the Great Commission and the Christian Life

	EVANGELISM		DISCIPLESHIP			
	1	**2**	**3**	**4**	**5**	**6**
Great Commission Emphasis	Luke 24:46-49 Proclamation of the gospel		Matthew 28:19-20, Discipleship— (1) Winning disciples, (2) Establishing others as disciples, (3) Being or becoming a disciple, and/or (4) Living as a disciple			
Recent Missional Cycle	1950s	1960s	1970s	1980s	1990s	2000s
Biggest Issue	Evangelism one's primary purpose in life	Evangelism and discipleship coequal	Discipleship and evangelism coequal	Using one's spiritual gift(s)	Practicing spiritual disciplines*	Finding one's purpose(s) in life
	Every believer a called evangelist, "All at it, always at it!"	Every Christian is to win and establish disciples	Every Christian is to establish disciples who will win others	May not include evangelism/ Slowly shift mission to a leadership emphasis; Great Commission now includes training qualified leaders to be on mission		
	One mission	Two missions		Many missions		
	Mere evangelism, saving souls	Evangelism and discipleship equal	Discipleship and evangelism equal	Evangelism (if considered) is one of a number of equal priorities		
	Discipleship a part of evangelism	Evangelism a part of discipleship process				
	Emphasize Souls		Emphasize a Balanced Approach; Greek Golden Mean, "Moderation in All Things"			
Orientation	Individualistic/Other-focused			Individualistic/Personal-focused/Leader-oriented		
Problem in Fulfilling "Great Commission"	Lack of boldness and zeal	Lack of boldness and zeal; lack of spiritual maturity	Lack of spiritual maturity; need for training, mentoring, and equipping	Ignorance of one's spiritual gift	Lack of discipline in seeking God	Ignorance of one's purpose(s) in life
Greatest Need to Fulfill Great Commission	Training in communicating the gospel	Training in communicating the gospel and discipleship	Discipling Christians; greater emphasis on mentoring	Spiritual gifts inventory with training in specific spiritual gift	Training in practicing the spiritual disciplines	Insight into life's purposes and training in fulfilling these
Life's Results	Souls saved	Souls saved and established	Christlike character	A fulfilled life using one's spiritual gifts	A personally spiritual disciplined life	A fulfilled life, living under God's purpose
			Leading others to the Savior; influencing others for Christ; showing Jesus to others			
Medieval Proponents	Waldenses, Albigenses, and Lollards					

*Confounding spiritual disciplines for the Great Commission is like confounding the maintenance of a racing car for the race itself.

5. Twelve Approaches to the Great Commission and the Christian Life (continued)

	CHRISTIAN STOICISM				CHRISTIAN SOCIALISM	
	7	**8**	**9**	**10**	**11**	**12**
Great Commission Emphasis	1 Corinthians 11:1 *Imitatio Christi*			John 13:34-35 Love one another		
Recent Missional Cycle				Emergent Churches?		
Biggest Issue	Christlikeness	Cost of discipleship	Living the virtues	Bonhoeffer, *Life Together*	Developing a loving church	Developing a Christian society
	Evangelism may or may not be a part of the imitation of Christ	Evangelism is theologically irrelevant	Conversion is a process; evangelism is unnecessary	Conversion is a process; evangelism may be necessary	Conversion to community, then to the King of community	Cultural Mandate, Genesis 1:26, 28
	Many missions Evangelism a part of Christlikeness only if believed to be a part of Christ's ministry	Evangelism is counter-productive	Evangelism is unnecessary	Evangelism is participation in community	Evangelism is love; love is evangelism	Evangelism to a Christian worldview; acceptance of Christian worldview is conversion
	Emphasize Balance	Emphasize Personal Self-Discipline			Emphasize Social Self-Discipline	
Orientation	Individualistic			Socialistic, Society, or Community-Focused		
Problem in Fulfilling Great Commission	Lack of Christlikeness	Lack of self-sacrifice on behalf of humanity's needs	Living the vices (cardinal sins) instead of the cardinal virtues	Selfish living	Lack of love; pharisaic; doctrinaire views; traditionalism	Reemphasis on man's goodness, achievements, and potential
Greatest Need to Fulfill Great Commission	Aspects of Christlikeness with training in emulating these	Understanding humanity's needs	Lists of the virtues with clues in living these	Training to subjugate one's selfishness to communal living	Emphasis on love in church	Emphasis on the good in man
Life's Results	Christlikeness Showing Jesus to others	Victory over the enemies of mankind's true humanity	Victory over the flesh	Victory over selfishness	Loving and growing churches	A positive society
Medieval Proponents	Franciscans (secondary inquisitors; contra-proclamational evangelists)		Dominicans (primary inquisitors; contra-proclamational evangelists)			Crusades to expand God's kingdom

6. Evangelism as the Main Idea

Evangelicals have long identified gospel proclamation as the main idea. But as evangelical theology matures other competing methodologies come to the fore. Bailey Smith calls these "subtle substitutes." He wrote: "The reason, then, for the word *subtle* being used so often is to express that because each of these other things is good, we can be fooled into believing they are best and final. Now let me say again that most of

	Main Idea	Biblical Focus	Sample Passages	Focus	Emphasis
1	**Proclamation**	Evangelism verses; verses on the cross	1 Pet 2:9-10; 1 Cor 2:2	Outward	Preaching/message oriented
2	**Soul-Winning (Disciple-Winning)**	Harvest verses	Matt 9:37-38; 1 Cor 9:19-23	Outward	Results oriented
3	**Church Growth**	People movement verses	Acts 2:41; 4:4; 5:14	Outward	Results oriented
4	**Christian Education**	Teaching verses	Deut 6:7; Matt 5:2; 28:19, "teaching"	Inward and outward	Mentoring oriented
5	**Glory of God**	Glory of God verses; sovereignty verses	Eph 1:6, 12, 14; Col 3:17	Inward, outward is duty	Philosophically oriented
6	**Discipleship (Establishing as Disciples)**	Discipleship and teaching verses	Matt 28:19-20; Acts 4:13; 2 Tim 2:2	Inward, then outward	Spiritual growth-oriented; spiritual mentoring
7	**Spiritual Gifts**	Spiritual gifts	1 Cor 12:7	Inward, knowing and using one's spiritual gift	Using one's spiritual gifts
8	**Spiritual Disciplines* (Living as a Disciple)**	Spiritual discipline verses	1 Tim 4:7-8	Inward, outward as discipline	Personal effort
9	**Christlikeness (Being a Disciple of Christ)**	Ministry of Christ	Luke 10:42; John 20:21	Inward	Parsing Jesus' "incarnational" ministry
10	**Prayer****	Verses on prayer	2 Chr 7:14; Jer 33:3	Inward (upward)	Personal prayer time
11	**Worship**	Verses on worship	Ps 100 (revise 1 Pet 2:9 to be worship?)	Inward (upward)	Formal worship

*Perhaps this is a renewal of the "Deeper Life" emphasis of the early Keswick movement.

**An emphasis on prayer as the sole acting agent of spiritual activity is sometimes detrimental to proclamation or taking the initiative in sharing the gospel (see Lewis Sperry Chafer, *True Evangelism or Winning Souls by Prayer* [1911]).

6. Evangelism as the Main Idea (continued)

the substitutes within themselves are good, but they are not good as substitutes for evangelism. Yet, they are becoming that, and the trend is extremely dangerous and very damaging to the fulfillment of the Great Commission" (Bailey E. Smith, *Real Evangelism: Exposing the Subtle Substitutes for That Evangelism* [Nashville: Broadman Press, 1978], ix).

	Possible Preferred Evangelism Method	Great Commission Emphasis	Possible Positive Results	Possible Negative Results	Bible Version*** or Creedal Emphasis
1	Personal, preaching, or street evangelism	Proclamational, emphasize Luke-Acts	Persons born from above	None	Wycliffe's 1st edition (1382), NASB, HCSB
2	Personal and crusade evangelism	Proclamational, emphasize Luke-Acts	Souls saved	Easy believism	
3	Invitational evangelism (inviting to church event)	Sociological, emphasize Matthew	Churches grow	Culture driven	
4	Teaching (normally within the church)	Teaching and training, emphasize Matthew	Christians trained	Inward focus; never ending need for maturity	Vulgate and KJV on Matt 28:19-20; Creed of Athanasius
5	Apologetic, dialogue, didactic, or reactive evangelism	Discipleship, emphasize Matthew	God focused	Not proclamationally driven; usually removes initiative	Wycliffe's 2nd ed (1388), Westminster Shorter Cat., KJV
6	Relational evangelism	Discipleship, emphasize Matthew	Persons trained in spiritual disciplines	Not proclamationally driven; lack of initiative	
7	Service evangelism	Discipleship, emphasize Matthew	All Christians mobilized to serve	Not proclamationally driven; lack of initiative	New Jerusalem Bible (Rom 1:1-2)
8	Relational evangelism	Discipleship, emphasize Matthew	Spiritual discipline, moral philosophy	Not proclamationally driven; lack of initiative	
9	Incarnational evangelism	Christlikeness, emphasize John	None (in and of itself)	Not proclamationally driven; lack of initiative	*The Message*
10	Prayer evangelism	Discipleship, emphasize Matthew	God focused	Not proclamationally driven; lack of initiative	
11	Worship evangelism	Discipleship, emphasize Matthew	God focused and praise focused	Not proclamationally driven; lack of initiative	New Jerusalem Bible (1 Pet 2:9); Apostles and Nicene Creed

***Bible translations have varying tendencies in translating proclamational or missional words (Matt 28:19, *mathēteuō*; 1 Pet 2:9, *exaggellō*; Acts 8:4, 12, 25, 35, 40 [and the other 47 uses], *euaggelizō*). See charts below.

7. Alternatives to Mere Proclamation

Often one or more of the fifty-seven alternatives are given to argue that mere proclamation of the gospel (à la 1 Pet 2:9-10) is not sufficient for the salvation of the sinner—or as the heart of the Great Commission (see Luke 24:46-47). Some of these alternatives provide arguments as to why the proclamation of the gospel is not enough for salvation, and/or give alternatives to the proclamation of the gospel to bring the sinner to faith in Christ.

These additions, and/or others, are added to the Great Commission given to the church, thus watering down

Reasons Against Mere Proclamation

Biblically Derived	1	"One thing necessary," other than evangelism	Luke 10:41-42: "Martha, Martha, you are worried and bothered about so many things; but only one thing is necessary, for Mary has chosen the good part, which shall not be taken away from her."
	2	More than "words only"	1 Thessalonians 1:5: "For our gospel did not come to you in word only, but also in power and in the Holy Spirit and with full conviction; just as you know what kind of men we proved to be among you for your sake."
	3	The need to wait before evangelizing	Based on Jesus' command to wait for the coming of the Holy Spirit, Christians should wait prior to sharing the gospel; Luke 24:49, "But you are to stay in the city until you are clothed with power from on high" (Acts 1:8).
	4	Multiplication of disciples is prioritative above the addition of converts	Based on translation "make disciples" (Matt 28:19-20), Christ's time with the 12 apostles (Acts 4:13), and human pedagogical principles, it appears more prudent to focus on a few (2 Tim 2:2) rather than to itinerate and indiscriminately evangelize the many (Luke 9:6).
	5	Possibility of multiplicity of means	Possible mistranslation of *pantōs* as "all means" (1 Cor 9:22) as implying a multiplicity of methods, more than just proclamation; "in everything" (1 Cor 10:33).
	6	Salt and light	Interpretation of Matt 5:13-16, "You are the salt of the earth . . . You are the light of the world" as explaining the dual responsibility of the Christian; salt in this case is interpreted as a preservative, rather than an antiseptic.
	7	Works salvation	Salvation is not based on faith alone, but includes or is solely based on being "poor in spirit," being one who "mourns," being "meek," and/or being a "peacemaker" (Matt 5:3-9); i.e., adding principles of Greek philosophy to the gospel.
	8	"Cultural mandate"	Based on Gen 1:26, 28, mere proclamation is too restrictive to the holistic purposes of kingdom of God and the transformation of society, i.e., the need is to proactively be a blessing to others (Gen 12:2-3).
	9	Populating the world	The most important thing, based on Gen 1:28, is to have as many children as possible to "multiply, and fill the earth."
	10	Jesus' ministry example and teaching above that of Paul	The ministry example of Jesus in the gospels is (1) different, (2) more holistic, and (3) more authoritative than the ministry example of Paul and the apostles in the book of Acts.
Nonbiblical	11	Cultural	Our culture is different from the Middle Eastern culture of Bible times, or of the *Pax Romana* period (or wherever proclamational evangelism is effective today).
	12	Sociological	One must take into account sociological differences (methods of communication or of thinking) of each people group in evangelism (i.e., sociology trumps biblical methodology).
	13	Historical apostolic era	New Testament evangelism is necessary only for the establishment of the church in society (apostolic era); once a church is established, apostolic evangelism is no longer needed (Gustav Warneck).

7. Alternatives to Mere Proclamation (continued)

the mandate for world evangelization. Once something is added to mere proclamation (such as a change in method of evangelism), the same is added to the order of salvation (soteriology). It necessarily follows that the Great Commission (i.e., purpose of the church) must be changed to allow for any addition to mere proclamation. It seems very likely that these additions are how evangelical churches (proclamation-centered churches) morph into becoming nonevangelical churches (nonproclamation-centered churches).

Reasons Against Mere Procl.				**Alternatives and/or Additions to Mere Proclamation**										
Nonbiblical				**Ecclesiological**									**Sacra-mental**	
14	**15**	**16**	**17**	**18**	**19**	**20**	**21**	**22**	**23**	**24**	**25**	**26**	**27**	**28**
Historical generational	Historical revisionism	Comparative religions	Psychological	Keys	Institutionalism	Orphanages	Unity	Giving	Worship	Teaching	Gospel authors as primary evangelists	Bringing a heretic back into the church	The Lord's Supper	Baptism
Society has evolved and is not open to New Testament evangelism as it once was, either: (1) "in the days of our denominational founders;" (2) during one of the Great Awakenings; (3) during the days of XYZ evangelist, or (4) one or two generations back.	History is rewritten (1) to exclude apostolic evangelism; as occurs for the Reformation (omit evangelistic work of Lambert d'Avignon and Guillaume Farel) or (2) to overemphasize social ministry (the social work of Wilberforce or Moody in the 19th century).	All religious systems contain a measure of truth, in fact (in this view) one may say that the Holy Spirit speaks to all peoples through their worship of the divine light that they have received (Ps 36:9; Rom 2:14-15).	Belief in mere proclamation is obsessive, truncated, and compartmentalized, stemming from emotional instability and Pharisaic literalism, and leading to dysfunctional relationships, Christians, and churches.	Matt 16:19; 18:18; Luke 22:29-30	Matt 16:18; Eph 1:22-23; 5:23-32	James 1:27; Sir 4:10	John 17:21, 23; Eph 4:3; Phil 2:1-2	Matt 6:4; John 12:1-8; Acts 4:36-5:2; 10:2, 4; Luke 6:35; 11:41; 21:5; 2 Cor 9:6	1 Cor 14:23; Eph 1:6, 12; 1 Pet 2:9 (if mistranslated); after receiving the Great Commission the disciples were continually in the Temple worshiping (Luke 24:53).	Matt 28:19-20; Col 1:28-29; 1 Tim 3:2; 2 Tim 2:2, 24	Narrow understanding of *Gospel* as primarily narratives of the life of Christ (Mark 1:1), presumes: (1) gift of the evangelist is ceased (Eph 4:11), (2) moral influence theory.	James 5:20; Jude 22-23	John 6:53-56; 1 Cor 11:26 (Luke 24:31, 35)	Mark 16:16; Acts 2:38; 1 Pet 3:21

7. Alternatives to Mere Proclamation (continued)

Alternatives to and/or Additions to Mere Proclamation													
Sacramental		Good Works									Miracles		
29	30	31	32	33	34	35	36	37	38	39	40	41	42
Confession	Prayer for another	Social justice	Voluntary poverty	Voluntary suffering	Vow of celibacy	Caring for the poor	Showing mercy	Serving	Good deeds	Doing good	Speaking in tongues	Baptism in the Spirit	Healings
Gal 6:2; James 5:16	James 5:15	Amos 5:24; Micah 6:8; Zech 7:9-10; James 1:27	Luke 14:33; 21:1-4; Phil 3:7-8; Heb 11:26 (Heb 10:34)	2 Tim 1:8; James 5:10-11; 1 Pet 2:19-21; e.g., Heb 11:36	Matt 19:12; 1 Cor 7:8; 9:5 (woman married to Christ; men married to the church, 1 Tim 3:2)	Luke 4:18; Gal 2:10	Matt 25:40; Luke 4:40; 6:35-36; 10:37	Matt 20:28; Mark 10:45	Matt 5:16; 25:40; Acts 9:36; Eph 2:10; Titus 2:14; 3:14; James 2:26; 1 Pet 2:12; 1 John 3:18	Acts 10:38; Gal 6:10	Mark 16:17; Acts 2:5-12; 10:46; 19:6; 1 Cor 14:5	Matt 3:11; Mark 1:8; Luke 3:16; John 1:33; Acts 1:5; 2:38; 11:16; 19:1-7	Matt 4:23; 9:35; Mark 6:13; 16:18; Luke 4:40; 9:2, 6

7. Alternatives to Mere Proclamation (continued)

Alternatives to and/or Additions to Mere Proclamation														
Miracles (cont)		Attitude			Spiritual Maturity									
43	44	45	46	47	48	49	50	51	52	53	54	55	56	57
Snake handling	Casting out demons or working miracles	Love	Compassion	Fruit of the Spirit	Community	Virtuous living	Cost of discipleship	Sanctification	Imitation of Christ	Prayer	Spiritual giftedness	Finding one's purpose(s)	Spiritual disciplines	Teaching only one's own children
Mark 16:18; Acts 28:3-6	Heb 2:3-4; Mark 16:20; Matt 7:22	Matt 10:37, 39; Mark 12:30-31; Luke 10:27; John 13:34-35; 1 Cor 13:13; 1 John 4:7-8, 12, 18	Matt 9:36; 25:31-46	Gal 5:22-23	Acts 2:46-47; 4:34-37; 5:12-13	1 Tim 3:2, 10; Titus 1:7; 2 Pet 2:7; 3:11, 16	Matt 10:38-39; Luke 14:27	1 Thess 4:7; Heb 12:14	John 13:34-35; 1 Cor 11:1; Eph 5:25; Col 3:13; Heb 13:2; 1 Pet 2:21; 1 John 2:6	Luke 11:1-4; Eph 6:18; 1 Thess 5:17	1 Cor 12:7, 11; Eph 4:7; 1 Pet 4:10	Matt 6:33; 1 Cor 12:7; Eph 1:5-6, 11-12	1 Thess 5:17; 1 Tim 4:7-8	Deut 6:4-9; Jos 24:15; Eph 6:4

8. Lessons from the Parable of the Sower

The parable of the sower, found in the first three Gospels (Matt 13:4-9, 18-23; Mark 4:3-9, 14-20; Luke 8:5-8, 11-15), provides teaching that can be a tremendous encouragement to the evangelist. In this parable Jesus spoke of some realities of evangelism and follow-up. These are truths that transcend the limitations of time and culture. Those who go forth with the gospel seed will encounter varied reactions. They will also face obstacles in the follow-up of new converts. Jesus shares this parable to prepare and encourage the evangelist for some of the realities of spiritual warfare.

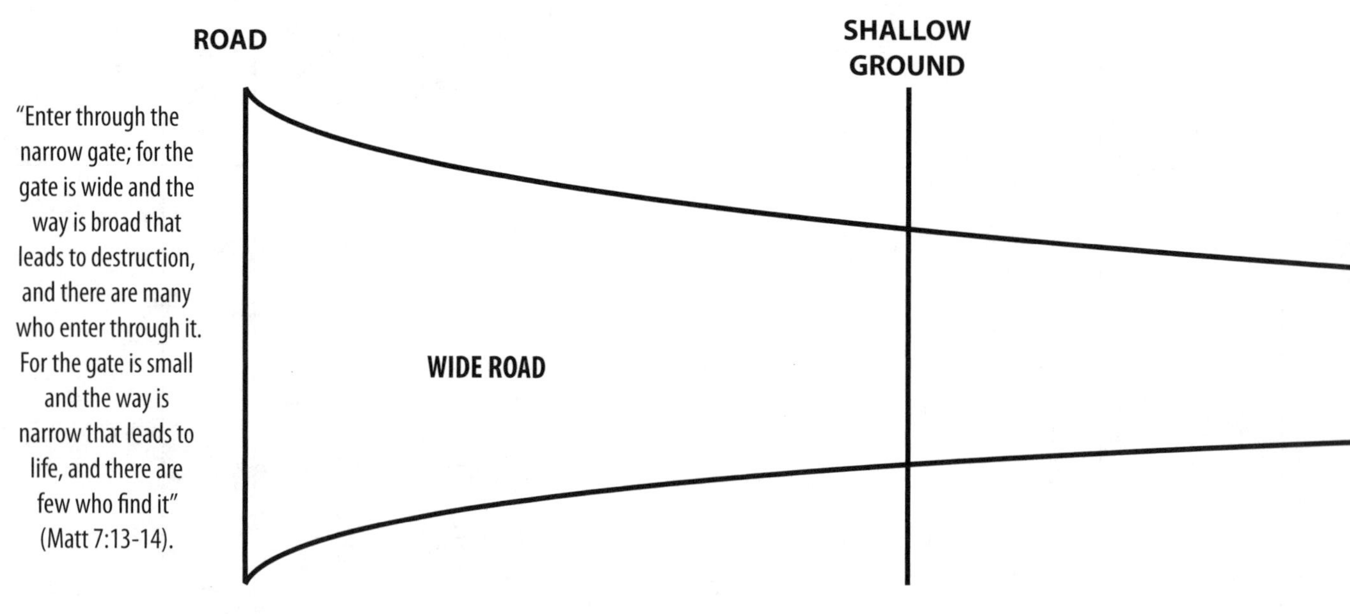
ROAD
SHALLOW GROUND
"Enter through the narrow gate; for the gate is wide and the way is broad that leads to destruction, and there are many who enter through it. For the gate is small and the way is narrow that leads to life, and there are few who find it" (Matt 7:13-14).
WIDE ROAD

ROAD	SHALLOW GROUND
Hears the Word; immediately Satan snatches the Word; person does not understand the Word	Hears the Word; understands the Word; receives it with joy; has no root in himself, but is short-lived; is persecuted and afflicted because of the Word. . . falls away
Most hearers will be on the wide road. Although we may not like it, it is a timeless truth—lest we change the gospel to accommodate to larger crowds, thus making ourselves better than our Master (Luke 11:29; John 6:66-67; 15:20)	Forgetting that part of the seed falls on shallow ground, some argue against crusade or street evangelism. They prove their point by saying that converts from these types of evangelism do not persevere in the faith. Could these not be the inevitable seed sown in shallow soil, predicted by Jesus? Will not seed sown in the shallow soil typify all genuine gospel proclamation (Matt 13:24-30)?

8. Lessons from the Parable of the Sower (continued)

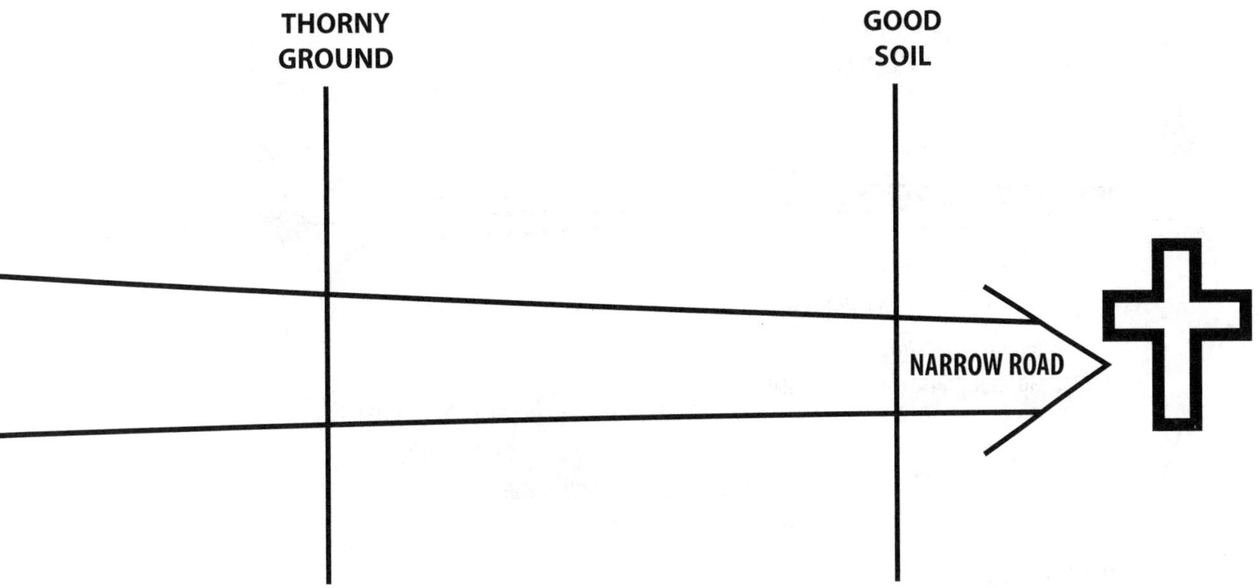

Hears the Word;
but the worries of the world, the deceitfulness of riches, and the desire for other things choke the word; bring no fruit to maturity

Some seed will necessarily be sown in weed-infested soil. If a perceived Christian does not bring fruit to maturity, is he a "carnal Christian" (1 Cor 3:12-15) or a branch not remaining in Christ (John 15:6-7)? Do these persons merely need further discipleship to be productive, or is this soil inevitable in evangelism?

Hears the Word;
accepts it;
bears fruit 30-, 60-, and 100-fold

Some seed will produce a return of "fruit." Is this fruit the "fruit of the Spirit" or is it souls saved? While Paul (Gal 5) and Jesus (Matt 7) did speak of "fruit" as character traits, the context of John 4:35-38 and 15:16 seems rather to address souls saved (1 Cor 9). Likewise, will not all true Christians necessarily reproduce themselves, 30-, 60-, or 100-fold? Are not all Christians to be "fishers of men" (Matt 4:19)?

9. Defining Evangelizing—Psalms

The following verbs (accompanied by the original Hebrew verb) are adapted from the New American Standard Bible translation (NASB).

Proclaim (*nagad*), 13 uses
Make known (*yada*), 5 uses
Utter (*hagah*), 2 uses
Proclaim (*basar*) 2 uses
Proclaim (*shama*), 1 use
Come [go] and declare (*bo + nagad*), 1 use
Teach (*lamad*), 1 use

Speak, declare (*sephar*), 21 uses
Speak (*amar*), 7 uses
Speak (*dabar*), 4 uses
Utter, flow [forth] (*naba*) 3 uses
Speak (*siach*), 1 use
Mention (*zakar*), 1 use

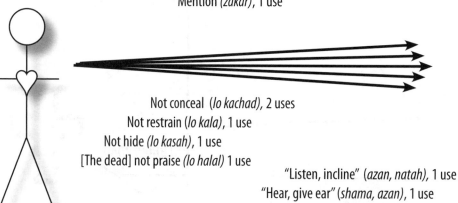

Not conceal (*lo kachad*), 2 uses
Not restrain (*lo kala*), 1 use
Not hide (*lo kasah*), 1 use
[The dead] not praise (*lo halal*) 1 use

"Listen, incline" (*azan, natah*), 1 use
"Hear, give ear" (*shama, azan*), 1 use
"Let them praise" (*halal*), 1 use
[The dead] not praise (*lo halal*) 1 use

Write (*kathab*), 1 use
Given banner, displayed (*kathab nes, nasas*), 1 use
Seen (*raah*), 1 use

Shout joyfully (*ranan*), 4 uses
Make music [sing praise] (*zamar*), 3 uses
Confess (*yadah*), 3 uses
Sing praise (*halal*) 3 uses
Praise, laud (*shabach*), 2 uses
Extol (*rum*), 2 uses
Sound His Praise abroad (*shama tehillah*), 1 use

Some Interesting Combinations

Confess (*yadah*) and sing praise (*zamar*), Ps 18:49
Come [go] (*bo*) and declare (*nagad*), Ps 22:31
Declare (*nagad*) and speak (*dabar*), Ps 40:5
Tell (*saphar*), come [go] (*bo*), make mention (*zakar*), declare (*nagad*), and declare (*nagad*), Ps 71:15-18
Give thanks (*yadah*), sing praise (*zamar*), and declare (*nagad*), Ps 92:1-2
Declare (*nagad*) and see (*raah*), Ps 97:6
Speak (*malal*) and announce (*shama*), Ps 106:2
Laud (*shabach*) and declare (*nagad*), Ps 145:4
Eagerly utter (*naba*) and shout joyfully (*ranan*), Ps 145:7

10. Defining Evangelizing—the Book of Acts

The following verbs for evangelization were used by Luke in the book of Acts to describe the evangelism in the NT church (NASB, except for "evangelize").

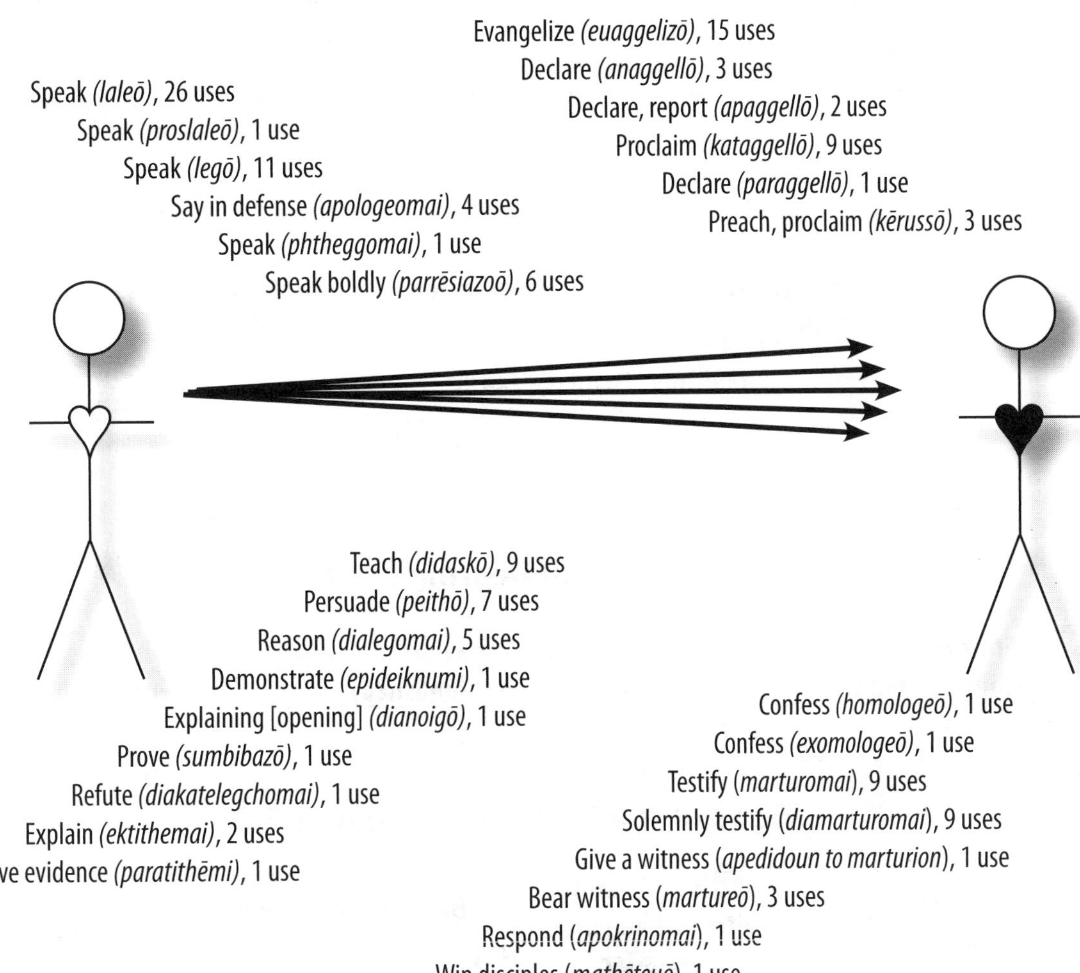

Some Interesting Combinations of These Verbs in Acts

Teach (*didaskō*) and evangelize (*euaggelizō*), Acts 5:42; 15:35 (Luke 20:1)
Evangelize (*euaggelizō*) and win disciples (*mathēteuō*), Acts 14:21 (NIV, "and won a large number of disciples")
Boldly speak (*parrēsiazoō*), reason (*dialegomai*), and persuade (*peithō*), Acts 19:8
Bear witness (*martureō*) and say (*legō*), Acts 26:22
Boldly speak (*parrēsiazoō*) and speak (*laleō*), Acts 26:26
Persuade (*peithō*) and say (*legō*), Acts 28:24
Preach (*kērussō*) and teach (*didaskō*), Acts 28:31

The Corresponding Dynamic Power of the Word of God in Acts

"The Word of God kept on spreading" (Acts 6:7).
"But the word of the Lord continued to grow and to be multiplied" (Acts 12:24).
"And the word of the Lord was being spread through the whole region" (Acts 13:49).
"So the word of the Lord was growing mightily and prevailing" (Acts 19:20).

11. Missional Translations and Interpretations

Brief History of the Translation of *mathēteuō*

Texts	Greek	Latin Vulgate	Wycliffe 2nd ed (1388)	KJV (1611/ 1769)	Young's Literal (1862/ 1898)	Darby's English (1884/ 1890)	ASV (1901)	NIV (1984)	Johns-ton's (2006)
Matt 28:19	*mathēteusate*	*docete*	teach	teach	disciple	make disciples	make disciples	make disciples	win disciples
Acts 14:[20]21	*mathēteu-santes*	*docuissent*	taught	had taught	having discipled	having made (many) disciples	had made (many) disciples	won (a large number of) disciples	won (many) disciples

Interpretations of "Win Disciples" in Matthew 28:19

Win disciples	Multiply disciples, "Teach"					Follow Christ	Imitate Christ
Win souls, Acts 14:21 [NIV]	Teach to win others	Teach to live and win	Teach to live a balanced life	Teach to teach others	Teach to lead others	Live as a disciple	Be a disciple

Views of Bearing Fruit

Fruit = Souls (fishing for men)	Fruit = Behaviors (justice versus bloodshed)	Fruit = Inner Virtues (Fruit of the Spirit)
John 4:36; 15:8, 16	Isaiah 5:1-7	Galatians 5:22-23

Views of "Be My Witness" in Acts 1:8

Initiating a witnessing conversation	Proactively bearing witness when in conversation	Bearing witness when asked	Living as a witness
Proactive Evangelism	Reactive Evangelism	Passive Evangelism, 1 Peter 3:15	Lifestyle Evangelism or Silent Evangelism

Approaches to "That I Might Win" in 1 Corinthians 9:19-22

God uses evangelist to intentionally win others to Christ ("Follow Me and I will make you fishers of men").	God uses evangelist to passively win others to Christ.	Winning others to Christ is only for those with the gift of the evangelist or evangelism.	Talking about "winning" sounds competitive, patronizing, and out of fashion.	God wins others to Christ on His own in some mysterious way.

Translations of *tas aretas exaggeilēte* in 1 Peter 2:9

Sing the praises	Show others the goodness of God	Shew forth the praises	Tell the virtues	Proclaim the excellencies
New Jerusalem Bible (1985)	New Living Translation (1996)	King James Bible (1611/1769)	Wycliffe, 2nd Edition (1388)	New American Standard (1977)

12. Variations in Translating "Evangelize"

The Greek verb for "evangelize" (*euaggelizō*) is found 54 times in the Greek NT (Luke-Acts, 25 times; Pauline, 21 times; etc.), and 20 times in the Septuagint (OT). The following show variations in the translation of this verb in the Bible.

Psalm 96:2

Shew forth his salvation from day to day	Tell of his salvation from day to day	Publish his salvation from day to day	Proclaim his salvation day after day	Proclaim good tidings of His salvation from day to day
King James Version (1611/1769)*	Revised Standard Version (1952)	English Darby Bible (1884/1890)	New International Version (1984)	New American Standard (1977)

*"Shew forth" is a KJV translation for the Hebrew *saphar, nagad,* and *bashar* (LXX: *anaggellō, exaggelloō,* and even *euaggelizō*), as also noted in Psalm 19:1; Isaiah 43:21; and the NT (1 Pet 2:9).

Luke 4:43

Mais il leur dit, Il me faut bien evangelizer auffi le royaume de Dieu aux autres villes: car je fuis envoyé pour cela	But he sayd vnto them, Surely I must also preach the kingdome of God to other cities: for therefore am I sent	But he said to them, I must needs announce the glad tidings of the kingdom of God to the other cities also, for for this I have been sent forth	But He said to them, "I must preach the kingdom of God to the other cities also, for I was sent for this purpose"	But He said to them, "I must evangelize the kingdom of God to other cities also, for I was sent for this purpose"
French Geneva Bible (1560)**	Geneva Bible (1599)	English Darby Bible (1884/1890)	New American Standard Update (1995)	Johnston's Evangelistic

**Calvin's French Geneva Bible, based on the 1535 Olivétan, translated "evangelize" 24 times, as did the revision of Martin in 1696.

Acts 8:25

Et ils évangélisaient plusieurs villages des Samaritains	Evangelizing many villages of the Samaritans	Preaching the gospel in many Samaritan villages	And they stopped in many Samaritan villages along the way to preach the Good News to them, too	Preaching the good news to a number of Samaritan villages
French Darby Bible (1885)***	Holman Christian Standard (2000)†	New International Version (1984)	New Living Translation (1996)	New Jerusalem Bible (1985)

***John Darby translated *euaggelizō* in the New Testament as "evangelize" 21 times in his 1885 French translation!

†The Holman Christian Standard is the *only* English Bible since Wycliffe's 1st edition (1382) to use the word *evangelize* (6 of 54 NT uses).

Acts 14:21

Quand ils eurent évangélisé cette ville et fait un certain nombre de disciples	After they had evangelized that town and made many disciples	And after they had preached the glad tidings of the Gospel to that citie, and had taught many	And when they had preached the gospel to that city, and had made many disciples	They preached the good news in that city and won a large number of disciples
French Louis Segond (1910)††	Holman Christian Standard (2000)	Geneva Bible (1599)	American Standard Version (1901)	New International Version (1984)

††The French 1910 Louis Segond used *évangéliser* only twice in Acts 8:40; 14:21. Similarly, some Portuguese versions use *evangelizar*.

13. Two Approaches to Evangelism—
A Look at 1 Corinthians 1-2

There are two essential approaches to evangelism: carnal and spiritual. Paul addresses these two clearly in 1 Corinthians 1–2. Later in 2 Corinthians he reminded the Corinthian believers, "For though we walk in the flesh [carnal], we do not war according to the flesh, for the weapons of our warfare are not of the flesh, but divinely powerful for the destruction of fortresses" (2 Cor 10:3-4).

CARNAL EVANGELISM

Special Method of Communication
Cleverness of speech, 1:17
Superiority of speech, 2:1
[Superiority] of wisdom, 2:1
Persuasive words of wisdom, 2:3

Special Adaptation of the Message to Human Wisdom
Wisdom of the world, 1:21
Wisdom, 1:22
Wisdom of men, 2:5
Wisdom of this age, 2:6
Wisdom of the rulers of this age who are passing away, 2:6

Special Sign Accompanying Communication
Signs (miracles or service), 1:22

Outward Symbol of Salvation
Baptism (adding ordinances or sacraments), 1:17

Result
Cross of Christ made void, 1:17
Faith rests on the wisdom of men, 2:5

SPIRITUAL EVANGELISM

Terms Emphasizing Method
Evangelize, 1:17
Preaching, 1:23; proclaiming, 2:1; speaking, 2:6

Terms Emphasizing Message
Cross of Christ, 1:17
Word of the cross, 1:18
Foolishness of the message preached, 1:21
Christ crucified, 1:23
Testimony of God, 2:1
Jesus Christ and Him crucified, 2:2
My message and my preaching, 2:3
Wisdom, not of this age… but of God, 2:6-7

Terms Emphasizing God's Sufficiency
Wisdom of God, 1:21, 24; 2:5

Terms Emphasizing God's Working
The power of God, 1:18, 24
Foolishness of God, 1:25
Weakness of God, 1:25
Demonstration of the Spirit and power, 2:5

Terms Emphasizing Man's Response
Stumbling block, 1:23
Foolishness, 1:18, 23

Terms Emphasizing Results
Are being saved, 1:18; to save, 1:21
Righteousness, and sanctification, and wisdom, 1:30
Faith rest in the power of God, 2:5

14. Three Approaches to Evangelism—Evaluating the Human Element

The following chart examines and illustrates some of the complexities of evangelism and the theological results of requiring a human element prior to verbally sharing the gospel. It is laid out as an experiment.

Two Prospects	Person A				Person B	Person C
Introduction of a Human Variable	Evangelism with "Positive" Human Preparation				Evangelism without Human Preparation	Evangelism with "Negative" Human Preparation
Variable: Seeing or Experiencing the Gospel—Positively, Not-At-All, or Negatively	**Lifestyle**	**Service**	**Friendship**	**Rational dialogue**	No prior witness of lifestyle, etc. (street evangelism or door to door)	Preaching Jesus from envy, strife, or selfish ambition (Phil 1:15-18)
Argued Constant: Hearing the Gospel	Hears the gospel				Hears the gospel	Hears the gospel
Argued Result of Added Human Variable	Supposed *higher* chance of: • Listening to the gospel • A hearing of faith • Being [truly] saved • Being [properly] followed up				Supposed *higher* chance of: • Rejecting the gospel • A carnal hearing • Manipulated conversion • Never being [properly] discipled	Supposed *lower* chance of: • Accepting the gospel • A hearing of faith • Any hope for conversion • Being [properly] discipled
Therefore ... Theologically Speaking	Higher chance of person A: • Being seed sown in the good soil • Being predestined unto salvation				Higher chance of person B: • Being seed sown on the road, or in the shallow or weed-infested soil • Not being predestined unto salvation	Higher chance of person C: • Being seed sown on the road • Not being predestined unto salvation
This is [Presumably]...	"Real-World" Evangelism				"Pie-in-the-Sky" Evangelism	"Hateful" Evangelism
Therefore ... Practically Speaking	Whereas Column C may typify truly "negative" evangelism, Column A communicates that evangelism is effective because of the human element, and rather than the spiritual elements of: • The power of the Word of God (Heb 4:12), which is the sword of the Spirit (Eph 6:17); and the power of the Word proclaimed (Gal 3:1-5), which does its work (1 Thess 2:13). • The power of the gospel (Rom 1:16); the word of the cross (1 Cor 1:18). • Those given by the Father (John 6:37); those drawn by the Father (John 6:44); those to whom it is granted (John 6:65); and those appointed to eternal life (Acts 13:48); "the Lord opened her heart to respond to the things spoken by Paul" (Acts 16:14)					

Disclaimer: While this chart represents the stark difference between the three approaches to evangelism, it does not seek to signify that God does not work through (1) existing relationships, (2) service rendered from a heart of love, or (3) caring discussion and dialogue. Rather, the issue is *requiring* these human elements prior to evangelism (i.e., "People don't care what you know, until they know that you care," or "Preach the gospel at all times, and if necessary use words").

Food for thought:

(1) Can this chart represent a practical drift which leads to the addition of the human [Pelagian] into a theology of salvation?

(2) May the Pelagian tendency of adding the human element in evangelism be the reason many adherents of the human additions consider a discussion of theology irrelevant?

(3) May the addition of the human in this way cause antagonism to doctrines which do not acknowledge the human, such as election, predestination, and total depravity?

(4) Could it be that some have an inconsistency between their theology and practice at this very point (call themselves Calvinists and adhere to or practice lifestyle evangelism)?

15. Comparing Lifestyle and Proclamation

	Expectant Evangelism	**Implications of Lifestyle Evangelism**
1	Instantaneous conversion (Acts 16:14; Rom 10:13)	Progressive conversion/gradual enlightenment
2	Substitutionary atonement (2 Cor 5:21)	Reconciliation model of the atonement
3	Faith comes by hearing (Rom 10:17)	Faith comes by experiencing and hearing
4	Instrument of salvation is word of God (Rom 1:17; 1 Pet 1:23)	Sharing the gospel must be preempted by relationship
5	Preaching Christ (2 Cor 4:5)	Preaching ourselves and Christ
6	Christ alone saves (Acts 4:12; Rom 5:8-10, et al.)	Christ's work needs human merits to be effective
7	Christ earned the right for proclamation (Rom 5:8; 1 Tim 1:15)	Christians must earn the right to share the gospel with others
8	Lifestyle and miracles of Christ did not lead to faith in all those who observed them (John 12:37)	Lifestyle of the Christian will lead the lost to become open to the message of the gospel
9	Harvest is ripe (Amos 9:13; Luke 10:2; John 4:35)	Harvest is not ripe; it needs cultivation
10	Must evangelize by faith (John 4:35)	Must evangelize by using natural relational rules
11	Christians' lives should be consistent with the gospel; Christians should live holy lives (1 Pet 1:14-16)	Christians must practice "radical identification" and "eat meat" (à la 1 Cor 10:23ff.) to relate to the lost.

Note: It is important to understand that, as within any movement, there are degrees of adherence to lifestyle evangelism. Various Scriptures are also cited by those adhering to lifestyle evangelism to affirm their position.

15. Comparing Lifestyle and Proclamation (continued)

	Expectant Evangelism	Implications of Lifestyle Evangelism
12	Christians will be hated by the world due to their association with Christ (John 15:18-21).	Christians are hated only because they are not culturally sensitive and open to the needs of the unsaved.
13	The gospel is a reproach (Heb 11:26; 1 Cor 1:23); it will be avoided by evildoers, lest their deeds be exposed (John 3:20-21).	The gospel need not be a reproach; natural man can and will accept Christianity's rational superiority with proper apologetics.
14	Satan has blinded the minds of unbelievers so that they cannot see Christ (John 3:20-21; 2 Cor 2:17; 4:3-4).	Man's sin has not fully blinded his mind; he can experience and discern certain spiritual truths if properly exemplified or communicated.
15	Rejection of gospel is due to spiritual blindness (Matt 13:19; 2 Cor 4:3-4); Christian only responsible to warn (Ezek 3:18-19), with patience (2 Tim 4:2) and gentleness (1 Pet 3:15).	Rejection of the gospel is due to a lack of relational cultivation; guilt is placed on the rejected Christian for his lack of cultivation, leading to a further fear of sharing the gospel.
16	Persecution is promised (2 Tim 3:12), and is a blessing (Matt 5:10-11; 1 Pet 4:12-14).	Persecution is a sign that the method of evangelism is faulty, needing modification.
17	Evangelism weapons are spiritual (2 Cor 10:3-5).	Must use both spiritual and carnal weapons.
18	Evangelism is urgent and preeminent for every Christian: (1) Jesus is coming back quickly (Matt 24:14). (2) Mankind is totally depraved (Rom 3:9-20). (3) Hell is real (Matt 25:46). (4) Christians are accountable (Ezek 3:16-21; Acts 20:26). (5) Time is short (Rev 22:20).	Evangelism is one of many aspects of the Christian life: (1) Emphasis on here and now. (2) Total depravity may be an overstatement. (3) Some question the reality of a literal hell. (4) Mentioning accountability is putting guilt trips on Christians. (5) Mentioning time adds unnecessary pressure.
19	The Bible is authoritative in both doctrine and practice (the work of evangelism) (2 Tim 3:16-17; 1 Cor 11:1).	The Bible is authoritative primarily for doctrine—the practice of evangelism must glean truth from culture.
20	Expectant evangelism is biblical and absolutely necessary for every Christian, and for the ministry of every local church: (1) Expectant and urgent evangelism is commanded in the Great Commission (Mark 16:15; Luke 24:46-47). (2) Expectant evangelism is exemplified (Acts 4:19-20; 5:29; 2 Tim 4:1-5).	Expectant evangelism is naive, simplistic, and counter-productive; it is negative to the world's view of the church (1 Cor 4:10): (1) Interpret Great Commission as primarily a slow and gradual process, stretch the words "make disciples" (Matt 28:19) into a prolonged process. (2) Adapt evangelism methodology to truths in anthropology, sociology, and psychology.

16. Spiritual and Carnal Evangelists

It seems that Luke (and the Holy Spirit) knew of the potential of evangelists to lapse into a carnal ministry. Thus we find in Acts 8, along with the ministry of Philip the evangelist, the antithetic of Simon the sorcerer.

	Philip the Evangelist	Simon the Sorcerer	False Teachers
Summary	A Spiritual Ministry	A Carnal Ministry	A Carnal Ministry
Ministry	Evangelist (Acts 21:8)	Formerly was practicing magic (Acts 8:9)	Peddling the word (2 Cor 2:17; Jer 23:30)
Length of ministry	Short time (Acts 8:5)	Long time (Acts 8:11)	Hidden reefs in your love feasts (Jude 12); from among your own selves (Acts 20:30)
Message	Christ (Acts 8:5)	Claiming to be someone great (Acts 8:9); "This man is what is called the Great Power of God" (Acts 8:10)	Many false prophets will arise, saying "I am *He*" and will mislead many (Mark 13:6; Eph 4:14; 1 Tim 4:1)
Audience	The crowds (Acts 8:6)	The people of Samaria (Acts 8:9); smallest to greatest (Acts 8:10)	Many false prophets will arise and will mislead many (Matt 24:11)
Appeal	Giving attention (Acts 8:6)	Giving attention (Acts 8:10, 11)	The appearance of wisdom (Col 2:23)
Signs	Performed signs (Acts 8:6); cast out unclean spirits, paralyzed and lame healed (Acts 8:7)	Magic arts (Acts 8:11)	Great signs and wonders (Matt 24:24; Mark 13:22)
Result of ministry	Rejoicing (Acts 8:8)	Astonishment (Acts 8:9)	Fall from your own steadfastness (2 Pet 3:17)

17. Five Approaches to the Leadership Roles in Ephesians 4:11

This chart provides a look at various views of leadership roles available in the church today. For example, charismatic and pentecostal churches often believe that all five of the leadership roles should be operating in every local congregation today.

Approaches to Leadership Positions	Apostle	Prophet	Evangelist	Pastor	Teacher
Charismatic or Pentecostal "Fivefold Ministry"—all currently in operation	Apostle	Prophet	Evangelist	Pastor	Teacher
Cessationist (1)	Office ceased; replaced by NT canon	Revivalist	Evangelist	Pastor	Teacher
Cessationist (2)	Office ceased; replaced by NT canon	Office ceased; replaced by OT canon	Evangelist	Pastor	Teacher
Cessationist (3), see Calvin's *Institutes*	Office ceased; replaced by NT canon	Office ceased; replaced by OT canon	Office ceased; it was only for (1) apostolic times, or (2) for non-evangelized peoples	Pastor	Teacher
Roman Catholic	Pope, from "Seat of Peter," speaks with absolute apostolic authority	Open to mystical apparitions of Mary, but antipentecostal	Office ceased; authors of the Gospels are the church's evangelists	Pope is "pastor of universal church"	Certain saints deemed "doctors of the church"; Aquinas, that "Angelic Doctor"

18. Placing Views of Evangelism on the Square of Opposition*

The Square of Opposition, used in logic to frame debates, provides a helpful tool to frame the questions and issues related to the theology and practice of evangelism.

18A. Should All Christians Evangelize?

Universal Affirmative
All Christians should evangelize.

Universal Negative
No Christians should evangelize.

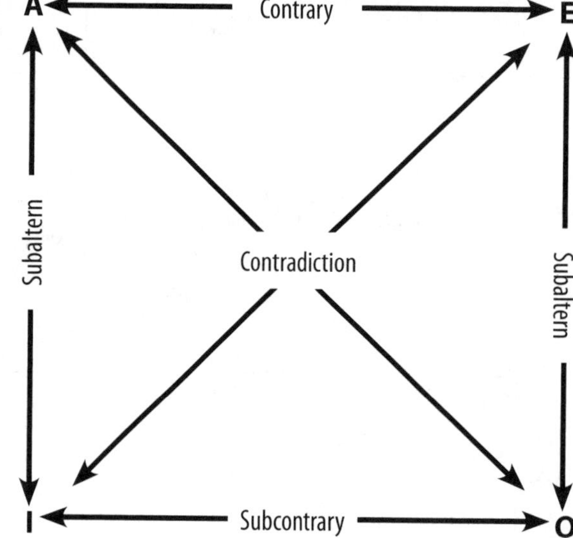

Particular Affirmative
Some Christians should evangelize (those with gift of evangelism).

Particular Negative
Some Christians should not evangelize (those without gift of evangelism).

18B. Evangelism and the Mission of the Church

Universal Affirmative
Evangelism is the only mission of the church.

Universal Negative
Evangelism is irrelevant and unimportant.

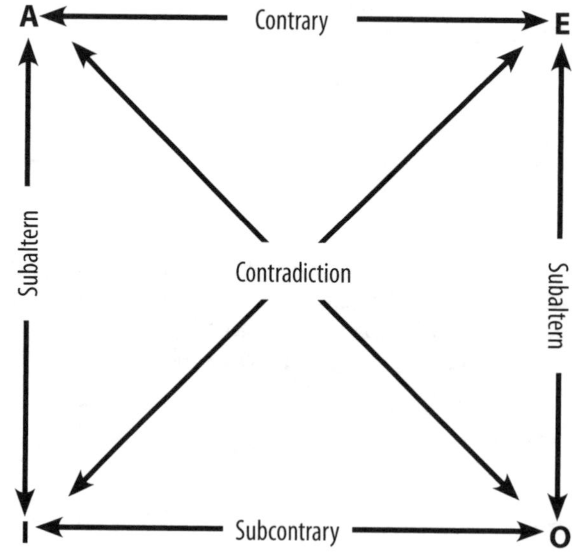

Particular Affirmative
Evangelism is the primary mission of the church.

Particular Negative
Evangelism is a secondary mission of the church.

*"Square of Opposition" adapted from Brand Blanshard, "Logic," *Collier's Encyclopedia,* 1961 ed.

18. Placing Views of Evangelism on the Square of Opposition (continued)

18C. Aldrich's Walk Around the Square of Opposition

(quotes are from Joseph Aldrich, *Life-Style Evangelism,* 78–79)

Universal Affirmative
Proclamational evangelism is absolutely necessary.

Universal Negative
"Furthermore, many are being kept from making an effective decision because of bad experiences with a zealous but insensitive witness."

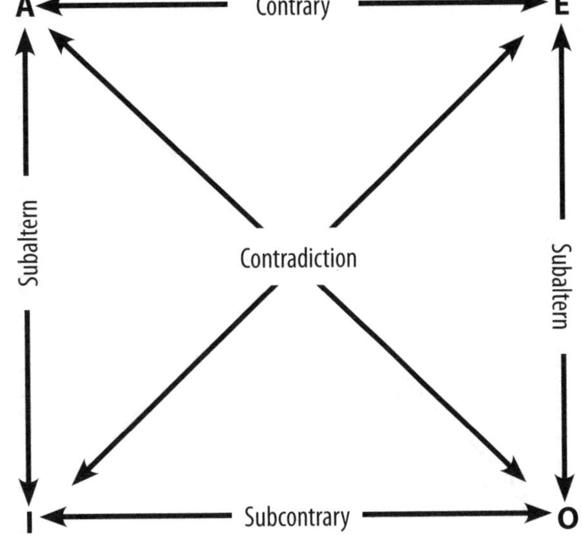

Particular Affirmative
"Although the proclamational approach to evangelism will have validity until Jesus comes. . ."

Particular Negative
". . .it [proclamation evangelism] is not the means by which the majority of Christians will reach their own private world." "The vast majority *do not* become Christians by confrontational, stranger-to-stranger evangelism."

18D. Stranger-to-Stranger Evangelism?

Universal Affirmative
Evangelism always involves sharing the gospel with a stranger.

Universal Negative
Evangelism never involves sharing the gospel with a stranger.

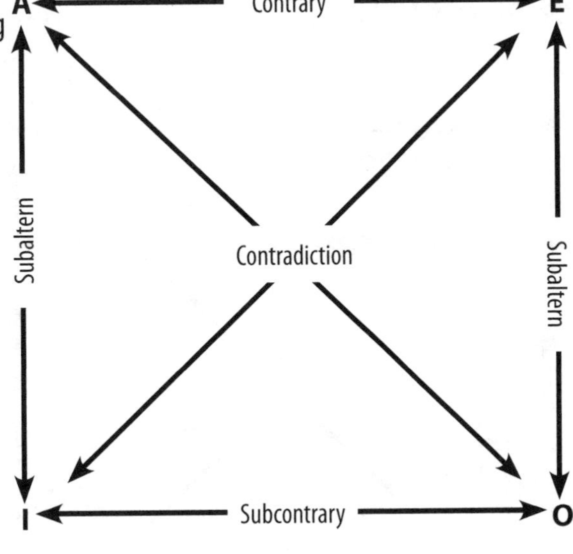

Particular Affirmative
Evangelism usually involves sharing the gospel with a stranger.

Particular Negative
Evangelism rarely involves sharing the gospel with a stranger.

18. Placing Views of Evangelism on the Square of Opposition (continued)

18E. Salvation and Hearing the Word of God

Universal Affirmative
The unsaved contact must hear the actual words of the Bible for the Holy Spirit to act on his heart.

Universal Negative
The unsaved contact need not hear the actual words of the Bible for the Holy Spirit to work on his heart.

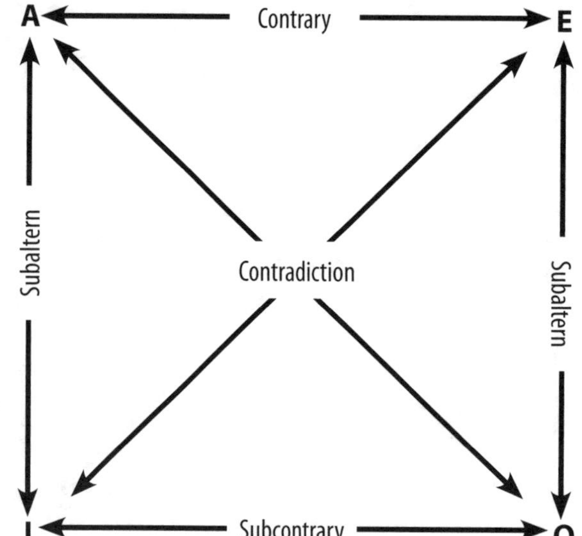

Particular Affirmative
The unsaved contact must usually hear the words of the Bible for the Holy Spirit to act on his heart.

Particular Negative
The unsaved contact need not usually hear the actual words of the Bible for the Holy Spirit to work on his heart.

18F. Call to Immediate Repentance?

Universal Affirmative
Evangelism always necessitates calling for an immediate repentance.

Universal Negative
Evangelism never involves calling for an immediate repentance.

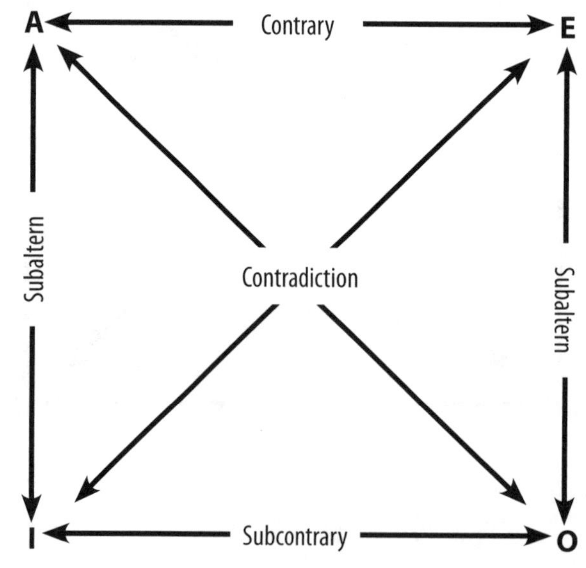

Particular Affirmative
Evangelism usually involves calling for an immediate repentance.

Particular Negative
Evangelism rarely involves calling for an immediate repentance.

18. Placing Views of Evangelism on the Square of Opposition (continued)

18G. Instantaneous or Gradual Conversion?

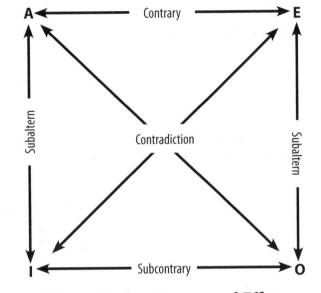

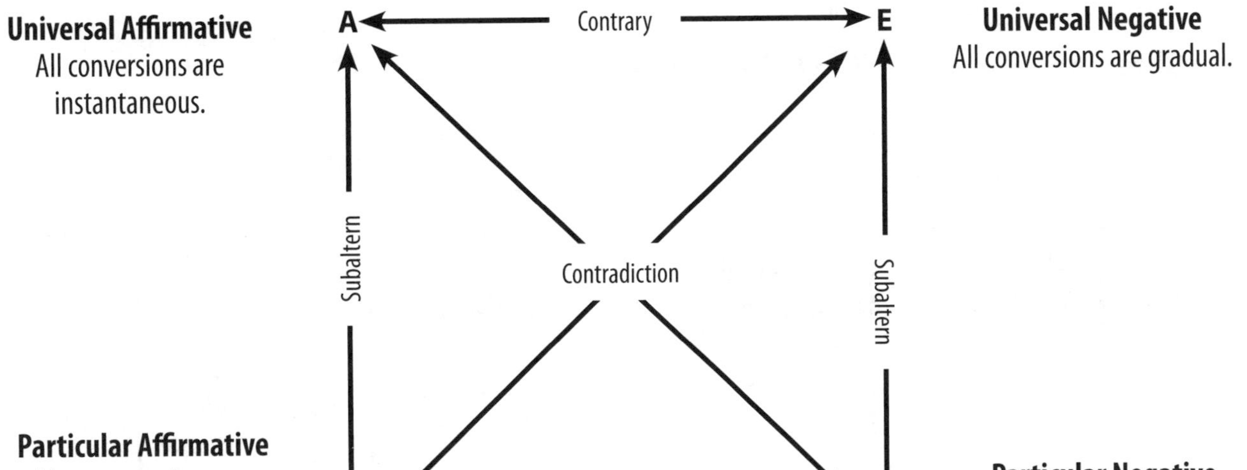

19. Revival as Cause and Effect

Is there a spiritual formula for evangelism, for revival, or for growing churches by which God is obligated or duty bound to respond, such as the following?

If … (protasis) then … (apodosis)

$$A + B + C + D \rightarrow E + F + G$$

When this formula approach is applied to 2 Chronicles 7:13-14 (including verse 13 which speaks of God's judgment), it looks something like this:

1 If I shut up the heavens so that there is no rain
2 Or if I command the locust to devour the land
3 Or if I send pestilence among My people
A And [if] My people who are called by My name
+ B Humble themselves and pray
+ C And seek My face
+ D And [if they] turn from their wicked ways
→ E Then I will hear from heaven
+ F Will forgive their sin
+ G And will heal their land

This formula approach can be applied rightly or wrongly to numerous promises in the Bible that contain a protasis and apodosis, such as Joshua 1:8; Matthew 6:33; John 14:13; 15:7, 16; James 5:15-16; and 1 John 5:14-15. These passages cover topics such as revival, answered prayer, prosperity, and healing. Proper interpretation requires the comparison of Scripture with Scripture (*sensus plenior*). While all God's promises are "Yes" in Christ Jesus (2 Cor 1:20), it is important not to ignore the conditional statements or to force God to answer his promises according to a man's finite understanding of some promises.

20. Differing Bridge Illustrations

The "Bridge Illustrations" are based primarily on the word *separation* (MT, *badal;* LXX *diistōsin*) in Isaiah 59:2, "But your iniquities have made a separation between you and your God," as well as the concept of reconciliation (*katallassō*) found in 2 Corinthians 5:18-20 and on other parts of the NT. The illustrations seem to show the theological emphases of their author.

20A. Simpson's Comparative Bridge Illustrations

(Taken from Michael L. Simpson, *Permission Evangelism: When to Talk, When to Walk,* 38)

MAN	1970s to 90s	GOD	GOD / MAN	Today's Seeker	CHURCH
How do I get to God?	Quest for purpose, value, and meaning based on childhood or cultural history with church	Evangelism Explosion: Do you know for sure...? If God were to ask you...?	How do I become a better person? • Not jugmental • Open to all ideas • Not a hypocrite	Quest for purpose, value, and meaning based on nonexistent or negative childhood church experience	

According to Simpson, the church needs to get back to where the people are (and where God is at work), and not sit back [separated] in its own culture.

20B. Relational Model of the Atonement with Four Human Preparations

(Taken from *Building a Contagious Church* by Mark Mittelberg. Copyright©2000 by Mark Mittelberg. Used by permission of Zondervan.)

In this model, four hurdles are portrayed as preparations *(preparatio evangelica)* prior to sharing the gospel.

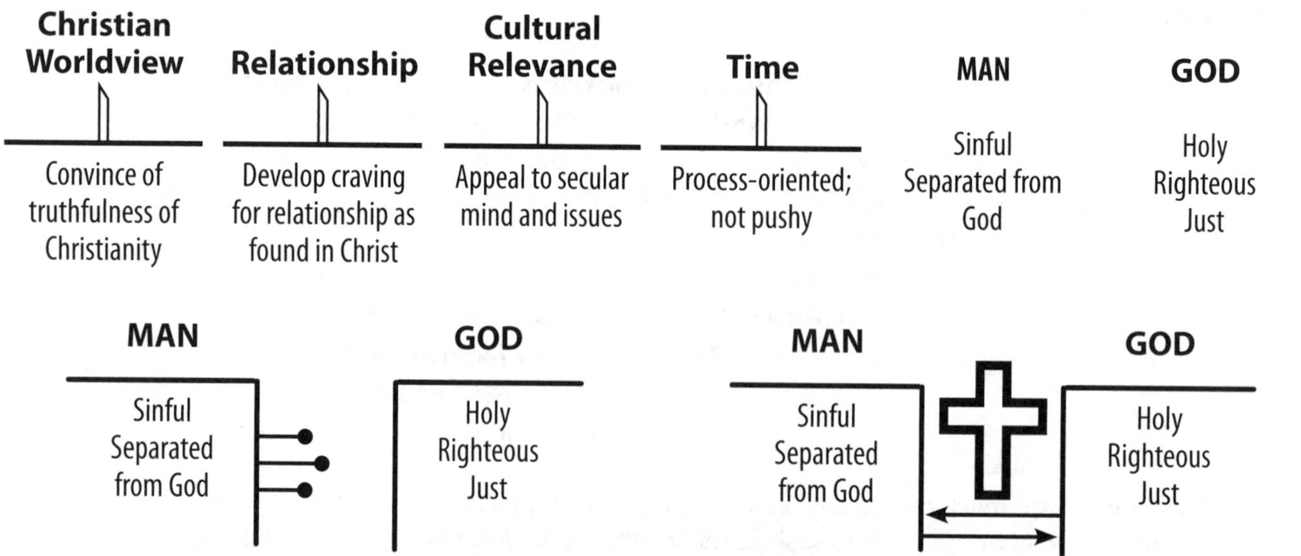

In Mittelberg's model, there seems to be a synergism of God and man working together in salvation, both in the evangelist paving the way for the gospel and in the recipient moving toward God prior to hearing the gospel.

20. Differing Bridge Illustrations (continued)

20C. Reconciliation/Substitionary Model of the Atonement

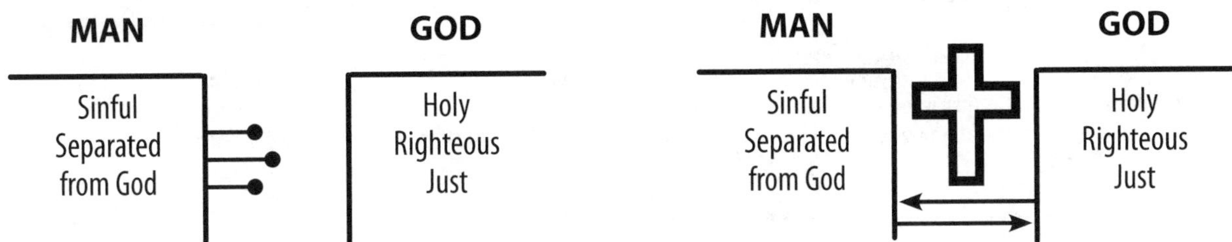

Illustration 20C can be interpreted and applied in two ways, through the relational view of the atonement, or by the substitutionary model. The important differences between the two are the verses used for sin and the terms used for the atonement. This type of Bridge Illustration is used in numerous gospel tracts, for example *The Four Laws Spiritual Laws, Steps to Peace with God,* and *Bridge to Life.*

20D. Horizontal Substitutionary Theory of the Atonement

Both illustrations 20D and 20E use substitutionary language when defining *sin*, while they show graphically that sin (rather than a vacuum or chasm) forms the separation between God and man, as clearly stated in Isaiah 59:2.

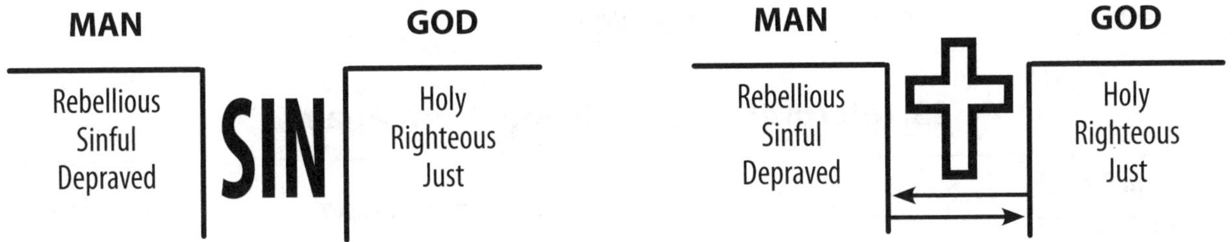

20E. Vertical Substitutionary Theory of the Atonement

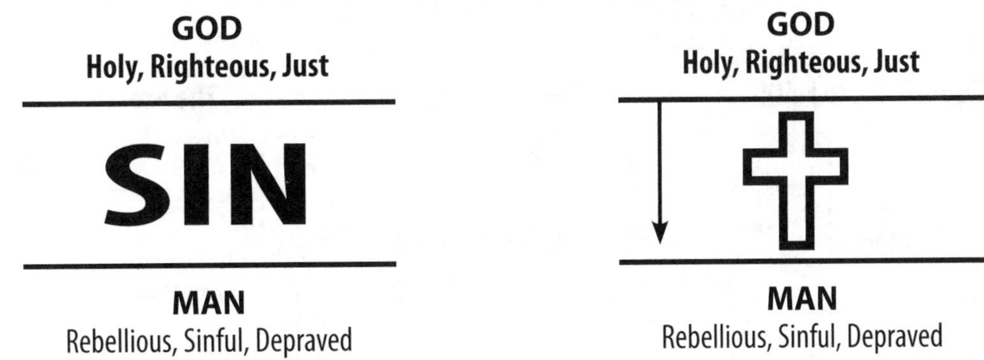

Something similar to Chart 20E is found in Darrell Robinson's *People Sharing Jesus,* 188–91, and in the Billy Graham School of Southern Baptist Theological Seminary's *Experiencing God's Grace,* 16 (see www.sbts.edu/pdf/GRACE.pdf).

21. Four Versions of the ABCs

	Substitutionary	Substitutionary/ Reconciliation	Reconciliation	Positive Thinking*
A	Admit that you are a sinner	Acknowledge that you have sinned	Admit that you need Jesus	**A—Affirm** Affirm that you can do it. . . . You must affirm: *I deserve to succeed.* You must affirm a second thing: *I have the ability to succeed. . . .*
B	Believe on Christ	Believe on Christ	Believe on Christ	**B—Believe** The A stands for affirmation or belief in yourself. B is a belief that you can make it happen, but not by yourself.... there is *someone* who has the wisdom you need that will turn the key to let you free.
C	Confess your faith to others	Confess Jesus before men	Confess Jesus as Lord	**C—Commit** When you affirm that you're created in the image of God, that you have latent abilities, and that you deserve to succeed as much as anybody else; when you begin to believe that somehow, some way, somewhere, some time, through someone, you can make it, then you get a dream. That dream is God throwing the ball back into your court. You have to hit it right back with a commitment.

*Taken from Robert Schuller, *Alphabet for Action! For Possibility Thinkers,* 5–8.

22. Interpretations of Being "Born Again"

Roman Catholic and Anglican	Psychological	Mainstream Protestant	Evangelical
Takes place at infant baptism	Decision to make a change or improvement in lifestyle or belief	Decision to believe in God's love and accept the reconciliatory role of Jesus Christ as exemplified in the cross	Decision to repent of one's sinfulness in response to the gospel and believe in the substitutionary work of Christ

23. Variations of Faith and Love

"From Faith to Faith"					to			"The Greatest Is Love"		
1	**2**	**3**	**4**	**5**	**6**	**7**	**8**	**9**	**10**	**11**
Faith in Christ as Savior	Faith in the love of Christ	Faith in power, glory, or deity of Christ	Faith in benefits of a Christian worldview	Faith in the power of faith	Faith in the act of prayer	Seeking to respond to God's love	Faith in the power of love	Love explains everything	Seeking to imitate God's love	Love as the highest virtue

24. Various Views of Preaching Assurance of Salvation

Groups	Preachers of Assurance Are...	Those Who Believe in Assurance...
Roman Catholic Church	Duping the masses	Have spiritual pride (first cardinal sin)
Mainstream Protestant	Misplacing the "here-and-now" emphasis of the message of Jesus	Are quaint, old-fashioned, too heavenly minded
Seeker-Sensitive and Emergent	Irrelevant	Are out of touch with culture and the "real" issues of the day
Wesleyan-Methodist	Avoiding the conditional passages of the New Testament	Are ignorant of the conditional passages of the New Testament
Experiential Calvinists	Biblical	Are certain of the "Blessed Hope"

25. What the Cross Is Not

A Mere Example of Extreme Self-Effacement	A Mere Example of Extreme Self-Discipline	A Mere Example of Extreme Selflessness	A Mere Example of Solidarity with the Human Predicament	A Mere Example to Be Worshiped—the Crucifix	A Mere Example to Be Imitated—the Stigmata	A Mere Example to Be Imitated—Addition of Other Merits to the Cross
Christianized Buddhism	Christianized Stoicism	Liberalized Christianity	Liberalized Christianity	Romanized Christianity	Romanized Christianity	Romanized Christianity
Gal 2:20	Gal 6:14	Phil 2:3-5	Matt 25:35-36	2 Kgs 18:4	Gal 6:17	Col 1:24

26. Views of Bearing One's Cross

(Matt 10:38; Mark 8:34; Luke 9:23; 14:27)

Literally	Literally	Figuratively	Figuratively	Figuratively	Figuratively	Figuratively	Figuratively
Bearing the sign of the passion, hence the stigmata	Picking up a cross and carrying it to identify with Christ's sufferings	Remembering the cross by wearing a cross or crucifix as jewelry	Remembering the cross by hanging a crucifix in every room in the house	Remembering the cross (and Trinity) by doing the sign of the cross before prayer	Patiently bearing the general difficulties of life in a fallen world	Bearing the reproach of Christ by living "Christianly" in a fallen world	Bearing the reproach of the gospel by accepting persecution for evangelizing

27. The Many and the Few

	Passages	Wide/All/Many	Narrow/Some/Few
Few Saved*	2 Chr 30:10-11	So the couriers passed from city to city through the country of Ephraim and Manasseh, and as far as Zebulun, but they laughed them to scorn and mocked them.	Nevertheless some men of Asher, Manasseh and Zebulun humbled themselves and came to Jerusalem.
	Matt 7:13-14	Enter through the narrow gate; for the gate is wide and the way is broad that leads to destruction, and there are many who enter through it.	For the gate is small and the way is narrow that leads to life, and there are few who find it
	Matt 7:21-23	Not everyone who says to Me, "Lord, Lord," will enter the kingdom of heaven, . . . Many will say to Me on that day, "Lord, Lord, did we not . . . ?" And then I will declare to them, "I never knew you; DEPART FROM ME, YOU WHO PRACTICE LAWLESSNESS."	but he who does the will of My Father who is in heaven *will enter.*
	1 Cor 9:22	I have become all things to all men, so that I may by all means . . .	. . . save some.
Many Deceived	Matt 24:5	For many will come in My name, saying, "I am the Christ," and will mislead many (Luke 21:8).	
	Matt 24:11, 13	Many false prophets will arise and will mislead many.	But the one who endures to the end, he will be saved.
	Mark 13:6	Many will come in My name, saying, "I am *He!*" and will mislead many.	
	2 Tim 3:13	But evil men and impostors will proceed *from bad* to worse, deceiving and being deceived.	
Few Workers	Matt 9:37	The harvest is plentiful . . .	. . . but the workers are few.
	Luke 10:2	The harvest is plentiful . . .	. . . but the laborers are few.
	Luke 21:8 et al	See to it that you are not misled; for many will come in My name, saying, "I am *He,*" and, "The time is near." Do not go after them.	
	1 Cor 16:8-9	A wide door for effective *service* has opened to me, and there are many adversaries.	
	2 Cor 2:17	For we are not like many, peddling the word of God,	but as from sincerity, but as from God, we speak in Christ in the sight of God.
	2 Cor 11:18	Since many boast according to the flesh . . .	
	Phil 3:18	For many walk, of whom I often told you, and now tell you even weeping, . . . enemies of the cross of Christ . . .	
	Titus 1:10-11	For there are many rebellious men, empty talkers and deceivers, especially those of the circumcision . . .	
	2 Pet 2:2	Many will follow their sensuality, and because of them the way of the truth will be maligned.	
	1 John 2:18	. . . even now many antichrists have appeared . . .	
	1 John 4:1	. . . because many false prophets have gone out into the world.	
	2 John 7	For many deceivers have gone out into the world . . .	

*Some verses are used to broaden the way of salvation, such as John 12:32; Romans 5:19; 8:29; Genesis 16:10; 22:17.

28. The Gospel and Eternal Life

A student once asked me, "Why are all gospel presentations fixated on eternal life?" As it turns out, the emphasis on eternal life comes primarily from the pages of the New Testament (quoting from the NASB)!

Concept	Terms	Author/Speaker
Eternal life	"Eternal life," 40 times in NT (none in OT)	Jesus (15 times in John); 6 times in 1 John
		Paul (9 times)
		Other (10 times)
	"Life eternal," 2 times in NT	John 4:36; 12:25
	"Everlasting life"	Dan 12:2
Eternal punishment	"Second death"	Rev 20:14; 21:8
	"Eternal destruction"	2 Thess 1:9
	"Eternal judgment"	Heb 6:2
	"Eternal punishment"	Matt 25:46
	"Eternal fire"	Matt 18:8; 25:41; Jude 7
	"Unquenchable fire"	Matt 3:12; Mark 9:43; Luke 3:17
	"Tormented day and night forever and ever"	Rev 20:10
	"And the smoke of their torment goes up forever and ever; they have no rest day and night"	Rev 14:11
	"Where their worm does not die, and the fire is not quenched"	Mark 9:48 (Isa 66:24)
Brevity of this life as compared to life eternal (also vanity of this life)	"As handbreaths . . . as nothing"	Ps 39:5
	"A mere breath"	Pss 39:5, 11; 144:4
	"A wind that passes and does not return"	Ps 78:39
	"A lengthened shadow," "a shadow when it lengthens," "a passing shadow"	Pss 102:11; 109:23; 144:4
	"A shadow"	1 Chron 29:15; Job 8:9; 14:2
	"A vapor"	James 4:14
	"Like the grass," "like grass," "all flesh is grass," "flowering grass"	Pss 37:2; 90:5-6; 92:7; 102:11; 103:15; Isa 40:6-8; 51:12; James 1:10-11; 1 Pet 1:24-25
	"Like a flower," "as a [like the] flower of the field"	Job 14:2; Ps 103:15-16; Isa 40:6-8
	"Like the locust"	Ps 109:23
	Reckoned in terms of years	Gen 6:3; Ps 90:10
	"In a moment they die"	Job 34:20
	"Short-lived"	Job 14:1
	"For soon it is gone and we fly away"	Ps 90:10
Focus should not be in this life	"Men of the world, whose portion is in *this* life"	Ps 17:14
	"Keep seeking the things above. . . . Set your mind on the things above, not on the things that are on earth"	Col 3:1-3
	"But as it is, they desire a better *country,* that is a heavenly one"	Heb 11:16

29. Sin and the Gospel

In his early ministry Billy Graham was accused of being obsessive in dealing with man's sin. Is a discussion of sin an add-on, or is it central and essential to the gospel? As it turns out, it is central to the gospel!

Concept	Passages	Term for sin	Term for Atonement
Definition of sin	1 John 3:4 (Lev 4:2, 27-28)	Everyone who practices sin also practices lawlessness; and sin is lawlessness.	
Images foreshadowing the substitutionary death of Jesus Christ	Exod 30:10	The blood of the sin offering of atonement	The blood of the sin offering [on the altar]
	Lev 4:27, 32,35 (1 John 4:10)	Now if anyone of the common people sins unintentionally in doing any of the things which the LORD has commanded not to be done, and becomes guilty	If he brings a lamb . . . Thus the priest shall make atonement for him . . . and he will be forgiven
	Lev 17:11 (Rev 1:5)	[Guilt]	For the life of the flesh is in the blood, and I have given it . . . to make atonement for your souls; for it is the blood by reason of the life that makes atonement.
	Isa 53:5 (Ps 32:1-2; 1 Pet 2:24; 3:18)	Transgressions, iniquities	But He was pierced through for our transgressions, He was crushed for our iniquities; . . . And by His scourging we are healed.
	Isa 53:12 (Isa 59:20)	Sin	Yet He Himself bore the sin of many.
Jesus as atoning sacrifice for sin	John 1:29 (Gal 1:4; 1 John 2:1-2)	Who takes away the sin of the world	Behold, the Lamb of God
	1 Cor 5:7 (2 Cor 5:21)	[Old leaven]	Christ our Passover

29. Sin and the Gospel (continued)

Concept	Passages	Term for sin	Term for Atonement
Jesus as atoning sacrifice for sin	Heb 9:7, 15, 22, 26, 28 (1 Cor 6:11; Heb 1:4; 2:17; 7:26-27)	Sins of the people . . . transgressions . . . sin . . . sins of many	And according to the Law . . . almost . . . all things are cleansed with blood, and without shedding of blood there is no forgiveness.
	Heb 10:12 (Heb 10:14)	Sins	But He, having offered one sacrifice for sins for all time. . .
	Rev 5:4, 12 (Rev 5:9-10)	No one was found worthy.	Worthy is the Lamb that was slain.
The gospel	Acts 2:38 (Acts 3:19; 5:31; 10:43; 13:38; 22:16; 26:18)	Sins	Repent, and each of you be baptized in the name of Jesus Christ for the forgiveness of your sins; and you will receive the gift of the Holy Spirit.
	Rom 6:10 (Rom 6:23)	Sin	For the death that He died, He died to sin once for all. . .
	Acts 3:26	Wicked ways	For you first, God raised up His Servant and sent Him to bless you by turning every one *of you* from your wicked ways.
	Acts 15:9	[Uncleanness]	cleansing their hearts by faith
	1 Cor 15:3 (Rom 3:24-25)	For our sins	Christ died.
	Col 1:13-14	Sins	For He rescued us from the domain of darkness, and transferred us to the kingdom of His beloved Son, in whom we have redemption, the forgiveness of sins.
Sin in the Great Commission	Luke 24:47	For forgiveness of sin	Repentance . . . would be proclaimed in His name.

30. Comparing Gospel Presentations

	Erasmus's Philosophical[1]	Luther's Three Points[2]	Pascal's Philosophical[3]	Spurgeon's "Ark of Safety"	Navigator's *Topical Memory*[4]	Roman Road
Date	**1503**	**1522**	**1653**	**1880s**	**1940s**	**1960s**
Introductory Questions or Issues	However, just as divine Scripture bears no great fruit if you persist in clinging only to the literal sense. . . . I would prefer, too, that you follow the Platonists among the philosophers, because in most of their ideas and in their very manner of speaking they come nearest to the beauty of the prophets and the gospels.	n/a	The first thing that God inspires in the soul that he deigns to truly touch, is a knowledge of and an extraordinary insight by which the soul considers things and itself in a completely new way. This new light gives her [soul] fear and brings her a troubled [spirit] that pierces the tranquility she found in the things that gave her pleasure.	n/a	n/a	n/a
Introductory Point		It is given to me to resound the Gospel in your ears. . . . These principles, they are the great doctrines of Christianity. . .		Lev 19:2; Exod 12:13; God's people are always safe. But God's people are only safe through *the blood.*	n/a	n/a
Sin	(1) Sin exists—using the platonic differentiation between the flesh and the spirit. (2) Sin must be resisted—emphasizing the use of Stoic means.	And first, that we are in our nature children of wrath and that all our thoughts, our affections and our works serve us as nothing, now there is a fundamental truth, Eph 2:3, *We are all,* says the Apostle, *children of wrath.*	She considers the perishable things as perishable and even as already perished. . . . In this way she will perfectly comprehend that her heart was only attached to things that are fragile and vain.	This blood is once shed for the remission of sin. The paschal lamb was slain every year, but Christ, once for all, hath put away sin by the offering of Himself. He has said, "It is finished."	(1) The fact of sin, Rom 3:23; 3:11, 12. (2) The price of sin, Rom 6:23; 5:12; Gal 3:10. (3) The price must be paid, Heb 9:27; Rom 2:12; Heb 2:2-3.	Need (Why?): God says that all are sinners, Rom 3:10, 23. God tells us the reason all are sinners, Rom 5:12. Consequence (What?): God tells us the result of sin, Rom 6:23.

1 Desiderius Erasmus, *The Enchiridion of Erasmus*, ed. Raymond Himelick, 51.

2 Martin Luther, "Fragment of the Discourse that Luther Pronounced at Wittenberg upon Returning from the Castle of Wartburg" [1522], from Franck Puaux, *Histoire de la Réformation Française*, 1:408-9. Translation mine.

3 Blaise Pascal, "Sur la Conversion du Pécheur," in *Pascal: Œuvres Complètes*, ed. Louis Lafuma, 290–91. Translation mine.

4 From Navigator's *Topical Memory System*.

30. Comparing Gospel Presentations (continued)

CCC's *Four Spiritual Laws*[5]	Navigator's *Bridge to Life*	Evangelism Explosion	*Your Most Important Relationship*	SBTS' *GRACE*[6]	Cameron and Comfort[7]	Cho's Fivefold Gospel[8]
1965	**1969**	**1977**	**1985**	**2003**	**2004**	**2005**
Have you heard of the four spiritual laws?	n/a	[Abbreviated questions] (1) If you died tonight, are you sure you would go to heaven? (2) If God said, "Why should I let you into My heaven?" what would you answer?	You were created with value and worth. God wants your life to count.	Are you experiencing God's GRACE?	[Comfort uses humor to guide persons into the gospel, often with a gospel tract or through street preaching]	The first pillar of the Fivefold Gospel is the Gospel of Regeneration [others are: "Gospel of. . ." (2) Fullness of the Holy Spirit, (3) Divine Healing, (4) Blessing, and (5) the Advent]. The rebirth is a prerequisite to salvation (John 3:3). As such, the Gospel of Regeneration can be called the Gospel of Salvation.
(1) God Loves You, and Offers a Wonderful Plan for Your Life, John 3:16; 10:10	1) The Bible teaches that God loves all men. . . . But man is separated from God and His love, 1 Tim 2:5	(a) Grace: [1] Heaven is a free gift; [2] It is not earned or deserved, Rom 6:23	(1) God loves you and created you to have a personal relationship with Him, Ps 139:13-14; John 3:16; 17:3	G . . . stands for God, Gen 1:1; Ps 19:1; Rev 4:11; 4:8; 1 Tim 6:15-16; Titus 3:4; Ps 8:4-6; Gen 1:27; Matt 4:4; 22:37-38	"Making Sinners Tremble" [by use of the Ten Commandments]	
(2) Man is Sinful and Separated from God. Therefore, He Cannot Know and Experience God's Love and Plan for His Life, Rom 3:23; 6:23	(2) Because he has sinned against God, Isa 59:2; Rom 3:23 3) This separation leads only to death and certain judgment, Heb 9:27; 2 Thess 1:8-9	(b) Man: [1] Is a sinner, Matt 5:48; Rom 3:23; [2] Cannot save himself, Eph 2:8-9	(2) Our sin keeps us from having a personal relationship with God, James 4:17; Rom 3:23; Isa 59:2; Rom 6:23	R . . . stands for Rebellion, Lev 19:2; Rom 3:23; 5:12; 1 John 1:8; Isa 59:2; Heb 9:27; Matt 25:31, 46	[Nathan's rebuke of David, as a precedent to eliciting true repentance, hence, "I have sinned against the Lord" (2 Sam 12:13; Acts 16:29-30), Comfort uses the 10 Comm]	(1) The Way to Regeneration. All men were destined to be born sinners (Rom 5:16), and were unable to reach the glory of God through his own means (Rom 3:23).

5 Campus Crusade for Christ, *Four Spiritual Laws.*

6 The Billy Graham School of Missions, Evangelism, and Church Growth of the Southern Baptist Theological Seminary, *Experiencing God's Grace* (www.sbts.edu/pdf/GRACE.pdf). This presentation was approved in a faculty meeting at Southern!

7 Taken from Kirk Cameron and Ray Comfort, *The School of Biblical Evangelism: 101 Lessons.*

8 David Yonggi Cho's "Gospel of Regeneration" (http://english.fgtv.com/ Gospel/fivefold.asp), an example of the "Full Gospel."

30. Comparing Gospel Presentations (continued)

	Erasmus's Philosophical	Luther's Three Points	Pascal's Philosophical	Spurgeon's "Ark of Safety"	Navigator's *Topical Memory*	Roman Road
Date	**1503**	**1522**	**1653**	**1880s**	**1940s**	**1960s**
Gospel	Christ has given us the example of resisting sin.	Secondly, the great and merciful Jehovah sent us his unique son, in order that we might believe in him, and that by faith in this Savior we would be freed from the law of sin and might become the children of God, John 1:12.	In this way by a holy humility, God reveals himself above the greatness, she begins to raise herself above the common of humanity. She condemns their conduct, she detests their maxims... She directs herself to seek true goodness. She understands that there must be two qualities, one which endures as long as she [the soul] and that cannot be taken from her without her consent, and the other that there is nothing else worth loving.	There is not—I repeat it again—the slightest atom of saving power anywhere but in the blood of Jesus. . . . The blood is to save thee, not thy tears; Christ's blood, not thy repentance.	(4) The price has been paid by Christ, Rom 5:8; 1 Pet 3:18; Gal 3:13.	Remedy (How?): God tells us of His concern for sinners, Rom 5:8-9.
Commitment	To resist sin, we must have faith in the Bible, faith in the example of Christ, follow His example and that of other role models of Stoicism in the Bible and in church history—as confirmed by the Roman Catholic Church.	n/a		This brings us to the one condition. "When I see the blood I will pass over you." Sinner, . . . if you feel the need of a Savior, that blood is able to save you, and you are bidden simply to trust in the blood, and you shall be saved.	(5) Salvation is a free gift, Eph 2:8-9; Rom 3:24; Titus 3:5 (6) Salvation must be received, John 1:12; Rev 3:20; Rom 10:9-10.	Condition (Who?): God's way of salvation is made plain, Rom 10:9-10, 13.
Commitment Questions	*Enchiridion* was written "to prescribe in a concise fashion some method of Christian living which might help you achieve a character acceptable to Christ."	n/a	n/a	See the Savior hanging on the cross; turn your eye to Him, and say, "Lord, I trust Thee; I have nothing else to trust in; sink or swim, my Savior, I trust Thee."	n/a	n/a

30. Comparing Gospel Presentations (continued)

CCC's *Four Spiritual Laws*	Navigator's *Bridge to Life*	Evangelism Explosion	*Your Most Important Relationship*	SBTS' *GRACE*	Cameron and Comfort	Cho's Fivefold Gospel
1965	**1969**	**1977**	**1985**	**2003**	**2004**	**2005**
(3) Jesus Christ is God's Only Provision for Man's Sin. Through Him You Can Know and Experience God's Love and Plan for Your Life, Rom 5:8; 1 Cor 15:3-6; John 14:6	(4) Jesus Christ, who died on the cross for our sins, is the way to God, 1 Tim 2:5-6; 1 Pet 3:18	(c) God: Is merciful—therefore doesn't want to punish; Is just—therefore must punish sin. (d) Jesus Christ: Who He is, John 1:1, 14; What He did, Isa 53:6, 10, 4, (John 14:2), Rom 6:23	(3) Only through Jesus Christ can we have a personal relationship with God, John 14:6; 1 Pet 3:18; 1 Cor 15:3-6 (continue bridge illustration)	A . . . stands for Atonement, John 3:16; Rom 5:1; John 1:14; Heb 4:15; Rom 5:8; 1 Pet 3:18; 2:24; 2 Cor 5:21; Acts 17:31 (uses substitutionary diagram)	[Comfort emphasizes the sufficient salvation found in Christ alone without giving a list of verses on the cross]	. . . Following Adam's rebellion, God prophesied the plan of salvation . . . cross has four meanings: result of sin; extent of God's love; value of each man; the cost of reconciliation.
(4) We Must Individually Receive Jesus Christ as Savior and Lord; Then We Can Know and Experience God's Love and Plan for Our Lives: John 1:12; Eph 2:8-9; Rev 3:20	(5) . . . Only those who personally receive Jesus Christ into their lives, trusting Him to forgive their sins, can cross this bridge, John 1:12; 6). Every-one must decide individually whether to receive Christ, Rev 3:20; John 14:14	(e) Faith: [1] What it is not—mere intellectual assent nor temporal faith, Eph 2:8; [2] What it is—"trusting in Jesus Christ alone for our salvation"	(4) You must personally respond by trusting Jesus Christ as Savior and Lord, Eph 2:8-9; Acts 3:19; John 1:12	C . . . Stands for Conversion, John 14:6; Acts 4:12; Acts 17:30; Luke 3:3; John 14:15; Rom 6:23; Eph 2:8-9; John 1:12; Rom 10:9, 13; Acts 16:31; Rom 1:16	[Comfort provides 101 memory passages which include a number of verses on repentance and confession]	The two conditions for regeneration are repentance and faith. Repentance and faith are one in the same as they are manifested simultaneously. The other condition is faith.
You can receive Christ right now through prayer [sample prayer] Does this prayer express the desire of your heart? If it does . . .	n/a	n/a	Where would you place yourself in this illustration? (using three stages in bridge illustration)	E . . . stands for Eternal Life, John 5:24; 1 John 5:12; 2 Cor 5:17; John 10:10; 16:33; 14:27; Rom 8:35, 37-38; 1 Thess 4:16-17; . . . ; Are you ready? Go to God in prayer.	Romans 10:9-10, etc.	When we realize our sins and repent, thereby accepting Jesus Christ as Savior.

30. Comparing Gospel Presentations (continued)

	Erasmus's Philosophical	Luther's Three Points	Pascal's Philosophical	Spurgeon's "Ark of Safety"	Navigator's *Topical Memory*	Roman Road
Date	**1503**	**1522**	**1653**	**1880s**	**1940s**	**1960s**
Assurance		But there is a third point. . . Jesus Christ, who showed us his love by his deeds. Without this love, the faith is a cold speculation and without any usefulness, 1 Cor 13:1; fourthly, continued Luther, we have need of patience. There must be persecutions.	Her reason assisted with the lights of graces shows her that there is nothing more lovable than God and that he can be taken only from those who reject him, because to desire him is to possess him, and to refuse him is to lose him.	And as surely, sinner, as thou canst put thy trust in Christ, thou art safe. He that believeth shall be saved, be his sins ever so many; he that believeth not shall be damned, be his sins ever so few, and his virtues ever so many. Trust in Jesus now, Jesus only.	n/a	Results: God tells us the results of salvation, Rom 5:1; 8:1. Assurance: God gives the saved sinner assurance, Rom 8:16.
Evaluation	Erasmus' work, which was used to evangelize the French Protestants, shows a complete syncretism with Platonic or stoic philosophy. Even today, gospel presentations syncretize with modern or ancient philosophers.	Interesting that Luther had (1) fundamental points of the gospel, (2) that they dealt with sin and salvation by faith alone, and (3) used verses of Scripture as texts to prove his points.	Pascal exemplifies the efforts of monks and nuns around the world; for Pascal, he mentioned neither the Word of God, nor the person of Christ, nor the cross; the supplicant is left without any hope outside his own efforts to respond to the light within.	An excellent tract on the blood atonement that includes a sinner's prayer	A simple arrangement of the simple gospel; emphasis is definitely on individual sin and an individual salvation.	A good arrangement of the simple gospel with an emphasis on verses found only in Romans; helpful as a memory tool; verses in other Bible books are helpful to buttress points.

30. Comparing Gospel Presentations (continued)

CCC's *Four Spiritual Laws*	Navigator's *Bridge to Life*	Evangelism Explosion	*Your Most Important Relationship*	SBTS' *GRACE*	Cameron and Comfort	Cho's Fivefold Gospel
1965	**1969**	**1977**	**1985**	**2003**	**2004**	**2005**
How do you know that Christ is in your life? Rev 3:20. The Bible promises eternal life to all who receive Christ, 1 John 5:11-13; Heb 13:5.	If you have invited Jesus Christ into your life, the Bible says that you now have eternal life, 1 John 5:11-12.	n/a	(5) Your trust in Jesus Christ begins a lifelong relationship: God commits Himself to you, John 14:20; Heb 13:5; Col 2:13-14; 1 John 5:13; Gal 5:25; You commit yourself to God, Col 2:6-7.	1 John 5:12-13; Living daily in God's grace, 2 Cor 5:15: Prayer; Worship; Bible study; Fellowship; Service; Witnessing	n/a	. . . What results from our repentance? The counselor Holy Spirit comes into us (Rom 8:11). We are freed from the law of sin and death (Rom 8:1-2). We receive the right to become children of God (John 1:12). We shall enjoy the great blessings God has prepared (3 John 1:2).
A certain emphasis on man's side of salvation, especially as regards the present life; weaker on sin as rebellion and the need for repentance; uses the Bridge illustration; portion between God and man is a vacuum and not sin itself.	Emphasis on the reconciliation model and the need for individual decision; weaker on sin as rebellion and the need for repentance; the Bridge illustration became commonplace in most gospel tracts following this model.	More of an intellectual presentation of the gospel; helpful theological explanations and illustrations; also provided a whole church organizational strategy.	A strong emphasis on a relational gospel, i.e., reconciliation model of the atonement; weak on the forensic elements of salvation (sin as rebellion, the cross as substitution).	GRACE marks a return to the substitutionary emphasis: sin as rebellion and man's need for repentance; uses vertical bridge illustration with sin as the barrier; GRACE provides a helpful mnemonic device.	Cameron and Comfort have an excellent method of bringing persons to see their sin; they do not seem to emphasize or explain the cross, and they do react against a sinner's prayer.	This gospel presentation leans toward a reconciliation model of the atonement; the addition of the other four "Gospels" does not seem to follow Luke 24:46-47; salvation seems a mere preparation for the other four "Gospels."

31. Comparing Follow-Up Tools

	Follow-Up Program	Paul's Spiritual Growth in Acts 9:18-25	R. A. Torrey, *How to Bring Men to Christ* (1910)	*Navigator Wheel* (1957)	Navigators, *Lessons in Assurance* (1957)	Ralph Neighbour, Jr., *Survival Kit* (1979)
1	Gospel/ Assurance of Salvation	(1–2) Blindness removed; regained sight, v. 18			(1) Assurance of salvation, 1 John 5:11-12	(6–7) Aspects of Salvation: Beginning, Completion, Daily Process
2	Public Profession of Christ: Baptism	(3) Was baptized, v. 18	(2) Be baptized and partake regularly of the Lord's Supper			
3	Public Confession of Christ: Evangelism	(6) Began to evangelize, v. 20 (sign of true disciple, Luke 12:8-9)	(1) Confess Christ with the mouth before men at every opportunity	(6) Witnessing		(10–11) Five and Five Principle: Five by Prayer; Five by Witnessing
4	Consequence of Evangelism: Persecution	(9) Organized persecution, v. 23				
5	Consequence of Salvation: Christ			(1) Christ the center		(1) The Indwelling Christ
6	Consequence of Salvation: Sins forgiven	(4) Broke his fast, gained strength, v. 19	(8) When you fall into sin, don't be discouraged	[spiritual breathing: confession and forgiveness]	(4) Assurance of Forgiveness, 1 John 1:9	
7	Consequence of Salvation: Victory/ Spirit's Infilling		(5) Put out of your life every sin, even the smallest	(2) The Obedient Christian in Action	(3) Assurance of Victory (over sin), 1 Cor 10:13	(4–5) Two Natures: New Nature; Old Nature
8	Spiritual Growth: Bible Study	(8) Grew spiritually, vv. 19-20 (Luke 1:80; 2:40, 52)	(3) Study the Word	(3) The Bible		(8–9) Sources of Authority: Three Inadequate; One True
9	Spiritual Growth: Prayer	[Acts 9:12]	(4) Pray daily, often and in every time of temptation	(4) Prayer	(2) Assurance of Answered Prayer, John 16:24	
10	Spiritual Growth: The Church	(5) With disciples, v 19; (10) Believers protect, v. 25	(6) Seek the society of Christians	(5) Fellowship		(2–3) The Body: Its Life; Its Service
11	Spiritual Growth: Direction	(7) Changed reputation, v. 21	(7) Go to work for Christ		(5) Assurance of Guidance, Prov 3:5-6	

31. Comparing Follow-Up Tools (continued)

	Billy Graham, *Living in Christ* (1980)	**Bill Bright, *Transferable Concepts* (1981)**	**George Patterson (Honduras, 1983)**	**Avery Willis, *MasterLife* (1985)**	**Billie Hanks Jr., *A Call to Joy* (1985)**	**NAMB, *Beginning Steps* (1993)**
1	(1) Knowing Christ	(1) Be sure you are a Christian	(1) Repent and believe, Mark 1:15		(1) The love of God	(1) Assurance of salvation
2			(2) Be baptized, Acts 2:38			(2) Public profession of Christ
3	(4) Witnessing for Christ	(7) Witness in the Spirit. (8) Introduce others to Christ. (9) Help fulfill the Great Commission.	(7) Witness, Matt 28:18-20			(3) Evangelism
4						
5	(2) Growing in Christ			(1) Disciple's Cross	(2) Learning to walk (3) Example	
6		(2) Experience God's love and forgiveness.				
7	(3) Obeying Christ (*My Heart Christ's Home*)	(3) Be filled with the Spirit.		(2) Personal Spiritual Inventory	(4) Secret of godliness (5) Living in victory	
8				(3) How to Have a Quiet Time		(4) Bible study
9		(6) How to pray	(5) Pray, John 16:24	(4) Use the Daily Master Communication Guide		(5) Prayer
10			(3) Love; (4) Lord's Supper; (6) Give			(6) The church
11		(4) Walk in the Spirit. (5) Love by faith.				(7) Direction

32. Paradigms for Spiritual Growth

32A. Johnston's Spiritual Passions

(Taken from Thomas P. Johnston, *The Mindset of Eternity* [Deerfield, Ill.: Evangelism Unlimited, 1998], 369)

The Spiritual Passions

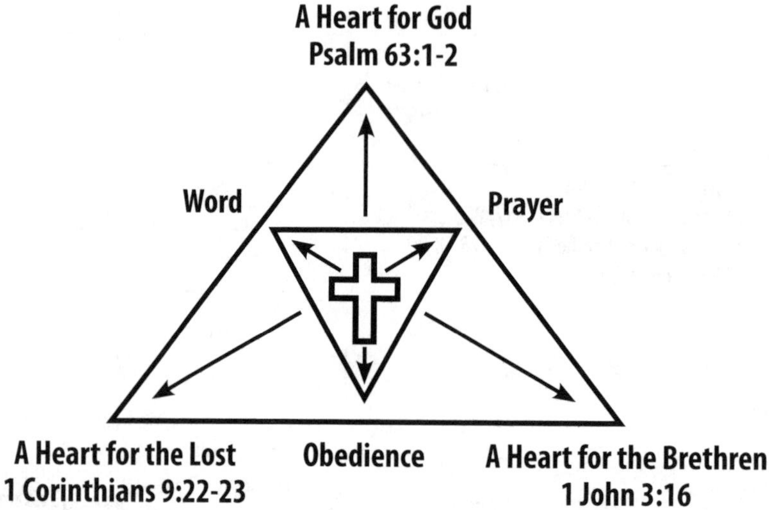

Note that, of the three spiritual passions, "a heart for the lost" is the driving focus of the Great Commission.

32B. The Navigator Wheel

(Taken from *Topical Memory System: Guidebook 1*)

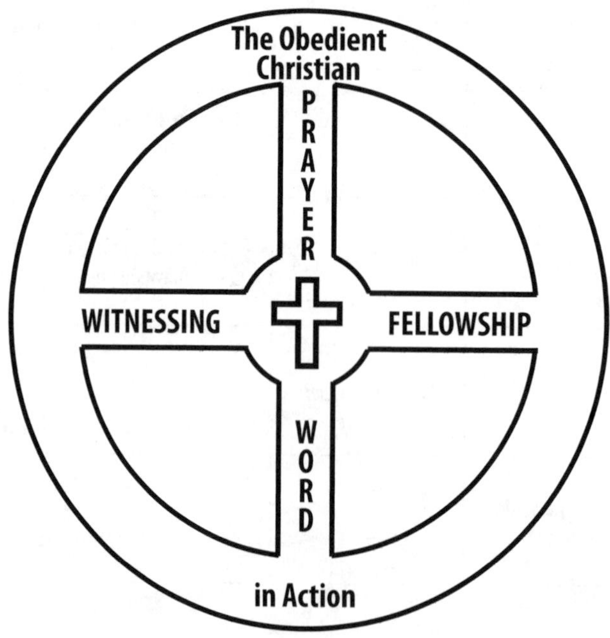

32. Paradigms for Spiritual Growth (continued)

32C. MasterLife's Disciple's Cross

(Adapted from Avery T. Willis, Jr., MasterLife *Day by Day: Personal Devotional* Guide, 3)

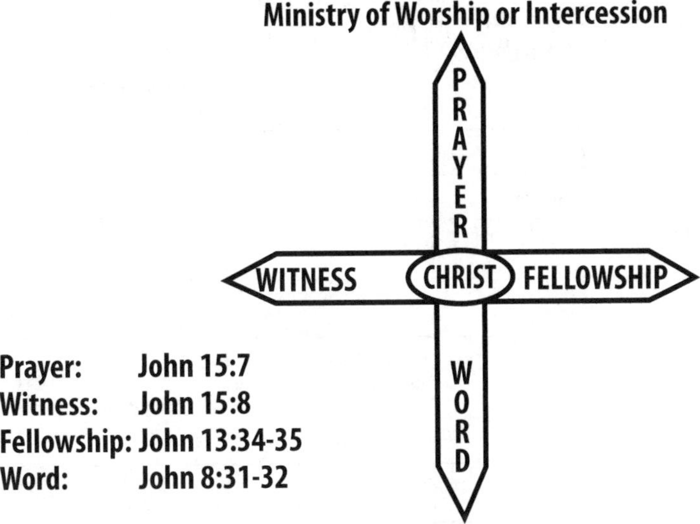

32D. Sonlife Discipleship Process

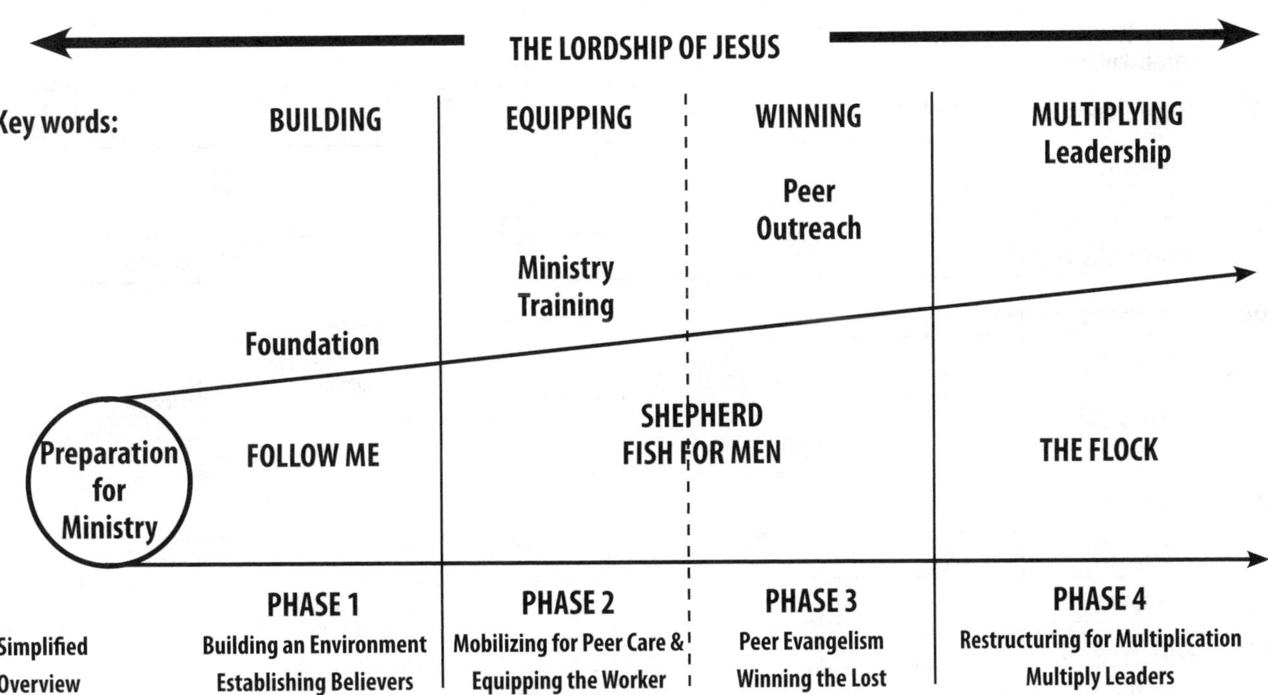

Bill Hull's "Discipleship Process" follows similar phases to that of Sonlife (*The Disciple Making Church*, 249).

33. Comparing Rules, Sacraments, and Disciplines for Christian Living

	Listing	Rule of Benedict (ca. 529)	Seven Mysteries of the Eastern Orthodox Church	Seven Sacraments* of the Roman Catholic Church	Lutheran Sacraments* (1530)	Navigator Wheel (1976)
1	New Birth				[Faith alone; Grace alone]	Assumed
2	Baptism		1. Baptism	1. Baptism	1. Baptism	Assumed
3	Confirmation		2. Chrismation	4. Confirmation		
4	Fellowship					4. Fellowship
5	Discipleship					
6	Penance		4. Penance	2. Penance/ Reconciliation (conversion or confession)	3. Absolution	
7	Prayer					1. Prayer
8	Silence and solitude					
9	Worship					
10	Bible study				[Scriptures alone]	2. Word
11	Scripture meditation					
12	Obedience	3. Obedience [to the abbot]				
13	Journaling					
14	Learning					
15	Evangelism					3. Witnessing
16	Ministry					
17	Eucharist		3. The Eucharist	3. Eucharist (Mass)	2. Lord's Supper (Communion)	
18	Physical exercise					
19	Fasting					
20	Chastity	2. Chastity				
21	Poverty	1. Poverty				
22	Stewardship					
23	Matrimony		6. Marriage	5. Matrimony		
24	Holy orders		5. The priesthood	6. Holy orders		
25	Extreme unction		7. The anointing of the sick	7. Extreme unction/ anointing of the sick		

*Sacraments can be defined as "a formal religious act conferring a specific grace [that which it represents] on those who receive it" (Webster's).

33. Comparing Rules, Sacraments, and Disciplines for Christian Living (continued)

	Coleman's Seven Disciplines (1984)	MasterLife's Disciple's Cross (1985)	Johnston's Three Spiritual Passions (1986)	Whitney's Ten Spiritual Disciplines (1991)	Rick Warren's Five Purposes (2003)	Seven Disciplines of an "Emergent Church" (2006)**
1	Assumed	Assumed	Assumed	Assumed	1. [as first act of] Worship	
2	Assumed	Assumed	Assumed	Assumed	Assumed	
3						
4	1. Fellowship	3. Fellowship			2. Fellowship	7. Fellowship and confession
5			3. Heart for the brethren		3. Discipleship	
6						7. Fellowship and confession
7	2. Personal devotion	1. Prayer	Prayer	2. Prayer		4. Prayer and study
8				8. Silence and solitude		1. Solicitude and silence
9			1. Heart for God	3. Worship	1. Worship	6. Worship and celebration
10	3. Bible study	4. Word	Bible	1. Bible intake		4. Prayer and study
11	4. Scripture meditation					
12			Obedience [to the Word]			5. Service and submission
13				9. Journaling		
14				10. Learning		
15		2. Witness	2. Heart for the lost	4. Evangelism	5. Evangelism	
16	5. Ministry			5. Serving	4. Ministry	3. Secrecy and sacrifice
17						
18	6. Physical exercise					
19	7. Abstinence			7. Fasting		2. Fasting and frugality
20						
21						
22				6. Stewardship		
23						
24						
25						

**Taken from www.watersedge.tv.

34. Terms for the Gospel in Acts

The following terms for the gospel in the book of Acts are clustered for thematic comparison. All the terms refer to the same gospel message, providing us synonyms to understand the parameters of the gospel.

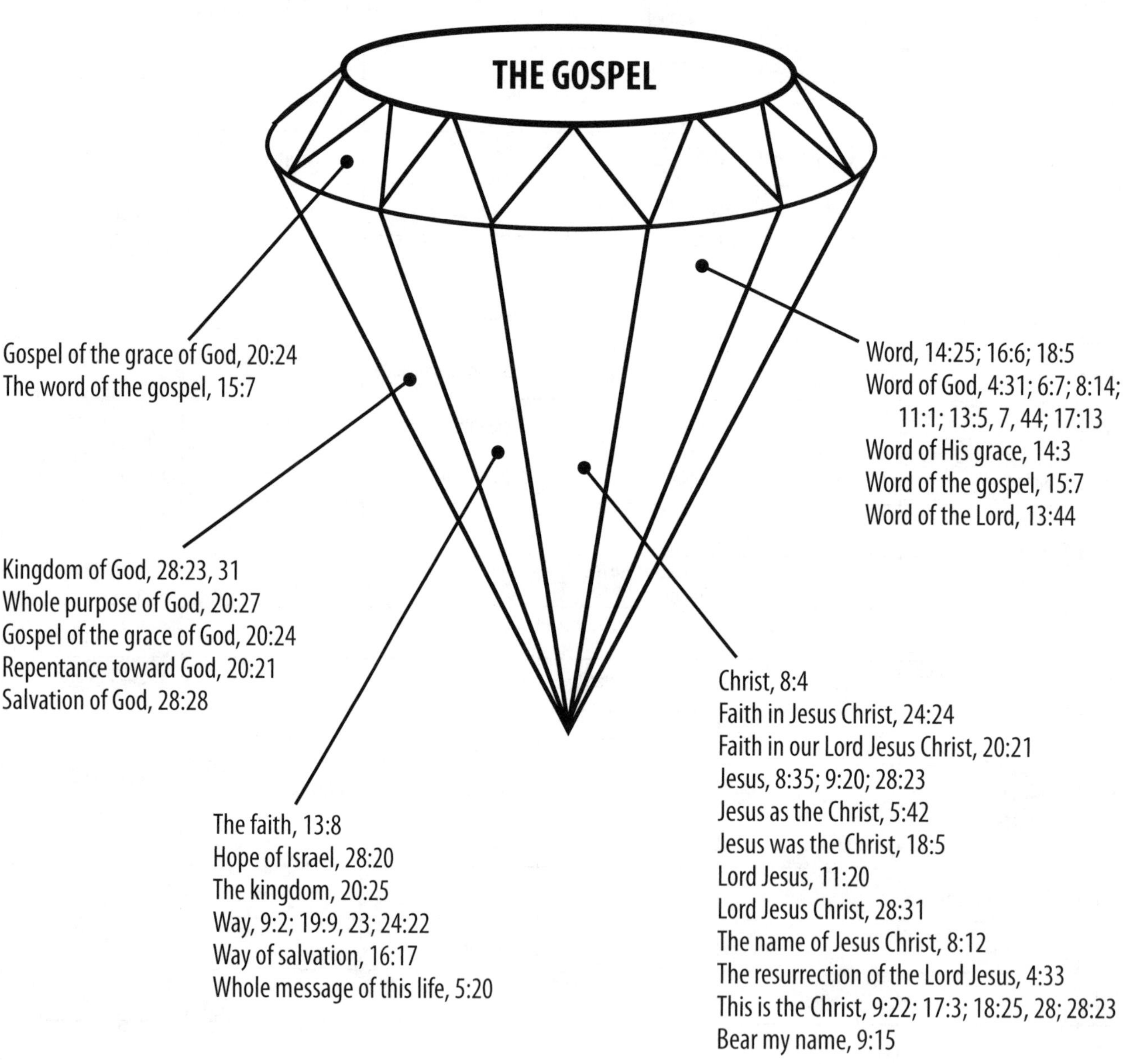

While the verb "evangelize" (*euaggelizō*) is found 15 times in the book of Acts, the noun "gospel" (*euaggelion*) is found only twice. This fact may be surprising, for the English reader will find "gospel" eight times in the book of Acts (NASB)—six of these are due to translating *evangelize* as "preach the gospel."

35. Context of the Gospel in Acts

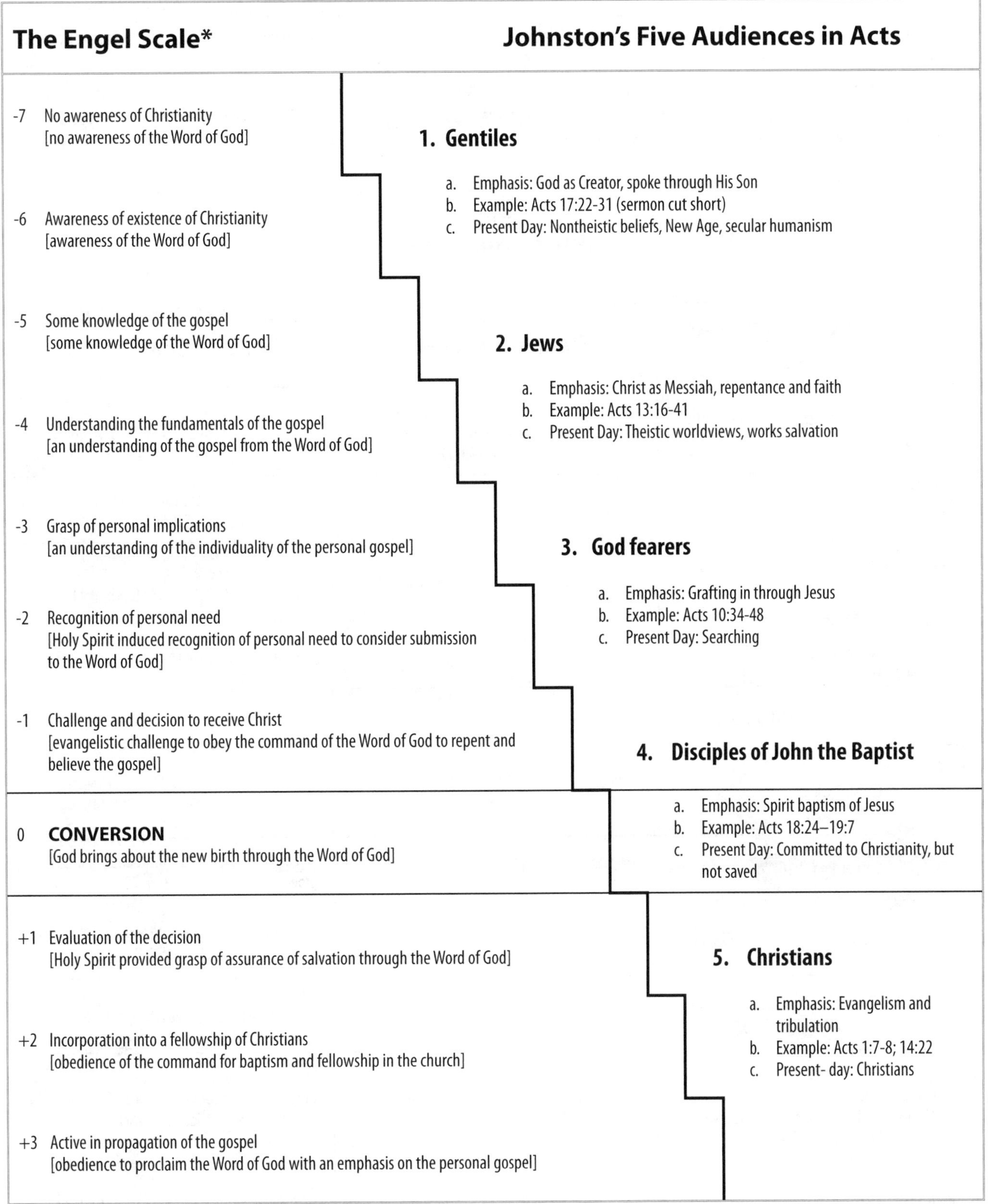

The Engel Scale*	Johnston's Five Audiences in Acts
-7 No awareness of Christianity [no awareness of the Word of God]	**1. Gentiles** a. Emphasis: God as Creator, spoke through His Son b. Example: Acts 17:22-31 (sermon cut short) c. Present Day: Nontheistic beliefs, New Age, secular humanism
-6 Awareness of existence of Christianity [awareness of the Word of God]	
-5 Some knowledge of the gospel [some knowledge of the Word of God]	**2. Jews** a. Emphasis: Christ as Messiah, repentance and faith b. Example: Acts 13:16-41 c. Present Day: Theistic worldviews, works salvation
-4 Understanding the fundamentals of the gospel [an understanding of the gospel from the Word of God]	
-3 Grasp of personal implications [an understanding of the individuality of the personal gospel]	**3. God fearers** a. Emphasis: Grafting in through Jesus b. Example: Acts 10:34-48 c. Present Day: Searching
-2 Recognition of personal need [Holy Spirit induced recognition of personal need to consider submission to the Word of God]	
-1 Challenge and decision to receive Christ [evangelistic challenge to obey the command of the Word of God to repent and believe the gospel]	**4. Disciples of John the Baptist**
0 **CONVERSION** [God brings about the new birth through the Word of God]	a. Emphasis: Spirit baptism of Jesus b. Example: Acts 18:24–19:7 c. Present Day: Committed to Christianity, but not saved
+1 Evaluation of the decision [Holy Spirit provided grasp of assurance of salvation through the Word of God]	**5. Christians** a. Emphasis: Evangelism and tribulation b. Example: Acts 1:7-8; 14:22 c. Present- day: Christians
+2 Incorporation into a fellowship of Christians [obedience of the command for baptism and fellowship in the church]	
+3 Active in propagation of the gospel [obedience to proclaim the Word of God with an emphasis on the personal gospel]	

*Engel Scale from Edward R. Dayton, "To Reach the Unreached" in Ralph D. Winter and Steven C. Hawthorne, eds., *Perspectives on the World Christian Movement: A Reader,* 591. The additions below each line are to provide focus on the role of God and His Word in the salvation process.

36. Select Instrumentalities of Salvation

The following chart seeks to juxtapose some conflicting instrumentalities of salvation. Please note that the historic evangelical instrumentalities are sometimes associated with "God-centered evangelism." One example of this conflict is noted in Chuck Colson's *How Now Shall We Live* (1999):

"It is our contention in this book that the Lord's cultural commission is inseparable from the Great Commission. That may be a jarring statement for many conservative Christians, who, through much of the twentieth century have shunned the notion of reforming culture, associating that concept with the

Historic Evangelical (Proclamational)		
Biblical Instrumentalities of Salvation from God Alone	**Gifts Given by God to the Elect/Redeemed**	**Necessary Proclamation of the Evangelist**
Word, 1 Pet 1:23 (Luther's *sola Scriptura,* Scriptures alone); Luke 24:25; John 6:68-69	Receive the Word, Matt 13:23; Mark 4:20; Luke 8:15; 1 Thess 2:13; by negation, Matt 13:19; Mark 4:15; Luke 8:11-12	Preach the Word, 1 Thess 2:13; 2 Tim 4:2
Law, Gal 3:24		Preach death from the Law, Rom 3:19-20; 10:1-4; Gal 2:16
Through Him forgiveness of sins is proclaimed, Acts 13:38	Repentance unto life, Acts 11:18	Preach repentance for forgiveness of sins, Luke 3:3; 24:47; Acts 2:38; 5:31 (Ezek 33:11)
Blood, 1 Pet 1:18-19		Preach the blood of Christ, Eph 1:7; Heb 9:22
Word of the cross, 1 Cor 1:18		Preach the cross of Christ, 1 Cor 1:17; 2:2; Gal 5:11
Christ, 1 Cor 1:24; 2:2	Recognize Christ, Matt 16:17; by negation, 2 Cor 4:3-4	Preach Christ and Him crucified, John 1:29; 1 John 4:10, 14
Gospel, Rom 1:16-17		Preach the gospel of justification by grace alone through faith alone, Rom 3:27-28; 4:5; 5:1; Gal 2:16
Death and resurrection of Christ, Luke 24:46		Preach the death, burial, and resurrection of Christ, 1 Cor 15:1-8
Grace, Eph 2:8; Titus 3:5 (Luther's *sola gracis,* grace alone)	Receive grace, Eph 2:8; Titus 3:5	Preach God's grace alone, Acts 15:11
A hearing of faith, Gal 1:2, 5; faith alone, Eph 2:8-9 (Luther's *sola fides,* faith alone); Luke 17:3; Acts 13:39, "through Him everyone who believes is freed from all things"	Faith from God, Mark 9:24; Acts 13:48; command to believe, Mark 1:15; John 12:36; 14:1, 11; Acts 16:31	Preach the need for faith, John 3:15-16, 36; 5:24; 6:40, 47; 1 John 5:13; Acts 11:21
Born again, 1 Pet 1:3, 23; Holy Spirit, Titus 3:5	Born of the Holy Spirit, John 3:6-8	Preach: "You must be born again," John 3:7

36. Select Instrumentalities of Salvation (continued)

liberal social gospel. The only task of the church, many fundamentalists and evangelicals believed, is to save as many lost souls as possible from a world literally going to hell. But this explicit denial of a Christian worldview is unbiblical and is the reason we have lost so much of our influence in the world. Salvation does not consist simply of freedom from sin; salvation also means being restored to the task we were given in the beginning—the job of creating culture" (295).

<table>
<tr><th colspan="2">Liberalizing Protestant (Incarnational: 50% divine/50% human)</th><th colspan="2">ROMAN Catholic (Sacramental-Incarnational)</th></tr>
<tr><td>Additional Instrumentalities of Salvation Provided by Men*</td><td>Necessary Evangelistic Efforts of Christians</td><td>Instrumentalities of Salvation Available Only through the Holy Roman Catholic Church</td><td>Necessary Evangelistic Efforts</td></tr>
<tr><td>Apologetics, 1 Pet 3:15</td><td>Apologetic evangelism; using the wisdom of man to defend the gospel, the resurrection, or the authority of the Bible (1 Cor 1:17-25)</td><td>Baptism, Mark 16:16; Acts 2:38; 1 Pet 3:21</td><td>Get people baptized (although the Trinitarian baptism of non-Catholics is accepted as salvific through the Catholic Church)</td></tr>
<tr><td>Love, John 13:34-35</td><td>Show love to all people (lifestyle, friendship, and service)</td><td rowspan="2">Sacrifice of the Mass or Eucharist, John 6:53-56; 1 Cor 11:26 (Leo XIII's Apostolicae Curae [1896] declared ordinations of Anglican Rite "invalid and void")</td><td rowspan="2">Teach people absolute necessity for and role of the Eucharist in salvation</td></tr>
<tr><td>Unity, John 17:21, 23</td><td>Work for unity among all churches (ecumenical movement)</td></tr>
<tr><td>Lifestyle, 1 Thess 1:5</td><td>Lifestyle evangelism</td><td>Confession and absolution, Gal 6:2; James 5:16</td><td>Teach people necessity of going to confession for absolution of sins</td></tr>
<tr><td>Good deeds, Matt 5:16; 1 Pet 2:12</td><td>Servant evangelism</td><td rowspan="2">Mary's role in the order of salvation as "Advocate, Auxiliatrix, Adjutrix and Mediatrix" . . . "the spiritual mother of all humanity and the advocate of grace" (John Paul II, Redemptoris Mater, 25 March 1987); Luke 1:28, 42</td><td rowspan="2">Teach the centrality and importance of Mary's continuing role in the salvation of all humanity</td></tr>
<tr><td>Providing physical and/or social assistance, Matt 25:34-46</td><td>Social action (feeding, clothing, housing, educating); political action (improving the lot of the poor or neglected)</td></tr>
<tr><td>Socio-political transformation, "Let My people go," Exod 5:1; 7:16; 8:1,8,20; 9:1,13; 10:3</td><td>Social action (feeding, clothing, housing, educating); political action (improving the lot of the poor or neglected)</td><td>Other distinctive theology: remaining sacraments, additional mediators, cardinal and venial sins, purgatory, submission to petrine succession and authority, etc.</td><td>Teach other distinctive theological dogmas as necessary for salvation</td></tr>
</table>

*Let the reader understand the context of including these aspects of Christianity as necessary instruments for the salvation of another person.

37. A Verbal Order of Salvation

Order of Decrees			General Revelation			Seeming Human Preparation	Additions—as Preparations for the Gospel	
							gracia preparatur or gracia prepareans	Prevenient Grace
God	God	God	Verses	God	Man (God)	Man (God)	God	God
Prov 8:22	The LORD possessed me [wisdom] at the beginning of His way, before His works of old	**Supralapsarian:** (1) Election; (2) Creation; (3) Fall; (4) Atonement	Ps 19:1-2; Rom 1:18-21	Nature	[Non-salvific] fear of God [a true understanding of God, but *not* a communication of the message of salvation]	Prayer for the Lost (Matt 5:44; Luke 6:28; Rom 10:1; 2 Thess 3:1-2)	Based on Isa 42:4 and parallels	Perhaps based on 2 Thess 2:6-7
			Rom 1:32	Sin and Hell				
Eph 1:4-5	He chose us in Him before the foundation of the world . . . predestined	**Infralapsarian:** (1) Creation; (2) Fall; (3) Election; (4) Atonement	Rom 2:14-15	Law of God; Conscience				
1 Pet 1:20 (Acts 2:23-24)	For He was foreknown before the foundation of the world		Ps 149:6-9; Ezek 25:5, 7, 11, 17; 26:6	God's Judgments				
Rev 13:8	. . . Whose name has not been written from the foundation of the world in the book of life	**Sublapsarian:** (1) Creation; (2) Fall; (3) Atonement; (4) Election	Job 33:15-18, 19-22	Dreams; Sickness and Pain				
			Prov 8, 9	Wisdom and Folly Are Constantly Calling Out				

Consider the order of these words: "But the word is very near you, in your mouth and in your heart, that you may observe it" (Deut 30:14)

37. A Verbal Order of Salvation (continued)

Additions—as Preparations for the Gospel		Hearing of the Word (Acts 15:7-9)				Confirmation of the Word		Addition Prior to Salvation
Signs or Miracles	Love, Unity, or Good Works	Necessary Evangelizing						Extended Time of Sorrow
Man (God)	Man (God)	Man (God)	Matt 7:13-14	God	God	God (Man)	Man (God)	Man (God)
Based on a shallow reading of the miracles in the Gospels and the book of Acts (cf. Mark 16:20)	Based on a shallow understanding of the witness to the world through Christian love (John 13:34-35), unity (John 17:21), or good works (Matt 5:16; 1 Pet 2:12)	Outward Word (Rom 10:14-15, 17) [Evangelism: speaking the gospel]	Wide Road	Natural Hearing (1 Cor 2:14)	Hardness of Heart	Based on the miracles in the Gospels and the book of Acts (Mark 16:20)	Based on the witness to the world through Christian love (John 13:34-35), unity (John 17:21), good works (Matt 5:16; 1 Pet 2:12), or rational arguments (1 Pet 3:15)	
					Non-salvific Fear of God			
					Fear of Judgment			
					Temporary			
			Narrow Road	Hearing of Faith (Rom 10:17; Gal 3:1-5; John 5:24; Acts 15:7; Eph 1:13)	[Salvific] Fear of God leading to a contrite heart (Ps 51:17 et al.)			Acts 9:9, 11, 19

37. A Verbal Order of Salvation (continued)

Repentance and Faith				Baptism (as addition)	Regeneration		Verbal Confession		Warning
				Prerequisite of Baptism			To God		
Verses	Man (God)	Man (God)	Man (God)	Man	God	God	Man (God)		Man (God)
John 1:10-11	Did not know him	Did not receive him		No believer's baptism = no salvation			Would not believe, Acts 28:24	Blasphemy and contradiction, Luke 5:21; Acts 13:45	[shake the dust off feet and say], Luke 10:10-11; Acts 13:51
Rom 9:32	Not by faith but by works	Stumbled over the stone							
Rom 10:3	Establishing their own righteousness	Not subject to God's righteousness							
1 Pet 2:7	Reject	Disbelieve					Many will say to Me on that day, "Lord, Lord," Matt 7:22	Deny before men, Luke 12:9 (Matt 10:33)	
1 Pet 2:8		Disobedient to the Word							Verbal warning, Acts 13:46-47
1 Cor 14:21		Would not listen (1 John 4:5)							
Mark 1:15	Repent	Believe		Based on a misreading of Mark 16:16; Acts 2:38, et al., baptism is deemed a necessary part of salvation				Matt 10:32; Luke 12:8	
Acts 2:38	Repent		Be baptized		Received the Holy Spirit				
Acts 15:7-9		Believed			Received Holy Spirit	Hearts cleansed	By faith		
Acts 20:21	Repentance toward God	Faith in our Lord Jesus Christ							
Rom 10:9-10		Believe in your heart/heart believes					With the mouth he confesses		
Rom 10:13							Calls on the name of the Lord		

The hearing of faith, regeneration, faith, conversion, verbal confession, salvation, and justification appear to be simultaneous as a part of instantaneous conversion. Love, unity, good works, or rational arguments are not necessary *preparatio evangelica* (preparations for the gospel) nor necessary confirmations of the gospel (Matt 13:58; Mark 6:6). The gospel is self-authenticating.

37. A Verbal Order of Salvation (continued)

Additions to Justification		Salvation/ Justification	Confirmations of Salvation		Addition to Sanctification	Sanctification			Addition Following Sanctification
Circumcision	Penance or Sacraments		Deeds	Words	Speaking in Tongues				Entire Sanctification
Man	Man	God	Man	Man	Man (God)	Verses	God	Man	God (Man)
		Practicing evil (Gal 5:21)	Matt 7:22-23	Matt 15:18-20; Mark 7:20		Rom 10:3		Seeking to establish their own . . . righteousness	
		Appointed doom (1 Pet 2:8)	1 Cor 6:9-10; Gal 5:19-21	Luke 19:22		John 3:20		Everyone who does evil hates the Light . . . his deeds will be exposed	
		Hardened (Rom 11:7)	Col 3:6-7	Matt 12:36					
The book of Galatians warns against Judaizing Christians, who wanted to force Gentiles believers to be circumcised, Gal 6:12-13.	Some require confession to be shared with a priest for penance and forgiveness to be granted; a misreading of James 5:16, etc.		Fruit of repentance, Matt 3:8; Luke 3:8	Catching men, Matt 4:19; Mark 1:17; Luke 5:10; Fruit that remains, John 4:36; 15:8,16	Speaking in tongues as the sign gift for receiving the Holy Spirit is often based upon the descriptive accounts in Acts and 1 Cor 14:18.	1 Cor 15:10	By the grace of God I am what I am; . . . not I, but the grace of God	His grace . . . not prove vain; but I labored even more than all of them	Entire sanctification is based on misinterpretation of verses such as Matt 5:48, etc.
		Shall be saved/ righteousness/ salvation				Phil 2:12-13	For . . . God . . . is at work in you, both to will and to work for *His* good pleasure	Work out your salvation with fear and trembling	
		Shall be saved				John 3:21	As having been wrought in God	That his deeds may be manifested	

Verses on hearing and not believing: Luke 8:12 (Mark 4:15); hearing and not understanding: Matt 13:13, 19; hearing and not acting: Matt 7:26-27 (Luke 6:49); on hearing and believing for a while: Luke 8:13; hears, receives with joy, is only temporary, Matt 13:20-21; Mark 4:16-17; on hearing and believing: John 5:24; Acts 4:4; 13:48; 15:7; 18:8; Rom 10:14; Eph 1:13 (John 4:42; 11:42); hearing and acting: Matt 7:24-25; Luke 6:47; on a verbal confession: (1) regarding the need to come to the Lord with words, Hosea 14:2-3; Heb 13:15; (2) regarding honoring God with the lips, and not with the heart, Isaiah 29:13 (Matt 15:8-9; Mark 7:6-7).

38. Preaching the Whole Counsel of God: Old Testament

"Positive and Encouraging Christianity" begs the question: what is negative or discouraging Christianity? It may be that certain aspects of Christianity that may be considered negative are not discussed. It seems that God's admonition to Jeremiah, "Do not omit a word" (Jer 26:2), also applies to all messengers of the gospel (1 Pet 4:11).

Interestingly, when Satan tempted Jesus, he used a positive apodosis from Psalm 91:11-12 about God sending His angels to guard His people. Jesus responded with a negative protasis (command) from Deuteronomy 6:16, which referred to a time when Israel questioned God's provision (positive apodosis) at Massah or Meribah (Exod 17:1-7). It was this sin that indicated a hardness of heart, which led God to abhor

The Four Quadrants	Protasis	Apodasis
Positive	**IX. Q1** **PROMISE** **Positive Condition:** Deut 28:1: "Now it shall be, if you diligently obey the Lord your God, being careful to do all His commandments which I command you today..." Jos 1:8: "This book of the law shall not depart from your mouth, but you shall meditate on it day and night..." Jer 17:7: "Blessed is the man who trusts in the Lord and whose trust is the Lord..."	**X. Q2** **BLESSING** **Positive Result:** Deut 28:1-6: "...the Lord your God will set you high above all the nations of the earth. All these blessings will come upon you and overtake you if you obey the LORD your God: Blessed *shall* you *be* in the city, and blessed *shall* you *be* in the country. Blessed *shall be* the offspring of your body and the produce of your ground... Blessed *shall be* your basket and your kneading bowl. Blessed *shall* you *be* when you come in, and blessed *shall* you *be* when you go out." [vv. 7-14 expand on these blessings] Jos 1:8: "...so that you may be careful to do according to all that is written in it; for then you will make your way prosperous, and then you will have success." Jer 17:8-9: "...for he will be like a tree planted by the water, that extends its roots by a stream..."
Negative	**XI. Q3** **WARNING** **Negative Condition:** Deut 28:15: "But it shall come about, if you do not obey the LORD your God, to observe to do all His commandments and His statutes with which I charge you today, that..." Deut 28:45-48: "So all these curses shall come on you and pursue you and overtake you until you are destroyed, because you would not obey the LORD your God by keeping His commandments and His statutes which He commanded you. They shall become a sign and a wonder on you and your descendants forever..." Deut 28:58-59: "If you are not careful to observe all the words of this law which are written in this book... the LORD your God, then the LORD will..." Jer 17:5: "Cursed is the man who trusts in mankind and makes flesh his strength, and whose heart turns away from the LORD..."	**XII. Q4** **CURSE** **Negative Result:** Deut 28:15-19: "...all these curses will come upon you and overtake you. Cursed *shall* you *be* in the city, and cursed *shall* you *be* in the country. Cursed *shall be* your basket and your kneading bowl. Cursed *shall be* the offspring of your body ... Cursed *shall* you *be* when you come in, and cursed *shall* you *be* when you go out." [vv. 20-44, 48-62, and 64-68 expand on these curses] Deut 28:63: "It shall come about that as the LORD delighted over you to prosper you, and multiply you, so the LORD will delight over you to make you perish and destroy you; and you will be torn from the land where you are entering to possess it." Jer 17:6: "For he will be like a bush in the desert and will not see when prosperity comes, but will live in stony wastes in the wilderness, a land of salt without inhabitant."

38. Preaching the Whole Counsel of God: New Testament

that generation (Ps 95:8-11; Heb 3:7-4:11). Perhaps similarly is preaching a belief in Jesus without repentance for sin. Jesus included both repentance and faith in His preaching (Mark 1:14-15). Likewise, it would seem that sometimes false teachers are fixated with the positive apodosis (Jer 23:17), thus rendering their message a "tickling the ears" which leads to a "turning away from the truth" (2 Tim 4:3-4; Ezek 33:30-33). The following texts are not exhaustive of this concept but are samples of some protases and apodoses in different contexts of Old and New Testament teaching.

The Four Quadrants	Protasis	Apodasis
Positive	**XIII. Q1** **PROMISE** **Positive Condition** Acts 2:38: "Repent, and each of you be baptized in the name of Jesus Christ" Acts 16:31: "Believe in the Lord Jesus" Luke 6:20-23: "Blessed are you who are poor..." "Blessed are you who hunger now..." "Blessed are you who weep now..." "Blessed are you when men hate you, and ostracize you, and insult you, and scorn your name as evil, for the sake of the Son of Man." 1 Cor 11:28, 31: "But a man must examine himself ... But if we judged ourselves rightly..." Rev 21:7: "He who overcomes..."	**XIV. Q2** **BLESSING** **Positive Result** Acts 2:38: "for the forgiveness of your sins; and you will receive the gift of the Holy Spirit." Acts 16:31: "and you will be saved, you and your household." Luke 6:20-23: "...for yours is the kingdom of God." "...for you shall be satisfied." "...for you shall laugh." "Be glad in that day, and leap for joy, for behold, your reward is great in heaven, for in the same way their fathers used to treat the prophets." 1 Cor 11:28, 31: "...and in so doing he is to eat of the bread and drink of the cup. ... we should not be judged." Rev 21:7: "...will inherit these things, and I will be his God and he will be My son."
Negative	**XV. Q3** **WARNING** **Negative Condition** Luke 6:24-26: "But woe to you who are rich..." "Woe to you who are well-fed now..." "Woe to you who laugh now..." "Woe to you when all men speak well of you..." 1 Cor 11:27: "Therefore whoever eats the bread or drinks the cup ... in an unworthy manner..." 1 Cor 11:29: "For he who eats and drinks ... if he does not judge the body rightly." 1 Cor 11:32: "... But when we are judged..." Rev 21:8: "But for the cowardly and unbelieving and abominable and murderers and immoral persons and sorcerers and idolaters and all liars..."	**XVI. Q1** **CURSE** **Negative Result** Luke 6:24-26: "...for you are receiving your comfort in full." "...for you shall be hungry." "...for you shall mourn and weep." "...for their fathers used to treat the false prophets in the same way." 1 Cor 11:28: "...shall be guilty of the body and blood of the Lord." 1 Cor 11:29: "...eats and drinks judgment to himself..." 1 Cor 11:30-32: "For this reason many among you are weak and sick, and a number sleep. ... We are disciplined by the Lord in order that we may not be condemned along with the world." Rev 21:8: "...their part will be in the lake that burns with fire and brimstone, which is the second death."

39. Hearing and Believing Selections in the New Testament

OT passages bring to light the continuity of hearing and believing into the New Testament.

	Passage	Recipient	Speaking	Hearing	Message	Response	Result
[1]	Gen 15:4, 6	{} Then [Abraham]		{Then behold, the [] came to him, saying, . . .}	[word of the LORD]	believed	. . . and He reckoned it to him as righteousness
[2]	Deut 32:1-2	Give ear, O heavens, [] let the earth	[and let me speak; and]	hear	the words of my mouth. Let my teaching. . . My speech. . .		. . . drop as the rain, . . . distill as the dew, as the droplets on the fresh grass and as the showers on the herb
[3]	Deut 30:14	you		is very near	But the word	in your mouth and in your heart	that you may observe it
[4]	Deut 32:47	for you			For it is not an idle word		indeed it is your life
[5]	Ps 19:7				The Law of the LORD is perfect,		restoring [*or converting*] the soul
1	Matt 7:24 (Luke 6:47)	Everyone		who hears	these words of Mine	and acts on them,	may be compared to a wise man who built his house on the rock
2	Matt 7:26 (Luke 6:49)	Everyone		who hears	these words of Mine	and does not act on them,	will be like a foolish man who built his house on the sand
3	Matt 13:23 (Mark 4:20; Luke 8:15)	And the one on whom seed was sown on the good soil, this is the man		who hears	the word	and understands it;	who indeed bears fruit and brings forth, some a hundredfold, some sixty, and some thirty

39. Hearing and Believing Selections in the New Testament (continued)

	Passage	Recipient	Speaking	Hearing	Message	Response	Result
4	John 4:39	From that city many of the Samaritans []	because of the word of the woman		who testified, "He told me all the things that I have done"	[believed in Him]	
5	John 4:41	Many more []		because of	His word	[believed]	
6	John 4:42	And they were saying to the woman,	"It is no longer because of what you said []	for we have heard for ourselves and		[that we believe,] . . . know that this One is indeed the Savior of the world"	
7	John 5:24	Truly, truly, I say to you, he		who hears	My word,	and believes Him who sent Me,	has eternal life, and does not come into judgment, but has passed out of death into life.
8	John 6:68-69	[We]	To whom shall we go? You have		words of {} <You are the Holy One of God>	[] have believed and have come to know that <>	{eternal Life}
9	John 17:20	I do not ask on behalf of these alone, but for those also	through their word			[who believe in Me]	
10	Acts 4:4			But many of those	who had heard the message	believed;	and the number of men came to be about five thousand
11	Acts 11:14	[To Cornelius]	He [Peter] will speak words to you				by which you will be saved, you and all your household

*The verbal form, *pisteuōn*, meaning "[he] who believes" is found 15 times in the book of John.

39. Hearing and Believing Selections in the New Testament (continued)

	Passage	Recipient	Speaking	Hearing	Message	Response	Result
12	Acts 13:48	When the Gentiles		heard	this [the statement of Paul],	they *began* rejoicing and glorifying the word of the Lord;	and as many as had been appointed to eternal life believed.
13	Acts 15:7-9	[] the Gentiles	[that by my mouth]	would hear	the word of the gospel	and believe . . .	giving them the Holy Spirit . . . cleansing their hearts by faith
14	Acts 16:14	woman named Lydia. . .	[spoken by Paul . . .]	was listening . . .	to the things []	and the Lord opened her heart to respond	
15	Acts 17:11-12	Now these were more noble-minded than those in Thessalonica		for they received [] with great eagerness, examining {} daily *to see* whether these things were so.	[the word] {the Scriptures}	. . . many of them believed, along with a number of prominent Greek women and men	
16	Acts 18:8	Crispus, the leader of the synagogue, [], and many of the Corinthians		when they heard		[believed in the Lord with all his household] . . . were believing	and being baptized
17	Acts 18:9-10	And the Lord said to Paul in the night by a vision,	"Do not be afraid *any longer,* but go on speaking and do not be silent			. . . for I have many people in this city"	
18	Acts 28:24	Some []	by the things spoken,			[were being persuaded] but others would not believe	

39. Hearing and Believing Selections in the New Testament (continued)

	Passage	Recipient	Speaking	Hearing	Message	Response	Result
19	Rom 10:14	How will they	{without a preacher?}	[whom they have not heard? And how will they hear]		believe in Him [] {}	
20	Rom 10:17			[from hearing, and hearing	by the word of Christ]		So faith *comes*
21	Eph 1:13	[you also]		In Him, [], after listening to	the message of truth, the gospel of your salvation—	having also believed,	you were sealed in Him with the Holy Spirit of promise
22	1 Thess 2:13	For this reason we also constantly thank God that when you	received the word of God	which you heard from us, []	not *as* the word of men, but *for* what it really is, the word of God,	[you accepted *it*]	which also performs its work in you who believe.
23	1 Thess 2:16	[to the Gentiles]	hindering us from speaking []			so that they may be saved	
24	Heb 4:2	For indeed we [], just as they also; ()	[have had {} preached to us]	they heard <>	{good news} (but the word)	because it was not united by faith in those who heard	<did not profit them>
25	1 Pet 1:23, 25		[] {} And this is the word which was preached to you		{not of seed which is perishable but imperishable, *that is*, through the living and enduring word of God.}		[for you have been born again]

Other verses attest that the verbally communicated Word of God was the focal evangelistic and soteriological commonality, Acts 4:18, 29, 31; 5:40; 8:14, 25; 9:27-28; 11:1; 13:5, 7, 44, 46; 14:1, 25; 15:35-36; 16:6, 32; 17:13; 18:11; 19:10 (Acts 28:31).

Other NT verses, such as 2 Timothy 3:16-17; Hebrews 4:12-13; 2 Peter 1:20-21, also speak to the inspiration, power, and authority of the Word of God, but do not mention faith or a response (2 Tim 3:15 does speak of "through faith").

40. Guide to Methodology Charts

This chart provides the overview of the 122 evangelism methods in the following 17 charts (41–57).

<table>
<tr><th></th><th colspan="9">Formal Evangelism</th><th colspan="8">Informal Evangelism</th></tr>
<tr><th>CHARTS 41-57</th><th>41. Preaching Evangelism</th><th>42. Worship Evangelism</th><th>43. Historic and State Church Evangelism</th><th>44. Presence Evangelism</th><th>45. Event Evangelism I</th><th>46. Event Evangelism II</th><th>47. Evangelism through Small Groups</th><th>48. Crusade Evangelism</th><th>49. Media Evangelism I</th><th>50. Media Evangelism II</th><th>51. Ministry-Based Evangelism</th><th>52. Prayer and Relational Evangelism</th><th>53. Contextual Evangelism</th><th>54. Apologetic Evangelism</th><th>55. Visitation Evangelism</th><th>56. Initiative Evangelism</th><th>57. New Testament Evangelism</th></tr>
<tr><td rowspan="2">Possible Greek Parallel Terms</td><td colspan="2" rowspan="2">kērussō</td><td colspan="2" rowspan="2">apologeō</td><td colspan="3" rowspan="2">martureō
koinōneō</td><td colspan="3" rowspan="2">euaggelizō
exaggellō
kataggellō
kērussō</td><td colspan="2" rowspan="2">martureō
koinōneō</td><td colspan="2">legō
didaskō
dialegomai</td><td colspan="3">laleō
euaggelizō</td></tr>
<tr><td colspan="5">kataggellō
diakatelegchomai
parrēsiazomai</td></tr>
<tr><td>Primary Emphasis</td><td colspan="7">Primarily Inside the Church</td><td colspan="10">Primarily Outside the Church</td></tr>
<tr><td>Audience</td><td colspan="12">Group Orientation</td><td colspan="5">Individual Orientation</td></tr>
<tr><td rowspan="2">Regularity</td><td colspan="4">Regular Recurring Items</td><td colspan="10">Special Events or Programs</td><td colspan="3">Regular Programs or Methods</td></tr>
<tr><td colspan="4">Regular Events</td><td colspan="3">Bridge Events</td><td colspan="4">Broad-Based Events</td><td colspan="6">Individual Events</td></tr>
</table>

41. Preaching Evangelism

The following stratifications of gospel preaching introduce the variety of views and practices involved.

	Stratifications of Gospel Preaching	Focus of Sermon						Content of Sermon				Inclusion of Simple Gospel				Use of Sinner's Prayer				Invitation to Receive Christ			Altar Call		
		Aimed only at elect	Aimed primarily at elect	Aimed primarily at saved	Aimed at saved and lost	Aimed at seekers	Aimed at all persons	Doctrinal sermons primary	Scriptural sermons primary	Topical sermons primary	Relevant topics primary	Rare presentation of simple gospel	Occasional presentation of simple gospel	Always presentation of simple gospel	Never a presentation of simple gospel	No sinner's prayer	Rare sinner's prayer	Occasional sinner's prayer	Always a sinner's prayer	No invitation to receive Christ	Occasional invitation to receive Christ	Always an invitation to receive Christ	No altar call	Occasional altar call	Always an altar call
1	Doctrinally driven	●						●				●				●				●			●		
2	Doctrinally focused		●						●				●			●					●		●		
3	Biblically driven			●					●				●				●				●			●	
4	Gospel focused				●				●					●				●				●		●	
5	Lost soul driven				●				●					●					●			●			●
6	Seeker sensitive				●					●				●					●			●			●
7	Seeker guided					●					●		●					●			●			●	
8	Culturally accommodated						●				●				●	●				●			●		

Some Examples in Church History

France, 1145: "He [Bernard of Clairveaux] preached on the day of St Peter (June 29, 1145), before a crowd whom he brought [agreed] to unanimously repress heresy [of the Albigenses] by raised hands" (Jean Duvernoy, *Le Catharisme: Histoire des Cathares,* 205; translation mine).

France, 1689: "When the sermon was over, the preacher [C. Brousson] asked whether there was any among his hearers wishing to be reconciled to God and His Church, and to re-enter the communion of saints.... Then, any who were so minded came forward and knelt before the preacher, who began to remonstrate with them and showed them how enormous was the sin they had committed in forsaking Christ" (Ruben Saillens, *The Soul of France,* 85–87).

Germany, 1720s: "I must preach that should someone hear me only once before he dies, he will have heard not just a part, but the entire way of salvation and in the proper way for it to take root in his heart" (A. H. Francke [1663–1727], quoted in Paulus Scharpff, *Three Hundred Years of Evangelism*, 46).

U.S., 1934: "If the church you attend does not have an invitation, find another church!" (Mordecai Ham in his revivals, from Vernon William Patterson, interviewed by Robert Schuster, Billy Graham Archives, Wheaton, Ill., 1985).

42. Worship Evangelism

9	10	11	12	13	14	15
Seeker Services	**Worship Evangelism**	**Liturgy as Evangelism**	**Creedal Evangelism**	**Lord's Supper as Evangelism**		**Baptism as Evangelism**
The shaping of the worship service to: (1) introduce persons to Christ, (2) give seekers the opportunity to worship God, and/or (3) allow seekers to experience Christian community	Experiencing true worship as evangelism	Experiencing God in worship; worshiping with the five senses: sight, smell, sound, taste, and touch	Recitation of creeds as true gospel proclamation; therefore leaning toward conversion as intellectual or cultural assent	The Lord's Supper as: (1) increasing grace, (2) providing grace	The Lord's Supper as true gospel proclamation	In many sacramental churches, baptism is regarded as the rite of entrance into the covenant family, and the first experience of grace; in Catholicism baptism is being "born again"
Mark Mittelberg, *Building a Contagious Church;* Jimmy Long, "Converted to Community"	1 Cor 14:23-25; Sally Morgenthaler, *Worship Evangelism,* worship is "more than just using the grey matter" (i.e. listening to sermons)	Robert Webber, *Worship Is a Verb*	High churches are creedal churches, where the recitation of creeds may be considered true evangelism	(1) Lutheran consubstantiation; (2) Roman Catholic transsubstantiation (*ex opere operato*)	1 Cor 11:26	In the Roman Catholic Church, the sacraments operate salvifically by virtue of what they represent (*ex opere operato*)

Food for Thought

Is participation in the Lord's Supper equivalent to telling a lost person about the death and resurrection of Christ, and the need for repentance for the forgiveness of sins?

If participating in the ordinances is salvific, are they therefore not necessarily evangelistic?

Can a person experience God through participating in Communion unworthily (as an unsaved person)?

Is it dangerous to allow unsaved persons to participate in Communion prior to their being born from above?

Can a person experience God through worship without a being born again (experiencing God in Communion)?

Is the reciting or singing of the Bible, prayers, creeds, or other truths a substitute for hearing and responding to the gospel preached (1 Cor 1:17-18)?

Should church and worship be framed primarily for the saved or for the lost?

Why have God's people gathered on the first day of the week? Is worship on Sunday (the Lord's day) a cultural issue? Should a church feel free to worship on Saturday or other days if it deems it helpful for outreach?

What ramifications are there for Christians who need to be fed, if their church is oriented primarily to seekers? Is this scattering and not gathering (Jer 23:1-2)?

43. Historic and State Church Evangelism

16	17	18	19	20	21	22	23
Catechetic Evangelism	**Evangelism through Marriage and Children**	**Pilgrimages as Evangelism**	**Sale of Indulgences as Evangelism**	**Crusades as Evangelism**	**Inquisition as Evangelism**	**"Giving" Providing True Salvation-Evangelism**	**Icons as Evangelism**
Evangelism of children and youth in the church through the mechanism of catechism or Christian education	Restricting mixed marriages to converted, with the vow that children will be reared in that faith	Visiting a physical location to gain a blessing from what the location represents	Purchasing a certificate of indulgence or an item of jewelry to which is given indulgence power	Gaining control of a city or territory as the "work of God"	Defending the faith from heresy using the sword of the state as the work of God	Giving to the Lord [thus his church], true witness to the gospel, with the benefit of forgiveness of sins	In Eastern Orthodox iconography, where holy icons are deemed true evangelism
Schleiermacher's *Brief Outline on the Study of Theology* included evangelism as a part of catechetics (i.e., Christian education)	See "Marriages Between Catholics and Other Christians" (Stransky and Sheerin, *Doing the Truth in Charity* [1982], chap. 7)	Most famous pilgrimage site is Lourdes, France, where healings are said to occur; also in North America at Ste-Anne-de-Beaupré, near Quebec-city	Dominican Tetzel sold indulgences to help build St. Peter's in Rome; this practice is based on verses like Tobit 12:9; on indulgences for the dead, see 2 Maccabees 12:40-45	2nd Lyons Council (1274) called crusades the "work of God"; 4th Lateran Council (1215) called on rulers to "defend the faith" from heretics as in Albi, France (1209–1229)	"Foulques constituted Brother Dominic and his companions preachers . . . to [1] extirpate heresy, [2] combat vice, [3] teach the faith, and [4] train men in good morals"	John 12:1-8; Luke 6:35; 21:5; Acts 4:36-5:2; 10:2, 4; 2 Cor 9:6; see especially Tobit 4:10; 12:9; Sirach 3:3-4, 30; 29:12; 40:17	Holy icons are said to contain a true witness of the gospel

Food for Thought

Martin Luther had his early defining conflicts with practitioners, such as Dominican friar Johann Tetzel who was selling indulgences, the proceeds of which were used to build St. Peter's Basilica in Rome. The issue of indulgences was one of the primary symptoms that caused Luther to voice conflict within the Roman Catholic Church and nail the "95 Theses" on the Wittenberg door in 1517. By the way, Luther's later disputes were not handled by practitioners but by theologians, such as the scholastic Johannes Eck:

- When Luther compared the sale of indulgences (as evangelism) with the evangelism in the book of Acts, did he not readily observe the differences taught in Galatians 1:8-9?
- Is not the sale of indulgences consistent with Catholic soteriology (Ratzinger, *Catechism,* § 1478-79)?
- Has Catholic soteriology changed since the days of Dominican Thomas Aquinas (John Paul II, "Mexico Ever Faithful" *Osservatore Romano* [5 Feb 1979])?
- Has Vatican II, 1993 *Catechism of the Catholic Church,* or the 1994 "Evangelicals and Catholics Together" statement changed Catholic soteriology?

Is the visible church the manifestation of God's kingdom? If so, how does this effect outreach? Should evangelism not then be the development of the organization of the visible church?

Are words such as *church, kingdom, worldview,* and *gospel* interchangeable?

44. Presence Evangelism

24	25	26	27	28	29	30	31
Religious Symbols as Evangelism	**Special Clothing as Evangelism**	**Architecture as Evangelism**	**Nomen-clature as Evangelism**	**Ecumenism as Evangelism**	**Mysterious Evangelism**	**Presence Evangelism**	**Fasting as Evangelism**
Wearing of religious symbols as a silent, outward, but true witness of the gospel	Wearing of unique clothing or uniform as a silent, outward, but true witness of the gospel	Building of elaborate places of worship to exclaim the glory of God, or the grandeur of the religion	Renaming of towns, roads, mountains, rivers, hospitals, and other facilities after religious figures	Based on John 17:21 and 23, "That the world may know," unity is considered a true witness of the gospel	Augustine who heard over a wall, "Pick up and read" (*tole lege*)	(1) Living as salt in a culture as a silent form of evangelization; (2) letting one's presence be felt through real estate	Fasting to be seen by men as evangelism; silent witness of solidarity with the sufferings of (1) Christ or (2) men
A cross, a crucifix, a fish (on a car), a WWJD bracelet	A headdress, uniform, or clerical collar (as priests, monks, nuns, or the Salvation Army)	Some 21st-century mainline Protestants consider architecture as evangelism, as do some church growth persons	The Catholic Church often makes its presence known by giving towns the names of patron saints, such as St. Jude, St. Anne, and Our Lady of ___	Striving for unity as a witness is the World Council of Churches' approach to true and effective evangelism, as well as that of many other unity efforts	Emphasizing God's supernatural calling, without outward evangelism; especially true of those who overemphasize election or predestination	(1) WCC's approach mission as conscientization; (2) sometimes the purchase of real estate can be marketed as evangelism, establishing a presence in a given location	Ash Wednesday in the Roman Catholic calendar, vows of poverty, or similarly to identify with the poor; note the austerity of Dominic

Food for Thought

Will preaching always be "foolishness" to the world, or can the gospel be framed so as not to be a reproach (Christianized Stoicism)?

Is it possible to be such an example, to serve so effectively, or to live such a good life that the gospel will no longer be considered foolishness?

Is it absolutely essential for the gospel to be verbally communicated for salvation?

Does saving faith always necessitate the prior hearing of the gospel?

In what way can real estate be considered evangelism? If it is, does not the gospel consist only or primarily of (1) the grandeur of God and/or (2) the prestige of a given church?

Further Food for Thought

Is it always necessary to share actual portions of Scripture in evangelism?

Can there be salvation outside of actually hearing the very words of the Bible? If so, how?

45. Event Evangelism I

32	33	34	35	36	37	38
Secular Education as Evangelism	**Sacred Education as Evangelism**	**Child and Youth Events**	**Camp Meeting Revival Method**	**Camp Ministry Evangelism**	**Rock Concert Evangelism**	**Music Evangelism**
Educating the heathen to show them through a secular education the rational superiority of a Christian worldview	Providing biblical, theological, and/or religious education to lead students to come to acknowledge the Christian worldview and its lifestyle as superior to other worldviews	Special age-oriented outreaches to draw children or youth and share the gospel with them	Planning extended meetings in a field where a stage is constructed, there is nonstop preaching, and families can set up tents to sleep	Running group excursions at a distance to maximize personal and community time, while providing opportunities for fun, adventure, worship, and Bible exposition	Gathering youth on a field to hear a series of Christian rock groups on various stages; they sleep in tents, etc.	(1) Viewing Christian music itself as evangelism with no preaching, or (2) Christian music concerts with preaching and/or a testimony of salvation
The Christian lifestyle of Ghandi or Martin Luther King Jr.	This view was encouraged by Harnack and Herrmann in *Essays on the Social Gospel* (1907)	Vacation Bible School, Backyard Bible Studies, and youth socials and outreaches; Child Evangelism Fellowship	A predominant Methodist approach to evangelism in U.S. in the 19th century; 1801 Cane Ridge Camp Meeting Revival	Numerous camping movements arose in the 20th century, often with an evangelistic flavor; Young Life's philosophy was that camps are where decisions are made for Christ	Combining a Woodstock-type music festival with the old-time camp revival meetings; since the mid-1970s 2–3 day Christian rock concerts have been held across the U.S.	Many Christian concerts include some type of testimony, often by the musician; popular musicians also provide a draw to enhance attendance at crusades

Food for Thought

Can Christianity be taught through long-term enculturation and education, without overtly preaching the gospel and calling for a decision?

Are there biblical examples in Acts of long-term enculturation or education resulting in conversions?

In what way is the style of music cultural, and in what way are the words of music cultural?

How do varying styles of music lend themselves to words and themes appropriate to the style of music?

Is there a difference between the words of the Bible set to music, biblical themes set to music, doctrinal themes set to music, or singing about real-life situations?

Further Food for Thought

Is the gospel relevant in and of itself, or does the evangelist need to "make a way for Jesus"?

Where is the line between cultural relevancy and allowing culture to frame the question rather than the Bible?

46. Event Evangelism II

39	40	41	42	43	44	45	46
Secular Event Evangelism	**Church Special Events**	**On-Campus Sports Evangelism**	**Off-Campus Sports Evangelism**	**Amusement Park Evangelism**	**Comedy as Evangelism**	**Coffee House Evangelism**	**Block Parties**
Sending evangelism teams to large events where many persons gather; local churches may reach out and/or partner with distant churches	Evangelism emphasizing either the Christian calendar or a culturally oriented interest or activity	On church campus, i.e., in a gymnasium owned and operated by the church	Off church campus, i.e., in various community sports leagues or through mission trips	Inviting youth for a free night at an amusement park in order to foster relationships	Inviting a Christian comedian to share the gospel, using comedy as a bridge	Offering youth a weekend or evening Christian entertainment alternative, with music and food	A planned carnival-type event with free food, music, and a festive atmosphere
Sending evangelism teams to the Super Bowl, the Kentucky Derby, the Olympics, or NASCAR events; sometimes renting a booth at the state fair or county fair, etc.	For example, Christmas pageants and Easter pageants; or Super Bowl parties, 4th of July parties; or fishing exhibitions, hot-rod car gatherings, etc.	Encouraging community participation in sports through using church facilities as an opportunity used to share Christ; Upward Basketball	Involvement in sports leagues as a church to provide a non-verbal and a verbal witness to others; YMCA, FCA, Sports Ambassadors, and Athletes in Action	Method used by Kansas City Youth for Christ and some churches, combines fellowship and relationship	Popularized by Mike Warnke et al.; now an accepted practice at youth conferences and in certain churches; evangelists may also feel led to use comedy	May or may not have intentional evangelism; common in the U.S. in the 1960s–70s and in Europe since the 1970s	May or may not have intentional evangelism; serves as an opening to share the gospel; www.church blockparty.com

Food for Thought

Are repentance from sin and eternal life irrelevant?

Must secondary issues be used to open a conversation to the gospel, such as life here-and-now issues? When does issue-driven evangelism lose its focus on the cross—Christ and His death as a substitution for sin?

Further Food for Thought

Does persecution mean that a method of evangelism is right or wrong?

Must persecution be avoided at all cost? Does the Bible teach or exemplify that the Christian should avoid or seek persecution?

How can persecution be understood as far as the commands to evangelize and admonitions to live peaceably?

47. Evangelism through Small Groups

47	48	49	50	51	52
Church Planting as Evangelism	**Sunday School Evangelism**	**Cell Group Evangelism**	**Home Evangelistic Bible Studies**	**Evangelistic Addiction Groups**	**Evangelistic Support Groups**
Starting up a new church in a given area; the urgency of planting a new congregation forces the church in its incipient stage to reach out to others, often evangelistically	Evangelism and follow-up efforts planned, promoted, and carried out by a Sunday School class	Evangelism through the ongoing hospitality of a home group of peers, sometimes involving whole families; a.k.a. Body Life Evangelism; small group evangelism; *oikos* evangelism	Combining hospitality, relationship, family, and evangelism through hosting periodic home evangelistic Bible studies	Gathering persons with addictions to hear the gospel and gain accountability through fellowship	Gathering persons with particular felt needs to support one another, may or may not be evangelistic
Planting new churches is "the single most effective evangelistic methodology under heaven" (C. Peter Wagner, *Church Planting for a Greater Harvest* [1990]).	Became a major Southern Baptist approach, Arthur Flake, *Building a Standard Sunday School* (1934)	Ralph Neighbour Jr., *Where Do We Go From Here?* (1987)	Acts 28:16; Bob and Betty Jacks, *Your Home a Lighthouse* (1986), Jerry Pipes, *Building a Successful Family* (2003)	Many churches use these types of ministries as evangelistic and discipleship opportunities (Alcoholics Anonymous, Narcotics Anonymous, and Gamblers Anonymous)	Autism support group, financial management support group, or home school support group

Food for Thought

Who can experience true Christian fellowship?
Can a nonbeliever fellowship with God or with believers?
When and how can fellowship be considered evangelism?
Does experiencing Christian hospitality or community (as in a small group, cell group, or home group):

- prepare for the hearing of the gospel,
- increase the salvific power of the gospel, or
- confirm the authenticity of the gospel message?

48. Crusade Evangelism[1]

53	54	55	56	57	58	59
Deeper Life Conferences	**Missionary Conferences**	**Single-Church Crusade**	**Multichurch Crusade**	**Simultaneous Revival**	**Citywide Crusade**	**Evangelistic Healing Services**
Gathering Christians to discuss issues of deeper spiritual living, such as holiness of life	Either single-church or multichurch meetings highlighting missionary activity around the world, often with a strong call to be involved in missions	A local church inviting a revivalist or evangelist to preach a (1) revival (aimed at the saved) or (2) crusade (emphasizing the lost)	Churches in a certain area from the same denomination (association of churches) will hold revival meetings	If multichurch crusades are held simultaneously with evangelists for each church or area, often a well-known evangelist is the driving force in a central church location	When a majority of churches in a given area join together to invite a well-known evangelist; cooperation becomes a complicating factor in citywide crusades	Typically a pentecostal or charismatic church or churches will invite healer-evangelists to preach a crusade
These meetings were common following the Holiness movement (in the U.S.) and the Keswick movement (in Great Britain)	Informative and helpful; sometimes the only evangelistic emphasis of some churches is vested in their missionary activity outside of their home country	Many full-time Southern Baptist evangelists go from church to church for this type of meeting (www.sbcevangelist.org); types of revivals are evangelistic, prayer, and teaching	Multichurch crusades may develop from pastor's networks and associational gatherings	The "Simultaneous Crusade" methodology pioneered by J. Wilbur Chapman was also used by the Southern Baptist Convention after 1947	Similar to D. L. Moody, J. Wilbur Chapman, Billy Sunday, Billy Graham, or Luis Palau crusades; Acts 8:6-8; citywide crusades may include evangelical and mainline denominations; some evangelists encourage Catholic participation	Mark 6:12-13; Luke 6:17-19; some evangelists- healers purchase time on television beginning in the 1970s; Aimee Semple McPherson, Kathryn Kuhlman, Oral Roberts, Benny Hinn

Food for Thought	**Further Food for Thought**
Are the days of citywide evangelism outreaches over? Are crusades historically confined (the Moody era)? Do crusades need a certain sociological context to be effective? Are crusade costs justified when renting large arenas, paying secular designers, and leasing sound and light equipment?	Must a new believer make a verbal commitment to Christ? Is it appropriate to ask a person to make a verbal commitment to Christ? Is a sinner's prayer valid?

1 Other names for Crusades include Preaching Missions, Revivals, Campaigns, Festivals, Encounters, Healing Missions.

49. Media Evangelism I

60	61	62	63	64	65	66
Issue-Oriented Christian Literature	**Gospel Magazines or Newspapers**	**Bible Distribution by Bible Colporteurs**	**Gospel Tract Distribution**	**Other Printed Media**	**Media Marketing**	**Media Evangelism**
Printing and disseminating of gospel intelligence through issue or topically oriented material	Printing and disseminating gospel intelligence through the medium of newspapers and magazines	The selling of Bibles door-to-door or the distribution of Bibles to prisons, schools, hotels, etc.	Conceiving, printing, and distributing gospel tracts, either for personal evangelism or for mass distribution	Printing and distributing other printed matter for evangelism: (1) books and (2) paraphernalia	Using mass media to advertise an evangelism venue, special event, or a church ministry	Using mass media to present the gospel or a relevant aspect of the gospel
Christian women's magazines, or children and youth magazines, such as are created by Focus on the Family	For example *Decision Magazine* had as its purpose the proclamation of the gospel, while informing about Billy Graham's ministry	Many Reformation-era Bible colporteurs were burned at the stake in France; the British and Foreign Bible Society (1804) distribution, and Gideon's	There are hundreds of Christian gospel tract societies and agencies, such as the American Tract Society, Chicago Tract Society, etc.	(1) Billy Graham books, Hal Lindsey's *Late Great Planet Earth*; (2) T-shirts, bracelets, neck bands, and such, with gospel messages	Billboard campaigns, television commercials, radio commercials, newspaper ads; sometimes including 1-800 numbers for follow-up	Billboard campaigns, television commercials, newspaper ads; similar to Jesus video (see under visitation)

Food for Thought	Further Food for Thought
Is it necessary to communicate the gospel of Jesus Christ with words (1 Cor 15:1-8) for valid evangelism? Are love (John 13:35), unity (John 17:21), or good works (Matt 5:16) a form of evangelism, sufficient in themselves unto salvation? Are the outward word and hearing of faith absolutely necessary for salvation?	Should personal evangelism be shunned if it produces stress, tension, fear, or is personally threatening? What of mental illness? At what point do family obligations override the command to evangelize (1 Cor 7:29)?

50. Media Evangelism II

67	68	69	70	71	72	73	74
Television or Radio Evangelism	**Internet Evangelism**			**Chat Room Evangelism**	**CB Evangelism**	**Telephone Marketing**	**Telephone Response Evangelism**
Regular preaching or evangelistic preaching on television or the radio	Web sites targeting gospel to specific audiences	Web sites that train Christians in evangelism	Web sites with generic gospel presentations	Interacting with lost persons through discussions in (1) public chat rooms or (2) those designed for outreach	CB Evangelism, sharing the gospel using CB radios (1970s–80s)	Telemarketing calls evangelizing others	Persons respond to ad campaigns by calling number, Christians share gospel over phone at a phone bank or at home
This method led to the founding of numerous Christian radio stations, such as WMBI from Moody Bible Institute and TBN television	For example: www.christiananswers.net; www.kidology.org; www.deceptioninthechurch.com; www.crosswayyosemite.com	For example: guide.gospelcom.net/resources/gospel.php; www.myfaith.com/evangelism/evangelize-evangelism training.htm	For example: www.sbc.net, www.acts1711.com, www.billygraham.org, www.ccc.net, www.fishthe.net, www.gotquestions.org, www.saved.com	Some individuals feel specifically called to this ministry; some chat rooms are set up for apologetic or general religious discussion	Beau Colle, *CB for Christians.* (Nashville: Broadman, 1976)	Norm Whan of "Phones for You" explained that a church in Texas planted a church in Montana using telemarketing	Passive telephone evangelism; numerous telephone response ads have been launched, such as 1-800-NEEDHIM; 1-888-JESUS-2000

Food for Thought	Further Food for Thought
Are there limits to the cost effectiveness of media evangelism, as far as purchasing television or radio time, developing Hollywood type of programming, etc.? When does the cost of a media make it cost prohibitive? Does the media provide the best "bang for the buck" in comparison to other types of evangelism? When is media evangelism merely marketing a church or ministry initiative?	Is impersonal media evangelism the best way to evangelize? Are media campaigns with 1-800 numbers effective when it comes to (1) sharing the gospel; (2) following up the convert; and (3) getting the convert into a local church for baptism and discipleship? What are media evangelism's strengths and weaknesses?

51. Ministry-Based Evangelism

75	76	77	78	79	80
Social Institu-tionalism	**Social Gospel**	**Incarnational Evangelism**	**Ministry Evangelism**	**Servant Evangelism**	**Servanthood Evangelism**
The founding of social institutions as evangelism, for example orphanages, schools, leprosaria, etc.	Meeting the social needs of man as the ultimate mission of the church	Seeking to combine social ministry and evangelism, with ministry as an end in itself, following a 50/50 incarnational pattern	Combining evangelism and social ministry together, while seeking to keep evangelism as the priority	Balancing individual service and personal evangelism, each as legitimate ends in themselves; may easily morph into marketing for the church	Using service as an entrée for personal evangelism
James 1:27; ministry of Mother Teresa in Calcutta	Harnack and Herrmann, *The Social Gospel* (1907), sought to develop a "balanced view," as did Harry Ward, *Social Evangelism* (1915)	Often without verbally sharing the gospel; showing the love of God and/or Christ; "giving back to the community"; "being salt and light"	Intentionally sharing the gospel, using ministry as an entrée (Titus 3:14); Atkinson/ Roesel, *Meeting Needs-Sharing Christ* (1995)	"Earning the right to be heard"; Sjogren's *Conspiracy of Kindness* (1993)	Reid and Wheeler, "Servanthood Evangelism" (1997)

Food for Thought

Does social service provide a salvific preparation for the gospel (Luke 16:30-31)?

Is practicing righteousness before men a substitute for actually sharing the gospel?

When does social service move from being the outcome of a reborn life, to a necessary partner with evangelism, to an end in itself?

Is social service a part of the Great Commission and/or a part of a definition of evangelism?

Does the 10:1 ratio of Luke 17:17 relate to service evangelism, or even the 5000:12 ratio of John 6:66?

Is the gospel sufficient as a message in itself, or must power be added to it by lifestyle or service (1 Cor 1:17; 2:2)?

Is a bridge necessary for the gospel to be most effectively communicated?

When does a bridge to the gospel become a tactic or use of "bait-and-switch"?

When does the bridge move from being the *a posteriori* to the *a priori,* or when does it move from being prevenient to salvific?

52. Prayer and Relational Evangelism

81	82	83	84	85	86	87
Prayer Evangelism/ Prayer Walking			**Warfare Prayer**	**Lifestyle Evangelism**	**Relational Evangelism**	
General prayer for the lost without verbally sharing the gospel; Augustine's mother?	Prayer "on site with insight" in target areas looking for specific spiritual needs but without overtly sharing the gospel	Prayer "on site with insight" in target areas looking for opportunities to share the gospel	Intentionally targeting spiritual strongholds for periods of prayer prior to, during, and after evangelism	Silent witness; nonverbal; such as monastic poverty	Intentional verbal testimony, with a gradual method of sharing; relationship can be evangelism	Intentional verbal testimony, with an instantaneous method of sharing, repeated as necessary
Praying for You (Kregel, 1991); Samuel Zwemer, "Prayer is not evangelism" (1944)	Combining prayer in difficult target areas with looking for opportunities to share Christ	Combining prayer in difficult target areas with looking for opportunities to share Christ	Especially emphasized among charismatic groups; Ed Silvoso	See Paul VI, *Evangelii Nuntiandi* (8 Dec. 1975); 13th century *vita evangelica* versus *vir evangelicus* versus *imitatio Christi*	Relationship is a necessary *preparatio evangelica;* Pippert (1979), Aldrich (1981); evangelism part of discipleship process	Jim Petersen, *Living Proof* (1985); Darrell Robinson, *People Sharing Jesus* (1997)

Food for Thought

Is stranger-to-stranger evangelism in the NT?

Is there biblical teaching against stranger-to-stranger evangelism?

Are there biblical examples or warnings against stranger-to-stranger evangelism?

Are there biblical teachings or examples requiring prior relationship to share the gospel?

Does adding relationship to the gospel change soteriology?

Is the gospel sufficient as a message in itself, or must power be added to it through relationship (1 Cor 1:17; 2:2)?

Is building a relationship really a necessary part of preevangelism, thus placing human relationship within the order of salvation?

Further Food for Thought

Do genuine evangelism and conversion always take prolonged time?

Are there biblical examples of one-time evangelism leading to instantaneous conversion?

Are there biblical examples of a prolonged period of testifying or a prolonged period of conversion?

Does the NT ever endorse a progressive-enlightenment-type of salvation either theologically or practically?

Does not a linear process approach to salvation undermine "you must be born again" and the substitutionary atonement?

53. Contextual Evangelism

88	89	90	91	92	93
Prison Ministry	**Prison Ministry**	**Whole Nation Evangelism; People Movements**	**Family Evangelism; Household Evangelism**	**Women's Evangelism**	**Urban Ministry**
Serving prisoners in their misery and need	Sharing the gospel with prisoners and meeting their needs as possible	Reaching whole nations through empowering people movements within the nation, often by sophisticated sociological analysis	Intentionally sharing the gospel with (1) members of one's own family or (2) members of an entire household (sometimes rather than individualistic approach)	Framing the gospel presentation to the specific needs of women	Applying principles of ministry and evangelism to the urban context (ethnicity, racism, crime, alcohol, drugs, addictions, prostitution, poverty, job skills, homelessness, and cults)
James 1:27; there are several various prison ministries that deal primarily with the social and emotional needs of prisoners	James 1:27; some prison ministries and individual churches reach into prisons with the gospel message to change souls	An outgrowth of Donald McGavran's missionary emphasis on people movements and church growth; perhaps a step toward a social emphasis	(1) Some Calvinistic churches emphasize reaching one's children; (2) developed missiologically as preferential for patriarchal societies	NAMB's "Heart 2 Heart" is an example of women's evangelism both in message and method	Harvie Conn, a champion of "balance" between individual and social within the urban context

Food for Thought

Is the book of Acts "descriptive but not prescriptive" relating to methods of evangelism?
Does the book of Acts provide a reliable evangelistic methodology of Paul imitating Jesus (1 Cor 11:1)?
Was Paul's evangelistic methodology (and hence his theology) different from that of Jesus?
Does "NT Evangelism" necessarily imply NT-based methodology?

Further Food for Thought

Does a contact "falling away" prove an ineffective or illegitimate gospel message, gospel presentation, or evangelism method?
Is it wrong to share the gospel with someone if human follow-up will be difficult or impossible?
If a "true disciple" of Jesus Christ is the ultimate goal, does this change the style of outreach (Acts 14:21)?

54. Apologetic Evangelism

94	95	96	97	98	99	100	101
Dialogue Evangelism	**Apologetic Evangelism**	**Narrative Evangelism**	**Analogical Evangelism**	**Dialogical Evangelism**	**Telling Our Story**	**Telling His Story**	**Chronological Storying or Story-Boarding**
Preparing for evangelism, by listening to show respect, honor their humanity, or acknowledge truth in their religion	Framing the gospel or the truth to meet perceived questions or worldview issues, using culture and/or Scripture	Relating truths about God through culture or life experiences; often indirectly evangelistic; considered "relevant"	Finding and using redemptive analogies in culture to relate the gospel with relevance	Engaging persons in conversations about relevant topics leading to a gospel presentation	Telling our story, either of conversion or God's working in a specific situation	Sharing the gospel through parable, Bible stories, or through directly sharing the gospel	Sharing the gospel beginning with the OT: to emphasize the themes of sin/ sacrifice, creation/ kingdom, or something else
Interreligious conversation with the view to learn and share truth; the warm sharing of ideas is often deemed sufficient, without a call to turn to Christ	Developing an awareness of the person's worldview to shape the gospel; Lee Strobel, *Inside the Mind of the Unchurched Harry and Mary* (1993)	Relating truths of the Bible to life experiences; often associated with postmodern evangelism	Missionary anthropologist Don Richardson's *Peace Child* (1975)	In John 4, Jesus and the Woman at the Well provides an example of dialogical evangelism, Darrell Robinson, *People Sharing Jesus* (1997)	Often this may be called a testimony; the difference lies in the emphasis on eternal life (substitution-ary) or life here and now (reconcilia-tion model)	Example of parable may be C. S. Lewis's Chronicles of Narnia; story may be anti-propositional truth; Jesus' parables hid the message, Matt 13:11	New Tribes Mission's chrono-logical method for unreached tribal groups; Matthias Media's "2 Ways 2 Live" tract (kingdom-oriented

Food for Thought

Can the gospel be savingly communicated through story (C. S. Lewis, Chronicles of Narnia; J. R. R. Tolkien, *Lord of the Rings)*?

Must some truths of the gospel necessarily be expressed as propositional truth?

Are not biblical truths regarding man's sin and the death of Christ on the cross propositional truth claims?

Did Jesus use parables [stories] to hide his message, rather than making it accessible (Matt 13:10-17; Mark 4:10-12; Luke 8:9-10)?

Was there not a continual misunderstanding of spiritual metaphors in the Gospel of John 3:4; 4:11, 15; 6:52?

Is not the gospel foolishness to Gentiles (1 Cor 1:18, 23)? Can this foolishness be removed through story?

Can a spiritually blind person truly understand a Christian worldview, propositional truths related to Christianity, or the gospel?

What is the role of apologetics in seeking to bring understanding to blinded hearts and minds (2 Cor 4:3-4)?

What is the role of God, the Word of God, and the Holy Spirit in bringing sight to blind spiritual eyes (2 Cor 3:15-16)?

55. Visitation Evangelism

102	103	104	105	106	107	108
Door-to-Door Public Relations	**Door-to-Door Distribution**	**Welcome Wagon Evangelism**	**Servanthood Visitation**	**Visiting Visitors**	**Visiting Prospects**	**Door-to-Door Sharing the Gospel**
Distributing non-spiritual things as a community service in the name of Christ or the local church (plants or batteries for smoke detectors) as public relations for church	Distributing (1) Bibles or gospel tracts, (2) Jesus videos, or (3) fliers to invite persons to an event such as Vacation Bible School, usually with no attempt to contact the residents or share the gospel	Finding a list of new persons in the community, through new water or telephone hook-ups, and contacting these people with information about the church	Door-to-door evangelism with a gift as a conversation opener, such as a bag of popcorn, a cookie, or a lightbulb	Visiting visitors to the church to either (1) show the love of God, (2) develop a relationship with them, or (3) share the gospel	Visiting acquaintances of church members or inactive members with the purpose of meeting spiritual needs and enfolding them back into the church	Going from house to house and door to door with the gospel message to whomever will listen; aka saturation evangelism or every home evangelism
This type of public relations is sometimes said to give the church a "presence" in the neighborhood	Campus Crusade for Christ promotes the distribution of the Jesus Video, with a repeat visit several weeks later	This method has become a standard approach used in church growth (GROW)	A recent wave of servanthood methods have developed which encourage or require the preparation of some type of service prior to sharing the gospel	Many church evangelism methodologies focus on sharing the gospel with visitors to church (EE, CCWT, LEO, WIN, CWT, and FAITH)	Often this strategy is used by new pastors who are seeking to revitalize an existing congregation that has lost members	Acts 5:42; sometimes called "cold turkey" (using sales-marketing terminology)

Food for Thought

Does not going door-to-door with a gift cost quite a bit of money?

What does going door-to-door with a gift item say about the sufficiency of the gospel?

When is door-to-door as public relations a bad use of time?

Is it wise to require a preparation for the gospel in visitation evangelism?

Should evangelism be limited only to the small percentage of people who will set foot in a given church? What about the many others in any given community?

If only visitors are visited, does this not make visiting a necessary prerequisite to hear the gospel?

Is it helpful to use the sales and marketing terminology, by calling initiative evangelism "cold turkey" evangelism?

Is there anyone whom the Holy Spirit cannot prepare without a human preparation to evangelism?

Is there any such thing as a "cold contact" with the Holy Spirit?

56. Initiative Evangelism

109	110	111	112	113	114
Personal Evangelism with Props	**Power Evangelism**	**Segmented or Targeted Evangelism**	**Initiative Evangelism**	**Expectant Evangelism**	**Urgent Evangelism**
Learning to share the gospel with a prop either as a (1) conversation starter, (2) to keep attention, or (3) a tool in sharing the gospel	Indicating that true apostolic evangelism often or always requires a manifestation of Holy Spirit power	Intentionally targeting a people group for evangelism by some sociological commonality	Initiating spiritual and gospel conversations with friends and strangers	Anticipating by faith that God will honor the promises of his Word (a ripe harvest, a lack of workers, and providing for our needs), as well as prepare hearts, empower His word, and make His gospel powerful	Sharing with divine urgency that Jesus is coming back quickly, the lost are really lost and headed for hell, the Christian is accountable, the harvest is white, and the time is short
Props may be: (1) lapel pins, (2) bracelets, (3) necklaces, (4) the EvangeCube or some other assistant for personal evangelism	Holy Spirit power may be manifested through a word of wisdom or knowledge, a miracle; John 4:16-18; Acts 3:1-10; 14:9-10; John Wimber, *Power Evangelism* (1986)	(1) By language group (People groups in missiology), (2) by religion (cult outreaches), or (3) by affinity group (Bikers for Christ or Exodus Int'l)	Acts 17:17; Bill Fay, *Share Jesus Without Fear* (1999); Bill Bright, *Witnessing Without Fear* (1987)	Hudson Taylor, "The Source of Power," *Ecumenical Missionary Conference* (1900), expected that some Chinese would respond to the gospel the first time they ever heard of Christ, and many did!	Urgent evangelism follows when Christians do not let persecution or death deter them from evangelizing; George Truett, *Quest for Souls* (1917); see also L. R. Scarborough and Roland Q. Leavell

Food for Thought	**Further Food for Thought**
Have the urgencies of evangelism changed? 1. Jesus is coming back quickly! 2. The lost are really lost and headed for hell! 3. The Christian is accountable for the lost he should reach! 4. Time is short, and the harvest is white! Do the urgencies of evangelism have any bearing on the methodology of evangelism?	Are supernatural miracles a necessary prerequisite for effective evangelism? Do power encounters automatically ensure: 1. a positive response of faith or 2. a better chance of a positive response for the subject of the miracle or in the onlookers? Consider Luke 16:30-31; 17:17-19; John 6:26-30

57. New Testament Evangelism

115	116	117	118	119	120	121	122
Passive or Reactive Evangelism	**Invitation-al Evange-lism**	**Everyday Evange-lism**	**House-to-House Evan-gelism**	**Temple or Synagogue Evange-lism**	**City-to-City Evangelism**	**Street Evangelism and Street Preaching**	**Countryside Evangelism**
Evangelism resulting from contact initiation, or being brought before kings; turning a conversation into an evangelism opportunity	Inviting the contact to meet another person who can share the gospel	The practice of daily personal evangelism	Most likely similar to door-to-door; personal evangelism from house-to-house	Preaching the gospel in the temple or in synagogues	Itinerant preaching from city-to-city; usually not from church-to-church, but rather outdoor evangelism	Preaching to groups of people on the streets of towns and cities	Preaching in fields and in the forest
Passive: John 3:1ff.; Acts 4:8ff.; 21:40-22:1ff.; 7:1ff.; Ezek 8:1; 14:1; 20:1; reactive: Luke 19:1ff.; Luke 23:39-43; John 4:7ff.	John 1:40-42, Andrew invited Peter; John 1:44-51, Philip invited Nathanael	Pss 34:1; 35:28; 40:16; 70:4; 71:8, 24; 75:9; Eccl 11:6; Acts 5:42; 17:17; D. L. Moody's example	Acts 5:42; 20:20-21; this was the Albigensian method in 12th–13th centuries (see http://jean.duvernoy.free.fr/text/ pdf/ bceaux. pdf)	Luke 20:1; Acts 3:11ff.; 5:42; 13:5, 14, 43; 14:1; Jer 7:2; 26:1-6	Matt 4:23; 11:1; Mark 6:12; Luke 4:42-44; 8:1-3; 9:6; 10:1; Acts 8:4, 25, 40; 2 Chron 30:6-11; Medieval *Wanderprediger* (*Vaudois,* Lollards); Farel-1530s; Methodist circuit riders-1700s	Street evangelism: Acts 17:17; street preaching: Acts 2:6ff.; 14:7; 17:17; Eph 5:15-16; Jer 11:6; 17:19-20	Matt 5-7; Luke 6; German Anabaptists; John Wesley and the circuit riders; Claude Brousson and 18th century French *église du désert*

Food for Thought

Are New Testament methods of evangelism obsolete because: (1) the church is now established (post-apostolic), or (2) the political, cultural, economic, or religious situation is different from that of the 1st century?

Do the biblical examples of evangelism provide normative approaches for a proper methodology of evangelism?

Does the argument, "These methods were good for 30 (or more) years ago, but are not valid now," indicate a move away from New Testament evangelism and/or a denomination's or a movement's incipient roots?

Further Food for Thought

Is the NT inerrant as far as the message of salvation only?

Does a NT gospel message necessarily imply a NT method of evangelism?

Does inerrant "in faith and practice" include inerrant in methodologies of evangelism, as well as in ecclesiology (NT church structures)?

Does a move in evangelism methodology not indicate or necessitate a corresponding move in biblical authority?

58. Fourteen Approaches to Apologetics

A fascination with apologetics carries with it some interesting challenges. Oliver Barclay made a poignant comment when he chronicled evangelicalism at Cambridge University in Cambridge, England: "Apologetics has always been a dangerous preoccupation and this generation [1900–1910] fell into the standard traps without realizing it" (Oliver R. Barclay, *Whatever Happened to the Jesus Lane Lot?* 54). This chart considers several points: (1) apologetic evangelism may mean different things to different people, depending on what is being discussed, for example, what aspect of evangelism is being discussed; (2) apologetics is one study which can easily turn the study of evangelism into the study of cultural or philosophical theology.

	1	2	3	4	5	6	7
Designation	**Biblical *Apologia* 1**	**Biblical *Apologia* 2**	**Justin Martyr's Defense of Christianity**	**Restoring Wayward Adherents**	**Mittelberg's Necessary *Preparatio Evangelica***	**Aquinas' Five Proofs of God's Existence**	**Finney's Moral Consistency**
Posture	**Apologetics as Judicial Defense**				**Apologetics and Proclamation**		
Expansion of Concept	Emphasizing protection of the church from false teaching	Emphasizing a legal defense before judges	Proving benefit of Christianity through social pragmatics	Teaching the distinctive doctrines in order to reabsorb the wayward	As a necessary worldview precursor to sharing the gospel	Proving God's existence from nature and reason	Proving God's existence from morality
Relation to Evangelism	Tangential to evangelism, part of pastoral ministry	Result of evangelism and persecution	Sociological and rational proofs of benefits of Christian worldview	As synonymous to evangelism; to reincorporate the wayward	To assure that worldviews are compatible prior to sharing	Rational or scientific proofs of the existence of God	Sociological proofs of cross-cultural morality
Impact on Gospel Presentation	Reasoned arguments do not add power to gospel	Allows gospel proclamation to rulers	Focus on sociological benefits of Christianity to prove the power of the gospel	Gospel presentation may be tangential, if focus is distinct church doctrines	Adds a necessary step prior to sharing the gospel	Scientific proofs logically precede or replace the need for the gospel proclamation	Appeal to cultural anthropology to affirm truth claims of Bible
Sample Proponents	Primary NT uses of *apologia* (8 NT uses) and *apologeomai* (9 NT uses); Calvin's *Institutes* were written to Francis I, king of France		Justin Martyr, *Apology*	French Jesuits used apologetics to reintegrate Huguenots into their faith	Mark Mittelberg, *Building a Contagious Church*	Thomas Aquinas, *Summa Theologica*	Charles Finney, *Systematic Theology* (1878)

58. Fourteen Approaches to Apologetics (continued)

Of consideration herein is the question of what truths are self-evident (or God-evident, Rom 1:18-21), and therefore emanate from general revelation, and what truths need to be taught to the natural man. Along with this issue comes the further question of what constitutes the "power of God unto salvation." Is it the rational arguments of man, no matter how true or how clear, or is it the gospel? If the former, then the power is in the wisdom of man; if the latter, then the power is in the Word of God. Paul wrote, "But a natural man does not accept the things of the Spirit of God, for they are foolishness to him; and he cannot understand them, because they are spiritually appraised" (1 Cor 2:14).

8	9	10	11	12	13	14
Dialogue	**Zacharias's Apologetic Approach**	**Pascal's Vacuum**	**Pascal's Wager**	**Kierkegaard's Leap of Faith**	**Harnack's and Herrmann's Social Gospel**	**More's *Utopia* and Schaff's *Theological Propædeutic***
Proclamation (cont.)		**Apologetics and a Call to Commitment**			**Results-Oriented Approach**	
Finding truth in another religion or worldview to show links with gospel	Finding points of relevance between culture and thought and the gospel (esp. moral argument)	An inner longing for something to satisfy a God-shaped void, need for joy, etc.	Proving belief in God is worth the risk of a wager	Belief in God takes a leap of faith	Emphasizing Christian Education to improve society	Rational superiority of Christianity noted in a triumphalist sense
To provide relevant context for and content of gospel	Apologetics as introduction to and affirmation of main points of the gospel	Inner longing drives the person to seek out God in some way	Appeal to benefit of Christian worldview	Whereas belief in God cannot be logically proven, it takes a leap of faith	Education is the *preparatio* for gradual conversion	Christian presence will result in its triumph as a religious system
May frame the gospel in a way that is not compatible with Scripture	Points of relevance add credibility and power to the gospel; thus, power not vested in Bible's words?	Challenges to gospel presentation: 1) reason may usurp need for gospel; 2) preach God, not Christ	Appeal to man's reason to show benefit of (1) belief in God, and (2) Christianity	Appeal to the need for a "leap of faith"—Give God a try	Education convinces of superiority of Christian worldview	Evangelism as a passive response (1 Pet 3:15; passive arrogance)
Newbigin, *The Gospel in a Pluralistic Society;* Vatican II, *Lumen Gentium*	Ravi Zacharias, "The Touch of Truth," in Carson, ed., *Telling the Truth*	Augustine, *Confessions*; Blaise Pascal, *Pensées*; C. S. Lewis, *Surprised by Joy*	Blaise Pascal, *Pensées*	Søren Kierkegaard, *Concluding Unscientific Postscript*	Adolf von Harnack and Wilhelm Herrmann, *Essays on the Social Gospel*	Thomas More, *Utopia*, and Philip Schaff, *Theological Propædeutic*

59. The Gospel and Philosophy

	Concepts	Usage	Biblical Understanding	Contextual, Integrational, or Syncretistic Understanding
Biblical Allusions	Job 9:8-10; 38:31-32; Isa 13:8; Amos 5:8; the Pleiades, Orion, and the Bear	Names of constellations	Descriptive of God's creation; explaining His creative power and glory; not to be worshiped (2 Kings 23:5)	Endorsement of astrological symbols; sometimes combined with magi account (Matt 2) to constitute a gospel witness
	Acts 17:18, "Epicurean and Stoic"	Two major forms of Greek philosophical thought	Describes persons who debated with Paul and mocked the gospel	Constitutes allusion to or endorsement of Greek philosophical systems, thereby allowing Greek philosophy to frame the main issues of theology
	Acts 28:11, "Twin Brothers"	Twin sons of Jupiter, Castor and Pollux	Descriptive of ship; no endorsement of Greek pantheon	Veiled endorsement of Greek pantheon
Biblical Omissions	Four personality types	Used to explain differences in human personality	No outright discussion of personality types in the Bible	Hailed as special insight into the human psyche—much like a hidden (or Gnostic) truth
	Socrates, Plato, and Aristotle	Some primary Greek philosophers	Never named in the Bible; though some are "sons of the east" (1 Kings 4:31)	Hailed as necessary for proper hermeneutic by scholastics and Erasmus
	Greek cardinal virtues	Plato had four virtues; Gregory I gave list of seven cardinal sins	Never mentioned in the Bible, though Beatitudes in Matthew are the closest	Formulate the essence of salvation; opposites form the essence of sin (hence, Rome's cardinal sins)
Biblical Categorizations	Eccl 1:17; 2:12-13, Wisdom, madness, and folly	Categorizations of human thought by Solomon	Provides a framework for philosophical thought	Not considered relevant as philosophical categorizations
	Eccl 7:25, Wisdom and an explanation, versus folly and madness	Analyses of the categorizations of Solomon	Provides interpretation of the philosophical framework set up by Solomon	Sometimes used in apologetics; often considered irrelevant to philosophical inquiry
	Eccl 10:12-14, Wisdom and folly compared	Results of following wisdom or folly	Provides end result of following two opposing views elucidated by Solomon	Often considered irrelevant to philosophical inquiry; philosophical views are often approached noncritically, as theologically neutral
	1 Cor 1:22, Greek and Hebrew systems compared	Greek naturalism compared to Hebrew supernaturalism	Shows two extremes in religion that were opposed to the gospel	Often considered irrelevant to philosophical inquiry
	Col 2:8, 20-23, Elementary principles versus Christ	Two opposing approaches to dealing with the sinful nature	Paul opposes a Christianized Stoicism, whereby the fleshly nature is controlled with human regulations	Often human regulations are encouraged and canonized in liberalizing and state-type churches
Several Cautions	1 Kings 12:33, Jeroboam instituted a religious feast (and golden calves)	Jeroboam instituted a feast "which he had devised in his own heart"	Jeroboam's sin of addition to Scripture was a stumbling block for centuries after his death	Often considered irrelevant to modern contextualization or integration
	Jer 23:13-32, Baal, dreams, or God's Word	Exposing the dangers of adding to Scriptures	Jeremiah opposed the false prophets of his day who added to Scripture	Often additions to Scripture are encouraged; remaining with Scripture alone is often considered naive, simplistic, and parochial

60. Five Interpretations of "Salt" in Matthew 5:13

Supernatural				Natural
A Blessing to Culture	**Seasoning within Culture**	**Antiseptic to Culture**	**Contractual Arrangement**	**Preservative of Culture**
"And in you all the families of the earth will be blessed," Gen 12:3	"They are the majestic ones," Ps 16:3; Job 6:6; Col 4:6	The cleansing through the word of Christ, John 15:3	"Salt of the covenant of your God," Lev 2:13; Num 18:19; 2 Chron 13:5	Turn blessings into commands; "Be the salt of the earth"

61. Views of Culture, the World, the Saved, and the Lost

Saved	Particularlist/ Few Saved	Median	Universalist/ Most Saved
Terms for Unsaved	Lost	Unchurched, Seekers	Pre-Christian
Culture	Basically evil	Neutral	Basically good
World	Evil (Rom 3:10-12)	Neutral	Good (Gen 1:31)
	"The worries of the world . . . enter in and choke the word, and it becomes unfruitful," Mark 4:19	"Of the sons of Issachar, men who understood the times, with knowledge of what Israel should do, their chiefs *were* two hundred; and all their kinsmen *were* at their command," 1 Chron 12:32	"By this all men will know that you are My disciples, if you have love for one another," John 13:35
	"Do not love the world nor the things in the world. If anyone loves the world, the love of the Father is not in him," 1 John 2:15	"And his master praised the unrighteous manager because he had acted shrewdly; for the sons of this age are more shrewd in relation to their own kind than the sons of light," Luke 16:8	"I do not ask on behalf of these alone, but for those also who believe in Me through their word; that they may all be one . . . so that the world may believe that You sent Me . . . I in them and You in Me, that they may be perfected in unity, so that the world may know that You sent Me, and loved them, even as You have loved Me." John 17:20-21, 23
Ministry	Save individual souls/ convert sinners	Save souls/ transform culture	Transform culture/ renew social order
Society	Saved are salt in society	Both/and	Saved must work to be salt in society
Use of Culture in Ministry	Shun culture (separate from it); seek NT ministry	Use cultural methods while seeking to maintain a NT message	Use culture as primary tool of influence; become mainstream; absorb culture

62. Niebuhr's *Christ and Culture* and Evangelism

H. Richard Niebuhr's *Christ and Culture* (1951) skillfully framed the evangelical (proclamational) view of soteriology out of the question. His work expanded on the social teaching of Ernst Troelsch (1912). Niebuhr both provides the theme of his book, as well as displays his bias, in the following quote: "Now that we have recognized the importance of the role played by anticultural Christians in the reform of culture, we must immediately point out that they never achieved these results alone or directly, but only through the mediation of believers who gave a different answer to the fundamental question" (Niebuhr, 67).

Fifty-two years later, John G. Stackhouse considered *Christ and Culture* "one of the most influential Christian books of the past century" (Leonard Sweet, ed. *The Church in Emerging Culture* [2003], 13). The words of Wolfhart Pannenberg, however, may bring nuance to the rhetoric of Niebuhr:

Niebuhr's Five Views	[Framed out of question]	Niebuhr 1	Niebuhr 4
Ethical Types	[Culture against Christ]	Christ against Culture [Niebuhr's, "anticultural Christians"]	Christ and Culture in Paradox
Issue	[World's hatred and crucifixion of Christ; promise of world's hatred and persecution of Christians]	Question framed as Christian's legalism and separation from the world	Duality and opposition between Christ and culture, hope of justification beyond history
Niebuhr's Proponents	[Hubmaier, Zwingli, Calvin, Knox]	Clement, Tertullian, Tolstoy, Mennonites	Marcion, Luther
Niebuhr's Analysis	[Not considered]	"Half-baked and muddle-headed men abound in the anticultural movement" (65). "Doubtless the individualistic ideal of soul-regeneration is not an adequate key to the attitude of radical Christians; but neither is the hope of social reform" (67).	"Cultural conservatives... were deeply concerned to bring change into only one of the great cultural institutions and sets of habits of their times—the religious" (187–88). "It is at this point that the conversionist *motif,* otherwise very similar to the dualist, emerges in distinction from it" (189)
Impact on Evangelism	[Persecution is to be expected in evangelism]	Evangelistic churches are anticultural and thus irrelevant to society	An overemphasis on conversion renders Christians too heavenly minded
Impact on Great Commission	[Proclamation is the primary thrust of the Great Commission]	Mere proclamation is problematic and idealistic	Proclamation + cultural change

62. Niebuhr's *Christ and Culture* and Evangelism (continued)

"It has frequently been noted that the mainline and accommodating churches are in decline, while conservative churches continue to grow. Evangelicals and fundamentalists are not embarrassed to challenge the prevailing patterns of thought and behavior associated with secularity. This growth, however, does not come without paying a price. That price includes a loss of openness to the human situation in all of its maddening variety, and a quenching of the unprejudiced search for truth. That said, the irony is that those churches that are dismissed as irrelevant by more 'sophisticated' Christians often turn out to be most relevant to our secular societies" (1991).

Niebuhr's Five Views	Niebuhr 5	Niebuhr 3	Niebuhr 2
Ethical Types	Christ the Redeemer of Culture [i.e., *Christus Victor*]	The Christ above Culture	The Christ of Culture
Issue	Conversionist solution: Christ is the converter of man in his culture and society	Synthesis: Christ the fulfillment of cultural aspirations, the restorer of the institutions of true society	Jesus the hero of human culture history, the greatest human achievement
Niebuhr's Proponents	Augustine; F. D. Maurice	Thomas Aquinas	Abelard, Ritschl
Niebuhr's Analysis	"The conversion of mankind from self-centeredness to Christ-centeredness was for Maurice the universal and present divine possibility. It was universal in the sense that it included all men; since all were members of the kingdom of Christ by their creation in the Word, by the actual spiritual constitution under which they lived" (225).	"Thomas also answers the question about Christ and culture with a 'both/and'; yet his Christ is far above culture, and he does not try to disguise the gulf that lies between them.... But he is a monk in the church which has become the guardian of culture, the fosterer of learning, the judge of the nations, the protector of the family, the governor of social religion" (129).	"Popular theology condenses the whole of Christian thought into the formula: the Fatherhood of God and the Brotherhood of Man" (101); "How often the Fundamentalist attack on so-called liberalism—by which cultural Christianity is meant—is itself an expression of cultural loyalty, a number of Fundamentalist interests indicate" (102).
Impact on Evangelism	If conversion is to be regrettably retained, it must move to the cultural order	Rather than convert society, efforts should aim to guard society	Efforts should be directed to recreate true culture
Impact on Great Commission	Cultural change = conversion of society	Church is the guardian of true culture and true humanity	Church is the Savior of human culture

63. Six Theological Circles in a Theology of Evangelism

In a theology of evangelism, there are clearly perceptible messages, means, and ends. The messages relate to the primary view of the atonement. The means relates to the method of furthering the work of the church. The ends relate to the result of the message and the means.

The lines of distinction are not always clearly delineated. Often there is a confusion of definitions and terms. An attempt is made to move conservative thinkers down the "square of opposition" to accept median views ("truth is nuanced"), thus affirming opposing (or paradoxical) views, and discounting the preeminence of the substitutionary atonement. A group or movement that slides away from the substitutionary atonement ceases to be evangelical. Phillip D. Jensen and Tony Payne wrote of the split of Intervarsity Christian Fellowship (IVCF) from the Student Christian Movement (SCM) in Cambridge, England in 1910:

> If we can be somewhat rude for a moment, it seems to us that many current evangelical student ministries have lost touch with their history on this matter. Many today have more in common with the SCM than with CICCU [Cambridge Intercollegiate Christian Union from which came IVCF]. They have not ceased believing in the cross and the atonement [earlier: "both sides subscribed to the doctrine of penal substitution"]. They have simply moved it off-center, and spent their time speaking about other things—things that are no doubt worthwhile and important in themselves but that are not the death of Christ for our sins. Their preaching could not be summarized as Christ crucified. If you lose that at the center of your ministry, then like the SCM you cease to be an evangelical ministry, and you are headed for disaster. It may only be a slight difference at first, but it is a watershed. The subsequent flow is in the wrong direction. The SCM, of course, became the World Council of Churches, which itself started out as an evangelical organization before degenerating into liberalism (Phillip D. Jensen and Tony Payne, "Church/ Campus Connections," in D. A. Carson, ed., *Telling the Truth: Evangelizing Postmoderns,* 198).

The move from the "Mere Proclamation" circle to the "Mere Relationship" circle is subtle but discernible. This first move toward relationship eases further moves toward a kingdom, community, or social emphasis, as the preeminence of the substitutionary atonement has been compromised. It must be noted that the word *kingdom* is an equivocal term, sometimes used in a biblical sense but often used with a social theology emphasis.

1. Mere Proclamation Circle

Message: Atonement as Mere Reconciliation

Great Commission as Mere Evangelism

Evangelism as Mere Friendship

Decision: "You Must Be Born Again!"

Salvation: Justification by Faith Alone

Result: A Blood-Bought Church

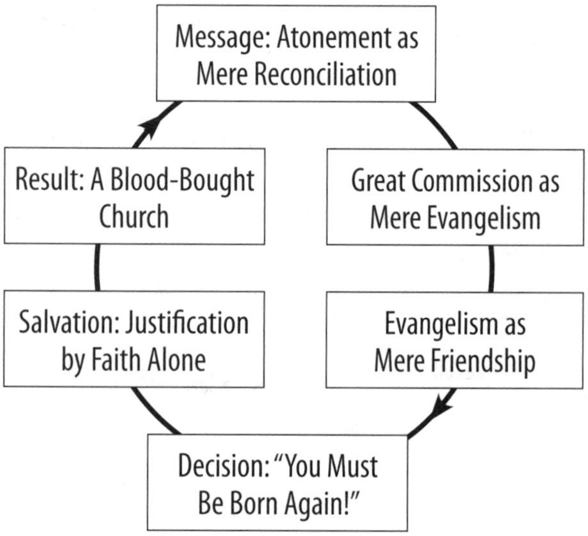

2. Mere Relationship Circle

Message: Atonement as Mere Substitution

Great Commission as Mere Relationship

Evangelism as Mere Proclamation

Decision: "Converted to Community"

Salvation: Justification by Relational Assent

Result: A Reconciled Community

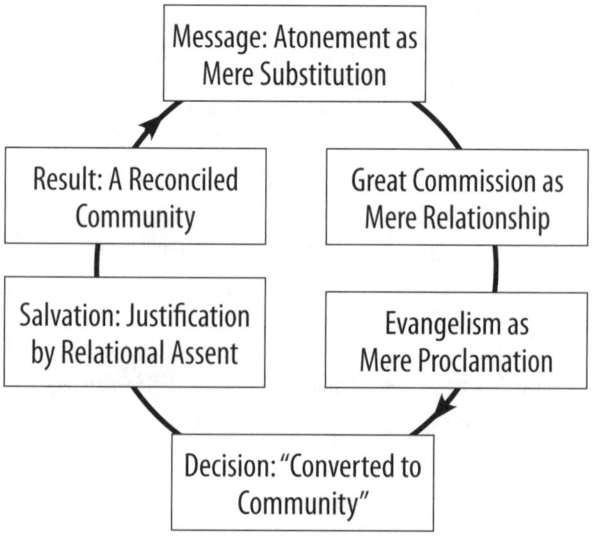

63. Six Theological Circles in a Theology of Evangelism (continued)

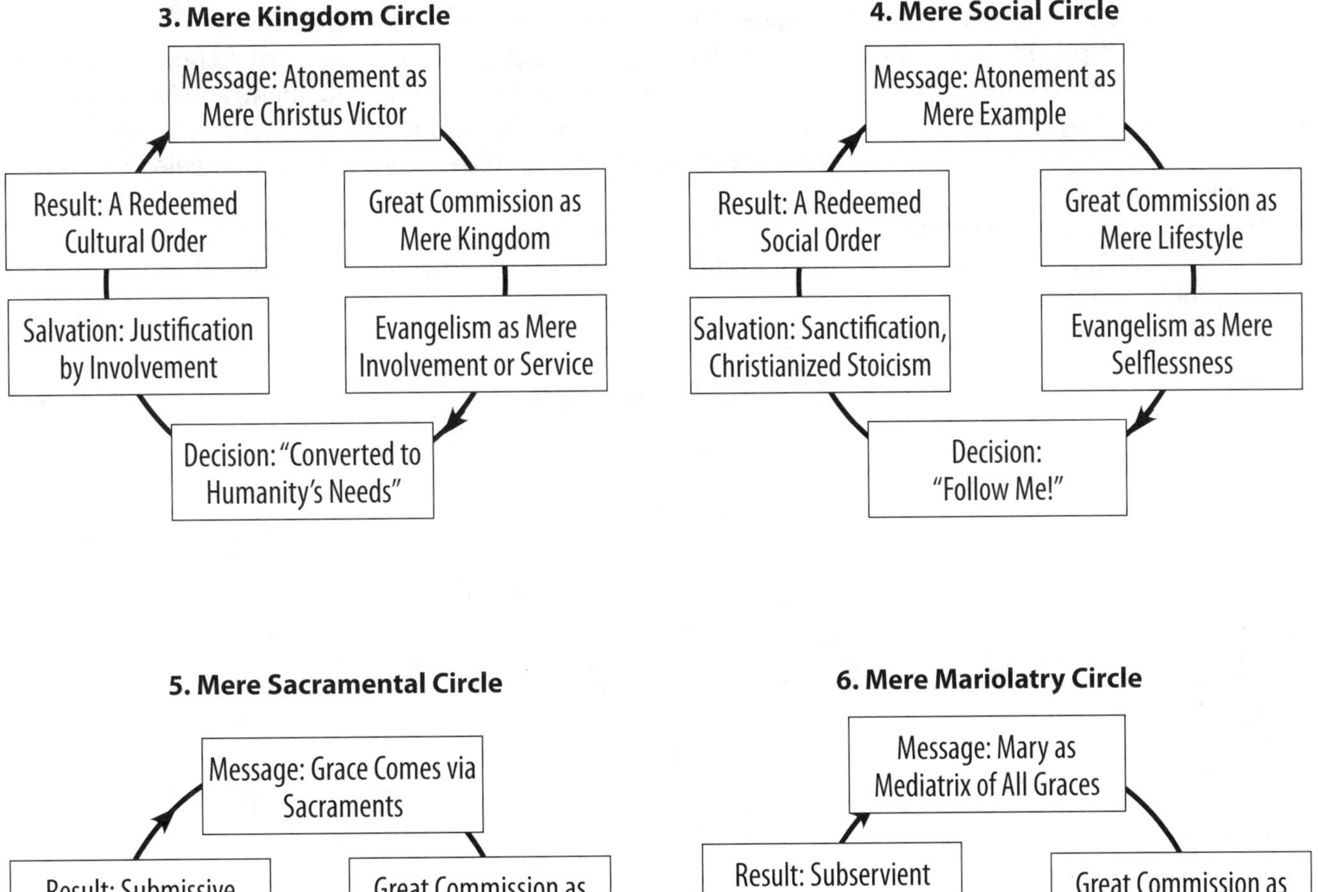

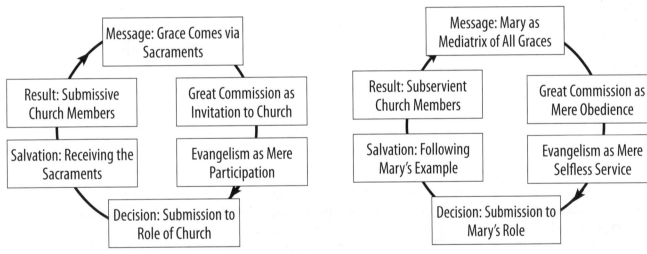

5. Mere Sacramental Circle

Message: Grace Comes via Sacraments
Great Commission as Invitation to Church
Evangelism as Mere Participation
Decision: Submission to Role of Church
Salvation: Receiving the Sacraments
Result: Submissive Church Members

6. Mere Mariolatry Circle

Message: Mary as Mediatrix of All Graces
Great Commission as Mere Obedience
Evangelism as Mere Selfless Service
Decision: Submission to Mary's Role
Salvation: Following Mary's Example
Result: Subservient Church Members

Some may seek to combine the "Mere Proclamation" circle with another theological scenario. In this case they fall prey to the waterslide mentioned by Phillip Jensen and Tony Payne, as they begin to walk down the "Square of Opposition." If a person, church, or movement is to remain distinctively evangelical, then they must preach Christ and Him crucified (1 Cor 1:17-18; 2:2). If and when they move from the preeminence of "Mere" Penal Substitution, they cease to be evangelical.

It seems that many attempts are made to forge median positions. The history of a theology of conversion and evangelism is replete with median positions. Is such an attempt not being "double-minded" (Ps 119:113)? Yes, "A little leaven leavens the whole lump of *dough*" (Gal 5:9).

64. Introducing the Evangelical Drift Portrayed in Charts 65–77

The following charts are the result of an extended journey into issues in a theology of evangelism. This brief introduction provides the framework in which they were created. Insights were gleaned from three areas of inquiry: (1) tensions inherent to a theology of evangelism; (2) theories of the atonement; and (3) twelve approaches to evangelism and social service. Charts 65–77, then, will provide a theoretical framework in which all of these were combined. The outcome of these charts is a step-by-step analysis of theological and methodological drift.

The inherit tensions in a theology of evangelism are precisely because evangelism often seeks to synthesizes theology and practice, the Bible and culture. The following chart seeks to explain the two progressions involved.

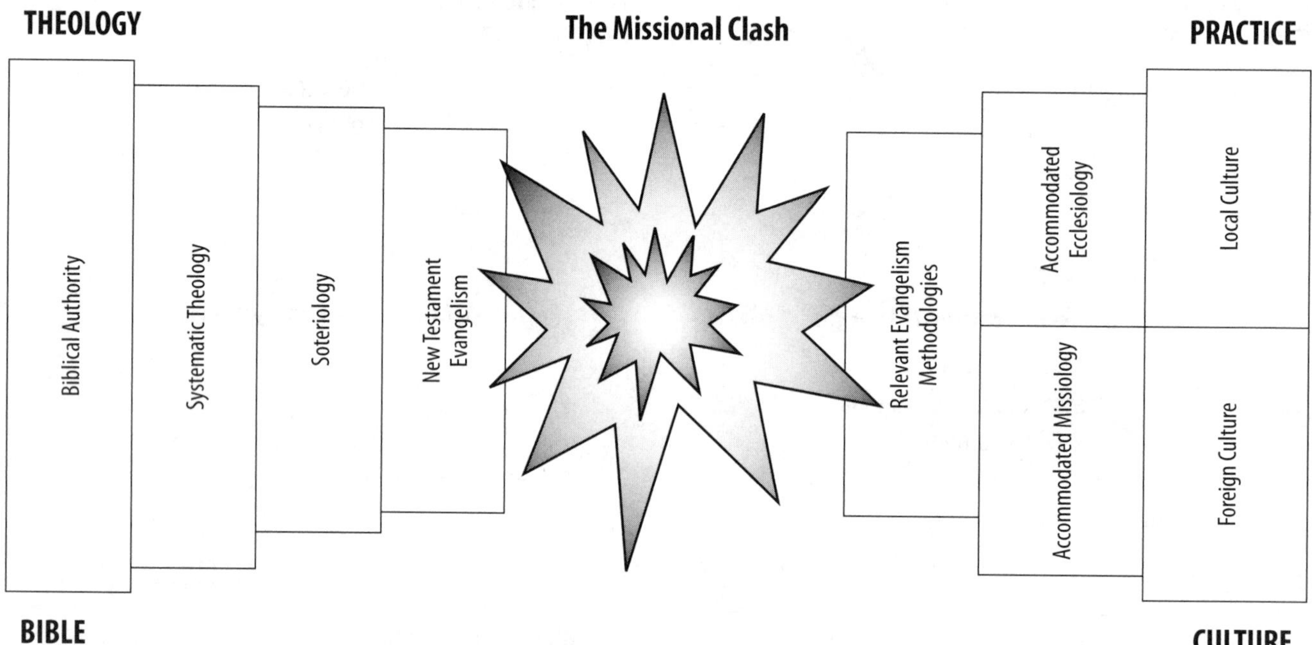

Biblically oriented evangelists begin with absolute biblical authority, which ought to lead them to a theology of salvation, as well as to New Testament evangelism. However, those who begin with culture as the starting point end up with a culturally guided view of evangelism. At this point the Bible and culture collide, and explosive disagreements ensue. The reason for the misunderstanding is often the amount of weight given either to the Bible or to culture.

In these tensions (often stratified by theologians through using Christological language), two poles are in evidence, Bible and culture or theology and practice. On the culture or practice pole, cultural context guides both missiology or ecclesiology toward paths of relevancy.

Most revolutionary to this discussion is the placing of theories of the atonement on these two poles.

Some theologians place the theories of the atonement in a circular position with the substitutionary theory as the central element of the death of Christ. Usually, however, when reading original autographs, competing theories to the substitutionary atonement discounted its validity as explaining the fullness of what Christ has done. These theologians rather posited a different theory of the atonement which they felt more clearly reflected the fullness of what Christ did on the cross. Therefore it is difficult to accept their competing views as complementary to the substitutionary atonement, as they were posited as an alternative to the substitutionary atonement! This reasoning, in part, guided my use of a linear approach to the models of the atonement.

64. Introducing the Evangelical Drift Portrayed in Charts 65–77 (continued)

Two factors led to my order of the views of the atonement. First, Gustav Aulén in his *Christus Victor* explained that there were in reality only two main theories of the atonement: objective (substitutionary) and subjective (moral-influence). He then posited a median position or a synthesis, *Christus Victor,* which he related to the ransom theory of the atonement. Aulén therefore left us with three main theories of the atonement, Substitutionary, *Christus Victor,* and Moral Influence, in that order.

Into this mix came a fourth view of the atonement provided to explain the changing theological language of Billy Graham, the reconciliation model. In my *Examining Billy Graham's Theology of Evangelism* (2003), I noted that Graham increasingly seemed to avoid using substitutionary language while opting for more relational or reconciliation language. My research found that Graham's terminology shifted most noticeably as regarded the sin nature of man.

Billy Graham on Sin

1947	1951	1955	1960	1977
Total Depravity	Depravity	Sin as a sickness	Sin as waywardness, degradation	The two faces of man, "his basic goodness and basic evil"

When looking at Graham's terminology from a theological perspective, the conclusion was clear. A change did take place. The question then became, a change from what to what? It was verifiable that Graham started off as a fundamentalist, as he stated the Five Fundamentals of the 1895 Nigara Bible Conference in a published sermon, "America's Hope," in *Calling Youth to Christ* (1947). Thirty years later, however, it would seem that Graham communicated a median point between the conservative and moderate camps of theology. Conservatives affirm that man is basically evil, while the moderates emphasize the basic goodness of man.

In so doing, Graham began to emphasize the reconciliation model of the atonement, much like that taught by the Scottish evangelist and theologian James Denney (see *The Christian Doctrine of Reconciliation* [1918]). If my evaluation is accurate, a fourth model of the atonement needs to be placed between the substitutionary model and *Christus Victor,* the reconciliation (relational) model of the atonement. The last missing element, so prevalent in 20th-century Protestantism, is the liberation theology model, which seems to be a practical outflow of *Christus Victor.*

To these five views of the atonement were added twelve different positions on the interrelationship of evangelism and social responsibility. I started with John R. W. Stott's explanation of three views in his analysis of the 1982 "Grand Rapids Consultation on Evangelism and Social Responsibility" (*Making Christ Known* [1996]):

- "Social activity is a *consequence* of evangelism."
- "Social activity can be a bridge to evangelism."
- "Social activity not only follows evangelism as its consequence and aim, and precedes it as its bridge, but it also accompanies it as its partner."

Beginning with Stott's three, I developed 12 positions on this continuum (listed as A-L in the following chart). The primary issue added to Stott's three views relates to aspects of *preparatio*: when and how does service become a necessary preparation for the gospel?

It was at this time that I began to posit a link between the theological and methodological charts, combining them into charts 66–75 that are before you for your consideration. In focusing primarily on 20th century North American evangelical drift, these charts seek to provide a paradigm for simultaneous drift both in theology and practice. It may be noted that theology and practice do go hand-in-hand. Charts 76–77 further propose four distinct drifts from the substitution model to *Christus Victor* via the reconciliation model of the atonement. The purpose of these charts is didactic and not polemic. They are not meant to describe every theologian or model, but rather to seek to explain spiritual drift.

65. Guide to Evangelical Drift Portrayed in Charts 66–75

	PROCLAMATION ⟷					
	A	**B**	**C**	**D**	**E**	**F**
Relationship of Service to Proclamation	Service is a supernatural outflow of proclamation.	Service is an opening for proclamation.	Service is a bridge to proclamation.	Service is a preparatory grace for proclamation.	Service is a preferred preparatory grace to proclamation.	Service is a necessary preparatory grace for proclamation.
Expansion of Relationship	Result of changed lives	To evangelize in closed countries	Allowing proximity for evangelism	Providing relevance to the gospel	Adding credibility to the gospel	Adding power to the gospel
Message	**Substitutionary Atonement**			**Reconciliation Model**		
Theology Charts	**66. Substitution's Theology**			**68. Reconciliation Model's Theology**		
Methodology Charts	**67. Substitution's Methodology**			**69. Reconciliation Model's Methodology**		

65. Guide to Evangelical Drift Portrayed in Charts 66-75 (continued)

<table>
<tr><th></th><th colspan="6">←→ SOCIAL SERVICE</th></tr>
<tr><th></th><th>G</th><th>H</th><th>I</th><th>J</th><th>K</th><th>L</th></tr>
<tr><td>Relationship of Service to Proclamation</td><td>Service is an equal partner to proclamation.</td><td>Service is an end in itself, apart from proclamation.</td><td>Service is primary over proclamation.</td><td colspan="3">Service is proclamational evangelism</td></tr>
<tr><td rowspan="2">Expansion of Relationship</td><td colspan="2">Two mandates (spiritual and social)</td><td rowspan="2">Conversion agenda secondary to social agenda</td><td colspan="2">Conversion agenda hinders social ends and means.</td><td>Conversion agenda hinders ecclesial ends.</td></tr>
<tr><td>Both necessary together</td><td>Need not be together</td><td>Proclamational evangelism unnecessary</td><td>Proclamational evangelism counterproductive</td><td>Proclamational evangelism is the method of heretics</td></tr>
<tr><td>Message</td><td colspan="2">Christus Victor Model</td><td colspan="2">Liberation Theology Model</td><td colspan="2">Moral Influence Theory</td></tr>
<tr><td>Theology Charts</td><td colspan="2">70. Christus Victor's Theology</td><td colspan="2">72. Liberation Model's Theology</td><td colspan="2">74. Moral Influence's Theology</td></tr>
<tr><td>Methodology Charts</td><td colspan="2">71. Christus Victor's Methodology</td><td colspan="2">73. Liberation Model's Methodology</td><td colspan="2">75. Moral Influence's Methodology</td></tr>
</table>

66. Substitution's Theology

A proposed starting point for revivalism's theology.

Examples	General Concepts
Emphasis	• Evangelism and conversion • Being "born again" • Salvation and eternal life; "soul winning" • Revival and godly living
Definition of Sin	Rebellion against the written Word of God
Extent of Sin	Total or utter depravity; i.e., total inability
Essence of the Message	Gospel is the death of Jesus Christ for sin, his burial, and his resurrection; his sufficient death for sin; the Word of God
Appeal to?	Heart regarding sin
Content of Preaching	Preach the Five Fundamentals: • Inerrancy • Virgin birth • Deity of Christ • Substitutionary atonement • Bodily resurrection Preach the six complementary convictions: • Urgent evangelism and perennial revival • Total depravity and total inability • Imputed righteousness • Need for the new birth, "You must be born again!" • Assurance of salvation • Imminent return of Christ and literal hell
Salvation/Conversion	Through the outward Word (*sola Scriptura*), the hearing of faith (*sola fides*), and by God's grace alone (*sola gracis*); salvation results in a complete change in nature
Mandate of the Church	Great Commission as [mere] proclamation of the Word of God (i.e., the gospel), and instantaneous conversion ("You must be born again.")
Priorities	Evangelism the preeminent priority
Cooperation, Ecumenism, and Separation	Cooperation with those who affirm the Five Fundamentals of the faith and share an evangelistic spirit
Faith-Reason Continuum	Faith—supernaturalistic
Inspiration/Authority of Scripture	Verbal inspiration; plenary inspiration Absolute inerrancy; full inerrancy
Eschatological Issues	Imminent return of Christ; premillennial; true heaven, literal hell with fire and brimstone
View of History	Linear: a beginning and an end; Cyclical: revival and apostasy
Christ-Culture Continuum	Culture against Christ; world hated and crucified Christ, world hates and persecutes Christians
Sample Morality Issues	For example: no social drinking; emphasizing proper separation from the world (however, separation is not one of the Five Fundamentals)
Favorite Scripture	Substitutionary portions: books of Leviticus, Acts, John, Romans (Pauline corpus)
Negative and Positive Evaluative Designations	Dualist, Heretic, *Parfait,* Wycliffite, Lutherite, Protesting, Schismatic, Sectarian, Dissenter, Pietist, Puritan, Revivalist, Dispensationalist, and Fundamentalist; Pauline; Legalistic, Pharisaical, Simplistic, Literalistic, Rationalistic, Individualistic, Personalistic, Conversionistic, Separatistic, and Immature; Conservative, Evangelistic, Fundamental, and "Toeing the line"

67. Substitution's Methodology

A proposed starting point for revivalism's evangelistic methodology.

Issues	Expansion
A. Presence	Long-term physical or social presence is unnecessary (Acts 8:11-12; 14:21).
B. Culture/Message	Biblically guided preaching is necessary for effective proclamation of the Word of God.
C. Relevance/Message	Simple gospel (Luke 24:46-47; 1 Cor 15:1-8) is primary and relevant.
D. Apologetics	Person's approach to truth or Bible does not change gospel; evangelism communicates objective truth.
E. Worldview	Clarifying and establishing Judeo-Christian worldview moves the focus from sin and the gospel.
F. Relationship	Relationship unnecessary, and sometimes may even hinder evangelism as "a prophet is not without honor except in his hometown" (Matt 13:57; Mark 6:4; Luke 4:24).
G. Lifestyle	Lifestyle is synonymous with works; its addition to evangelism process diffuses proclamation and confuses a definition of evangelism.
H. Community	Loving church is commended in Scripture; does not prove the vitality of Christianity.
I. Miracles	Miracles are helpful but not determinative for power; many misunderstand miracles (John 6).
J. Initiative	The proclaimer must take the initiative in sharing the gospel; passive or reactive evangelism are the exception, not the rule.
K. Urgency	There is an urgency and immediacy involved in evangelism; "now" and "today" are biblical emphases (2 Cor 6:2; Heb 4:7).
L. Dialogue	Dialogue, or listening to understand, is helpful and important, but not normative for effective evangelism.
M. Worship	As doctrinally sound worship includes references to the gospel, it provides a context for evangelism, but it usually requires the observer to enter a formal worship service; worship in the local church is primarily for believers.
N. Scripture	The very words of Scripture must be used in evangelism to unleash the power of the Word of God (Prov 30:5).
O. Sacraments	The sacraments have no role in evangelism; both baptism and the Lord's Supper are for believers only.
P. Process	Conversion is a punctiliar experience: "You must be born again!" (John 3:3); death to life; darkness to light; blind to seeing; lost to found.
Q. Commitment	A verbal commitment to Christ is required for salvation (Rom 10:9-10); the evangelist should urge for a response to the gospel.
R. Follow-up	While follow-up is important and necessary, it is not a part of evangelism.
S. Discipleship	While discipleship is important to spiritual growth, it does not minimize the importance of proclamation for immediate conversion.

68. Reconciliation Model's Theology

A proposed first point of drift in revivalism's theological foundations.

Examples	General Concepts
Emphasis	• Mending broken relationship with God and/or Christ • Finding meaning and purpose in this life • Worshiping Christ, without mentioning His crucifixion for sin • Local church, its programs and its influence • Knowing and communicating truth or a Christian worldview • Excellence in all things because God is a God of excellence
Definition of Sin	Sin as alienation from God, lack of purpose or lack of meaning in this life
Extent of Sin	Moral depravity or moral degradation; man's mind and will are tainted but not totally incapacitated
Essence of the Message	Gospel is (1) truth; emphasis on (2) establishing a relationship with Christ; (3) finding purpose in or meaning to life; (4) the glory of God; excellence in all things
Appeal to?	Mind regarding truth; reason for living
Content of Preaching	Begin avoiding the more thorny of the Five Fundamentals and six convictions: • Urgent evangelism and perennial revival • Total depravity and total inability • Imminent return of Christ and literal hell Simultaneously begin avoiding: • Inerrancy (as regards [1] New Testament methodology of evangelism, and [2] New Testament ecclesiology) • Need for the new birth, "You must be born again!"
Salvation/Conversion	Primary means of communication becomes relational model of the gospel (friendship) and/or radical discipleship (lifestyle); salvation may include a certain change in nature but more importantly a change in relationship
Mandate of the Church	Great Commission as discipleship (focusing on Matt 28:18-20; spiritual formation or relationship) and/or Great Commission plus Great Commandment (Matt 22:37)
Priorities	Evangelism either the most important of several biblical priorities or one of a number of priorities; definition of evangelism becomes an issue
Cooperation, Ecumenism, and Separation	Broaden cooperation to Christians who believe the deity of Christ and hold to a similar social agenda
Faith-Reason Continuum	Dynamic Synthesis I (Christologically speaking); reason is valid in and of itself
Inspiration/Authority of Scripture	Dynamic Equivalence I (Christologically speaking); limited inerrancy; infallibility
Eschatological Issues	Imminent return of Christ; premillennial/amillennial; hell may be figurative ("separation from God")
View of History	Pendulum swings between revival and apostasy; take the middle road between the two
Christ-Culture Continuum	Christ and culture in paradox
Sample Morality Issues	May emphasize grace versus legalism (i.e. avoiding the "letter of the law"; Pippert and Aldrich, "eating meat and evangelizing")
Favorite Scripture	"Nuanced" portions: book of Hebrews and Gospels; Luke 15, "Prodigal Son"
Positive and Negative Evaluative Designations	Truth is nuanced; "positive" or "encouraging" Christianity; growing in maturity; culturally sensitive; seeker-sensitive; sample statements: "We can't go back 30–50 years"; *contra* "No longer toeing the line," compromising.

69. Reconciliation Model's Methodology

A proposed first point of drift in revivalism's methodology of evangelism.

Issues	Expansion
A. Presence	Long-term physical or social presence assists evangelism.
B. Culture/Message	Culturally guided message is helpful for proclamation of biblical principles; look for truth in culture.
C. Relevance/Message	Simple gospel is not relevant; more important is preaching life here-and-now, than sin, substitution and eternal life.
D. Apologetics	Apologetics precedes and accompanies evangelism.
E. Worldview	Worldview issues need addressing prior to objective points of the simple gospel.
F. Relationship	The gospel is primarily relational, and is best communicated as relationship along relational lines.
G. Lifestyle	Lifestyle precedes proclamation as a necessary preparatory grace.
H. Community	A loving church provides a foundation to modelling the love of God and the relevance of the gospel of love.
I. Miracles	Miracles add to the power and credibility of the gospel.
J. Initiative	It is preferred for the unsaved to be gradually drawn to the gospel; the unsaved should take the initiative in asking about Christ.
K. Urgency	The urgency of evangelism must be tempered with the realities of communication and building trust.
L. Dialogue	It is preferable for the gospel to be shared with points of relevance identified through dialogue.
M. Worship	Worship provides an effective platform for effective evangelism, as pre-Christians experience and connect with God.
N. Scripture	While the words of Scripture are important, it is the clear and relevant communication of the words that gives them power.
O. Sacraments	The sacraments provide a context for pre-Christians to develop a proper relationship with God.
P. Process	While admittedly conversion is point-of-time, discipleship, however, is a process; relationships take time to develop.
Q. Commitment	Asking for a "now" decision can alienate a person who later may become open to a relationship with God.
R. Follow-up	Without follow-up, evangelism is almost a waste of time.
S. Discipleship	The primary emphasis of the Great Commission is discipleship.

70. Ransom's [*Christus Victor*] Theology

A proposed median point for revivalism's theological drift.

Examples	General Concepts
Emphasis	The kingdom of God here and now Engaging the culture using its methods and arguments Worshiping God's sovereignty, His kingdom, His rule, and His reign Living a balanced life
Definition of Sin	Sin as an antithesis: lack of love, righteousness, or goodness; sin as irrationality
Extent of Sin	Basic goodness and basic evil of man; man's reason is infected but good
Essence of the Message	Message is (1) incarnation of Christ, (2) rule of Christ, and (3) responding to the love of God
Appeal to?	Mind regarding Christian worldview (Socinian moral philosophy)
Content of Preaching	Drop three more of the Five Fundamentals and three convictions: Inerrancy Need for the new birth, "You must be born again!" Bodily resurrection Substitutionary atonement Imputed righteousness Assurance of salvation Preaching the Bible alone is not relevant Find and preach truth in culture and/or philosophy and history Preach a Christian worldview (Socinian moral philosophy), which includes social and political concerns
Salvation/Conversion	Social service and social liberation provide hope for others in this life—after all service is an end in itself; extending the rule of Christ through His visible church which incarnationally ministers to world needs; conversion is to Christ and to His kingdom program; no change in nature, rather change in ownership (as ransomed)
Mandate of the Church	Great Commission (emphasizing John 20:21) includes both spiritual and nonspiritual: (1) Great Commandment; (2) cultural mandate (Gen 1:26); (3) love (John 13:34-35); and/or (4) unity (John 17:21, 23)
Priorities	Evangelism is one of a number of equal biblical priorities; definition of *evangelism* differs markedly from New Testament evangelism (with complimentary reasonings)
Cooperation, Ecumenism, and Separation	Broaden cooperation with those who hold to a similar social agenda; emphasizing those within a broadly [Christian] religious perspective; cooperate with conversionists to protect constituency; decry proselytism of other "Christians"
Faith-Reason Continuum	Dynamic Synthesis II (Christologically speaking); reason is untainted
Inspiration/Authority of Scripture	Dynamic Equivalence II (Christologically speaking); infallibility; inerrancy of purpose
Eschatological Issues	Return of Christ less relevant; amillennial; hell is figurative, "separation from God"; open to annihilationism or conditional mortality
View of History	Hegelian dialectic/constant synthesizing of opposites
Christ-Culture Continuum	Christ the redeemer of culture
Sample Morality Issues	Moral dynamic equivalence when addressing moral gray areas in the Bible
Favorite Scripture	"Balanced" portions: Sermon on the Mount; sheep and the goats (Matt 25)
Positive and Negative Evaluative Designations	Open-minded; mature; balanced; wholistic or holistic; incarnational (50%–50%); emerging, emergent; sample statements: Greek Golden Mean—"moderation in all things"; "he's ahead of his time"; liberal and compromised; culturally accommodated

71. Ransom's [*Christus Victor*] Methodology

A proposed median point for revivalism's methodological drift.

Issues	Expansion
A. Presence	Long-term physical or social presence is essential for effective and lasting proclamation of the gospel.
B. Culture/Message	Culture provides context and content of proclamation (and therefore, culture trumps theology).
C. Relevance/Message	Simple gospel is not relevant; must find and preach truth in culture to be relevant.
D. Apologetics	Apologetics is a part of interreligious dialogue and should inform evangelism.
E. Worldview	Worldview issues need addressing prior to objective points of the simple gospel.
F. Relationship	Must move from microrelationships (God and the individual) to consider macrorelationships; from individualism to include societal change.
G. Lifestyle	Lifestyle is a living witness, with or without a verbal witness.
H. Community	Community is a living witness of Christ; we are His hands and His feet (Matt 25:37-40).
I. Miracles	Miracles add to the credibility, power, and effectiveness of gospel proclamation.
J. Initiative	It is necessary for the unsaved to be gradually drawn to the gospel; the Christian's role is to live an attractive life before the unsaved; shun proselytism.
K. Urgency	The urgencies of evangelism are actually negative, as they place the emphasis on the eternal and make the evangelist overly aggressive.
L. Dialogue	Dialogue provides the content of the message of the gospel, as truth principles can be drawn out of unsaved man and his culture.
M. Worship	Worship is effective proclamational evangelism.
N. Scripture	It is the ideas and stories of Scripture that make it cogent to the unsaved mind.
O. Sacraments	The sacraments are true proclamation of the gospel (1 Cor 11:26).
P. Process	Conversion is instantaneous, but it is also a process; both must be emphasized equally.
Q. Commitment	Conversion may not be very useful language to explain the totality of a relationship with Christ.
R. Follow-up	Distinguishing between evangelism and follow-up is a misunderstanding of the salvation process.
S. Discipleship	Distinguishing between evangelism and discipleship is a misunderstanding of the salvation process.

72. Liberation Model's Theology

A proposed continuation of revivalism's drift away from its theological foundation.

Examples	General Concepts
Emphasis	• Addressing and meeting sociopolitical and economic needs • Mental and emotional health
Definition of Sin	Sin is primarily and/or uniquely social (horizontal): man to man; racism and poverty.
Extent of Sin	Man's racism and social exploitation of others is his primary sin problem.
Essence of the Message	Message is freedom and solidarity in Christ; establishing Christ's reign of freedom and liberation over the social order; substitution is no longer the issue, Rauschenbusch wrote, "These traditional theological explanations of the death of Christ have less authority that we are accustomed to suppose. The fundamental terms and ideas—'satisfaction,' 'substitution,' 'imputation,' 'merit'—are post-biblical ideas, and are alien from the spirit of the gospel" (*Theology of the Social Gospel,* 242–43).
Appeal to?	Heart regarding inner social conscience; heart regarding the brotherhood of man
Content of Preaching	Preaching is for the purpose of self-actualization and to awaken the social conscience to social action. Drop the last two Fundamentals: • Virgin birth • Deity of Christ
Salvation/Conversion	The means is the end; socioeconomic-political equality is the goal; no change in nature or ownership, rather change in perspective
Mandate of the Church	Great Commission as evangelism is irrelevant; cultural mandate rules
Priorities	Evangelism is tertiary to the present issues of this life; evangelism's essence continues to undergo drastic redefinition; decry proselytism
Cooperation, Ecumenism, and Separation	Cooperate with those who hold a similar social agenda, even across religious lines; shun those who have a conversionistic agenda
Faith-Reason Continuum	Faith without works is irrelevant, other than as a means of human betterment; reason rules
Inspiration/Authority of Scripture	Illumination and/or intuition theories of inspiration; accommodated revelation; nonpropositional revelation
Eschatological Issues	Emphasis on return of Christ shows an improper approach to biblical interpretation; postmillennial; hell is figurative (i.e., universal salvation)
View of History	Linear view toward a constant improvement of humankind, and Hegelian to explain the maddening complexity of life issues
Christ-Culture Continuum	Christ above culture
Sample Morality Issues	For example, may include openness to homosexuality (Episcopal Church in U.S.)
Favorite Scripture	"Social" writings: Exodus event, social messages of Minor Prophets, portions of the words of Jesus, and James
Positive and Negative Evaluative Designations	Relevant; up-to-date; forward thinking; dealing with contemporary issues; W. Pannenberg, "Openness to the human situation in all of its maddening variety"; Liberal, socialistic, social gospel

73. Liberation Model's Methodology

A proposed continuation of revivalism's drift away from its methodological foundation.

Issues	Expansion
A. Presence	Long-term physical, psychological, or social presence is evangelism; shows solidarity with the human predicament.
B. Culture/Message	Message determined by cultural norms as viewed by proclaimer; seek to transform culture through biblical sociology.
C. Relevance/Message	Social, political, and economic needs are relevant; once these needs are met, then may discuss implications of the gospel to life and lifestyle.
D. Apologetics	Apologetics is education, to raise the social standards of disadvantaged persons.
E. Worldview	Worldview is the basis by which people are enslaved and exploited; must challenge individualistic economic worldviews to change the oppressive capitalistic forces in a culture.
F. Relationship	Relationships stem from an individualistic emphasis; rather need to look at societal structures that oppress the poor.
G. Lifestyle	Simple lifestyle is encouraged as an example and to show solidarity with the poor and oppressed throughout the world.
H. Community	Community is the reason for, method of, and goal for "evangelism."
I. Miracles	Don't believe in biblical miracles or in miraculous spiritual gifts; God uses natural means to accomplish his will.
J. Initiative	Christians must take the initiative to change the structures of society by fighting for world peace and equality.
K. Urgency	There is an urgency to fight for world peace and equality.
L. Dialogue	Dialogue between races and religions will bring "on earth peace, good will toward men" (Luke 2:14, KJV) along with racial harmony and socioeconomic equality.
M. Worship	Ecumenical worship (along with taking the Lord's Supper) can help break down unhealthy theological and political barriers and prejudices.
N. Scripture	Saved and unsaved are not helpful categories; Scriptures show us the importance of equality and peace.
O. Sacraments	The sacraments point to the ecumenical unity of all Christians, who ought to be striving together to stamp out racial oppression and economic usury of every kind.
P. Process	Conversion is best understood as the process of transforming societal structures of prejudice and inequality.
Q. Commitment	God calls His people to discard individualistic capitalistic selfishness and rather to adopt an unselfish lifestyle of understanding and improving all the "maddening" needs of mankind, including poverty, hunger, disease, and exploitation of every kind.
R. Follow-up	Proclamation of the gospel is less important, rather follow-up is to educate Christians to awaken their sleeping or misinformed social consciousness.
S. Discipleship	Evangelism and discipleship are synonymous, both with a social orientation.

74. Moral Influence's Theology

A proposed endpoint for revivalism's theological drift.

Examples	General Concepts
Emphasis	• Church institution and its politically corrected history • Sacraments and good works • Other distinctive theology (Marian veneration, prayer to the saints, cleansing fires of purgatory, etc.)
Definition of Sin	Sin is human weakness.
Extent of Sin	Possibility of living a holy life through one's own efforts, and thereby be an example to others (as the saints)
Essence of the Message	Emphasis on following the example of Christ, Mary, and the saints
Appeal to?	Man's personhood; the Catholic Church as the institution for ultimate human achievement and social betterment
Content of Preaching	Preaching a works salvation, devoid of instantaneous conversion; begin adopting mystical aspects of Christianity: • Veneration of Mary and the saints • Bank of salvific merits in heaven (merits of Jesus, Mary, and the saints) • Petrine succession as holding the keys (of who receives grace or not) • Indulgences, purgatory, transubstantiation, etc. Adoption of Thomas Aquinas's philosophical system and sacramental theology, whereby the organized hierarchy of the Roman Catholic Church is needed to deliver the means of grace—the seven sacraments of the church
Salvation/Conversion	The means is the means (*ex opere operato*); the sacraments (properly administered by the duly ordained priests) are the means of salvation.
Mandate of the Church	Great Commission equals increasing membership to and participation in the Roman Catholic Church; as a people become increasingly submissive to Catholic dictates, this equals the infusion of the kingdom of God into that culture.
Priorities	Evangelism is rarely discussed, unless it is for the sake of ecumenical discussion; evangelism is apologetics, bringing the "imperfect" baptized back into the church (Ratzinger, *Dominus Iesus* [16 June 2000/6 Aug 2000]).
Cooperation, Ecumenism, and Separation	Ecclesiologically isolationistic (Roman Catholics until 1938); recent cooperative efforts seem to be for self-serving purposes only, such as absorbing "imperfect" Christians back into the church (Leo XIII, "Return Model of Unity").
Faith-Reason Continuum	Reason—naturalistic; faith in traditions of human institution
Inspiration/Authority of Scripture	Dictation theory; living inerrancy of church's interpretation
Eschatological Issues	Hell is separation from God (i.e., figurative); purgatory undermines a "living hope."
View of History	Linear toward gradual assimilation of all into the kingdom of God, which is the church
Christ-Culture Continuum	Christ of culture
Sample Morality Issues	See indulgences, *Taxe de la chancellerie Romaine* (Rome: Vatican, 1471, 1484, 1492, 1503, 1508, 1509, 1512, 1514, etc.); *Catechism* (2003), § 1478-79.
Favorite Scripture	Philosophical, priestly (OT), and "sacramental" portions; books of Leviticus, Job, Ecclesiastes, Tobit, Sirach, Maccabees, and James
Positive and Negative Evaluative Designations	Established; stable; well grounded; historically rooted; "the old church"; heretical, persecutor of the true church, "Babylon," pope as the "Antichrist," "synagogue of Satan"

75. Moral Influence's Methodology

A proposed end point to revivalism's methodological drift.

Issues	Expansion
A. Presence	Long-term physical, psychological, or social presence is evangelism.
B. Culture/Message	Church tradition provides cultural norms to be accepted by inductees; church (=Kingdom) seeks to change culture through gradually increasing control and/or submission to authority.
C. Relevance/Message	The church as the depository of God's grace is the point of relevance in history.
D. Apologetics	Apologetics is evangelism; evangelism is apologetics.
E. Worldview	Submission to the authority of church tradition is the beginning of a proper understanding of a Christian worldview.
F. Relationship	Enter into relationship with church hierarchy, Mary, and the saints to gain the benefits of their grace and merits.
G. Lifestyle	Lifestyle is true and effective proclamation.
H. Community	Conversion is found only in, with, and by community in the church, "The world cannot be saved from the outside" (Paul VI, *Ecclesiam Suam*).
I. Miracles	Certain miracles are viewed as signs from God.
J. Initiative	Taking the initiative to share the simple gospel is a sure sign of a heretical view of conversion: (1) since "ecclesial communities which have not preserved the valid Episcopate and the genuine and integral substance of the Eucharistic mystery, are not Churches in the proper sense" (Ratzinger, *Dominus Iesus*); and (2) baptism (not faith) is the means of becoming a Christian: "those who are baptized in these communities are, by Baptism, incorporated in Christ and thus are in a certain communion, albeit imperfect, with the Church" (*ibid.*).
K. Urgency	There is an urgency to maintain one's salvation according to the dictates of the church.
L. Dialogue	Dialogue is a method to bring the "separated brethren" back into the church, as well as the method for constructive relationship building with those of other faiths.
M. Worship	Worship, especially the Eucharist as celebrated in the Mass, is true evangelism and the impartation of grace.
N. Scripture	Scriptures must be interpreted and taught according to the creeds, canons, and encyclicals of the church; an overemphasis on the Scripture and individualistic interpretation has long been anathematized as heretical in councils and encyclicals.
O. Sacraments	The sacraments provide the sure source for the communication of saving grace.
P. Process	Conversion is a lifelong process of discipleship.
Q. Commitment	Commitment must be made to the absolute authority, role, and veracity of the Roman Catholic Church.
R. Follow-up	"Evangelism" (or apologetics), follow-up, and discipleship are all a part of the lifelong sacramental salvation beginning at infant baptism and ending with extreme unction.
S. Discipleship	

76. Considering Four Directions of Evangelical Drift—Expanded in Chart 77

<table>
<tr><th></th><th>1</th><th>2</th><th>3</th><th>4</th><th>5</th><th>6</th><th>7</th><th>8</th><th>9</th><th>10</th><th>11</th><th>12</th><th>13</th><th>14</th><th>15</th><th>16</th><th>17</th></tr>
<tr><td>Approaches to Theology</td><td>Reformed Experiential</td><td>Reformed Rationalistic</td><td>Extreme Discipleship</td><td>Tongues Oriented</td><td>Individual Relational</td><td>Apologetic Rationalistic</td><td>Health and Wholeness</td><td>Purpose Driven</td><td>Existential/ Postmodern</td><td>Rationalistic Experiential</td><td>Health and Wealth</td><td>Demon Centered</td><td>Psychological</td><td>Positive Thinking</td><td>Social Relational</td><td>Love Oriented</td><td>Kingdom Oriented</td></tr>
<tr><td rowspan="4">Theological Designations of Sin; Sin = Root Problem Based on Primary Descriptors Used by Adherents</td><td colspan="4">Adam as Federal Head</td><td colspan="4">Adam as Natural Head (outside locus of sin)</td><td colspan="9">"The Paradox of Man"—
Basic Goodness and Basic Evil of Man</td></tr>
<tr><td colspan="4" rowspan="3">Sin as Total Depravity</td><td colspan="4" rowspan="3">Sin as Depravity
Sin as Degradation</td><td colspan="9">Sin as Deprivation</td></tr>
<tr><td colspan="9">Sin as an Antithetic</td></tr>
<tr><td colspan="9">Sin as a Sickness</td></tr>
<tr><td rowspan="2">Implied Spiritual Orientation</td><td>God Centered; God Oriented</td><td colspan="3">God Centered; Man Oriented</td><td colspan="4">Man Centered; God Oriented</td><td colspan="9">Man Centered; Man Oriented</td></tr>
<tr><td colspan="14">Individualistic</td><td colspan="3">Socialistic</td></tr>
<tr><td>Focus of Gospel</td><td colspan="6">Eternal Life</td><td colspan="11">Life Here and Now</td></tr>
</table>

Four Directions of Downgrade
A. Possible sequence of relational/social drift
B. Possible sequence of rationalistic drift
C. Possible sequence of emotive drift
D. Possible sequence of charismatic drift

Disclaimer: Titles of approaches to theology are attempts to show the variations in views of the atonement and do not correspond to any one person or theological method. Correspondingly, each view includes a variety of permutations, some more helpful than others. A biblical concept to consider: "A little leaven leavens the whole lump of *dough*" (1 Cor 5:6; Gal 5:9).

77. Four Directions of Theological and Methodological Downgrade

Model of the Atonement	Substitutionary Atonement				Substitutionary/ Reconciliation
	1	2	3	4	5
	Reformed Experiential	Reformed Rationalistic	Extreme Discipleship	Tongues Oriented	Individual Relational
Theological Designation of Sin; Sin = Root Problem Based on Primary Descriptors Used by Adherents	Adam as Federal Head				Natural Headship
	Sin as Total Depravity				Sin as Depravity
	Total Inability	Mind Tainted	Will Tainted	Will Tainted	Severed Relationship with God
Implied Spiritual Orientation	God Centered; God Oriented	God Centered; Man Oriented			Man Centered; God oriented
	Individualistic				
Appeal of Gospel	Forgiveness of Sin; Peace with God; Eternal Life	Submission to Glory of God	Appeal of Spiritual Disciplines	Appeal of Anointing of God	Severed Relationship with God
Focus of Gospel	Eternal Life				
	Death, Burial, and Resurrection of Christ	Sovereignty of God	Man's Efforts Joining with God's Grace	Gospel and Speaking in Tongues	Reconciled Relationship with God (Prodigal Son)
Decision	Repent and Believe	Repent and Believe	Repent and Believe	Repent and Believe	Repent and Believe
Preferred Methodology	Proclamation	Apologetic Evangelism	Lifestyle Evangelism	Worship Evangelism	Relational Evangelism
Tendencies of Sample Gospel Presentations, Methodologies, and/or Writings	"Roman Road"; Navigators *Topical Memory System;* NAMB's *Eternal Life;* Southern Baptist Theo Sem's *GRACE;* and Johnston's *There Is Hope*	"Evangelism Explosion" (D. James Kennedy, *Evangelism Explosion*)	Seems to expound a stoicism, an isolated spiritual growth bereft of a focus on the lost, lacking becoming "fishers of men"	A "Full Gospel" presentation: (1) sin; (2) the cross; (3) decision; and (4) speaking in tongues, 1 Cor 14:5; Luke 11:13	"Bridge to Life" Illustration: Navigator's *Bridge to Life,* Campus Crusade's *Four Spiritual Laws,* and Billy Graham's *Steps to Peace with God*

77. Four Directions of Theological and Methodological Downgrade (continued)

Model of the Atonement	Substitutionary Atonement/Reconciliation Language			Reconciliation Language/ Moving to *Christus Victor*	
	6	7	8	9	10
	Apologetic Rationalistic	Health and Wholeness	Purpose Driven	Existential/ Postmodern	Rationalistic Experiential
Theological Designation of Sin; Sin = Root Problem Based on Primary Descriptors Used by Adherents	Adam as Natural Head (outside locus of sin)			"The Paradox of Man"—Man's Basic Goodness and Evil	
	Sin as Degradation			Sin as Deprivation, an Antithetic, and/or a Sickness	
	Sin as Irrationality and Ignorance	Lack of Spiritual and Physical Wholeness	Sin as Selfishness; Ignorance of God's Purposes	God Not a Reality in Life	God Not the Object of Worship
Implied Spiritual Orientation	Man Centered; God Oriented			Man Centered; Man Oriented	
	Individualistic				
Appeal of Gospel	Logic of Christian Worldview	Lack of Physical and Spiritual Wholeness	Obtaining Purpose in Life	Gaining Meaning in Life (actualization)	True Lasting Joy (fulfillment)
Focus of Gospel	Eternal Life	Life Here and Now			
	Christian Worldview and Truth	Physical Health and Acceptance by God	Meaning and Purpose from God	Connecting with God	Recovery of Meaning in Life
Decision	Believe	Believe	Believe	Intellectual Assent	Intellectual Assent
Preferred Methodology	Apologetic Evangelism	Power Evangelism	Telling Our Story	Narrative Evangelism	Dialogue
Tendencies of Sample Gospel Presentations, Methodologies, and/or Writings	Augustine's *Confessions;* Charles Finney's *Systematic Theology* (1878); Ravi Zacharias in D. A. Carson, ed., *Telling the Truth*	"With his stripes we are healed," Isa 53:5, KJV; "I *am* the Lord that healeth thee," Ex 15:26, KJV; Ps 103:3	Rick Warren's *Purpose-Driven Life* (2003), Erasmus' *Enchiridion* (1503)	C. S. Lewis, *Surprised by Joy;* and Brian McLaren, *A Generous Orthodoxy*	Pascal's Vacuum and Wager, and Kierkegaard's Leap of Faith

77. Four Directions of Theological and Methodological Downgrade (continued)

Reconciliation Language/ Moving toward a *Christus Victor* (cosmic battle/kingdom of this world) Emphasis						*Christus Victor*
11	**12**	**13**	**14**	**15**	**16**	**17**
Health and Wealth	**Demon Centered**	**Psychological**	**Positive Thinking**	**Social Relational**	**Love Oriented**	**Kingdom Oriented**
"The Paradox of Man"—Basic Goodness and Basic Evil of Man						
Sin as Deprivation; Sin as an Antithetic; and/or Sin as a Sickness						
Sickness and Poverty Are Signs of Spiritual Death	Sickness, Evil, and Pain are from Demonic affliction	Sin Leaves Man Broken, Empty, and Emotionally Scarred	Sin Is Negative Thinking—Stinkin' Thinkin'	Problem Is Lack of Community	Sin Is a Lack of Love	Social Sin against God, God's Kingdom and Man
Man-Centered; Man-Oriented						
Individualistic				Socialistic		
Health and Financial Prosperity	Emphasis on Supernatural	Recovery of Wholeness in Life	Personal Sense of Self-Worth	Entrance into Divine Community	Need for and Appreciation of Love	Social Benefits of Christianity
Life Here and Now						
Health and Financial Prosperity	Deliverance from Demonic	Recovery of Wholeness in Life	Personal Sense of Self-Worth	The Church as Real Community	Need for and Appreciation of Love	Social Benefits of Christianity
Believe and Act	Believe and Act	Changed Thinking Proves Faith	Changed Thinking Proves Faith	To Join Christian Community	Changed Thinking Proves Faith	Changed Thinking Proves Faith
Healing Evangelism	Power Encounters	Incarnational Evangelism	Incarnational Evangelism	Communal Evangelism	Social Evangelism	Social Gospel
"Then you will make your way prosperous, and then you will have success," Josh 1:8; Jer 29:11	"I have given you authority to tread on serpents and scorpions, and over all the power of the enemy," Luke 10:19	Carl Jung, emptiness as root problem, Isa 61:1-3; Luke 4:18-19	Norman Vincent Peale, Robert Schuler, Joel Osteen	Celek and Zander, *Inside the Soul of a New Generation;* Jimmy Long, "Postmodern Order of Salvation"	Horace Bushnell, *The Vicarious Sacrifice*	Gustav Aulén's *Christus Victor,* aka ransom theory of the atonement

78. Ten Conceptions of Sin

	Personage	View of Evil	View of Salvation	Way of Salvation
1	**Plato**	Evil is the absence of good.	Living the virtues	Make conscious of goodness within.
2	**Pelagius**	Man is basically good.	Salvation as recognizing that goodness	Make conscious of reality of goodness.
3	**Horace Bushnell**	Sin is the absence of love.	Salvation as exemplifying/teaching love	Exemplify Christ's love (social action).
4	**Harry Ward***	"It now remains to carry these efforts and tendencies to their conclusion, to direct the forces of evangelism toward every part of the social order that remains unregenerate" (24).	"The call to repentance opens the gospel of the Kingdom and the first social task of evangelism is to show men their social sins that they may turn from them, to arouse and develop a social conscience" (95).	". . . for the most part the most effective social preaching is indirect, the natural and continuous unfolding of the whole gospel" (94). "Social repentance must be no vague sentiment that will permit the individual to escape responsibility" (97).
5	**Adolf von Harnack and Wilhelm Herrmann***	"Jesus does not distinguish rigidly between sickness of the body and of the soul; he takes them both as different expressions of *one* supreme ailment in humanity" (122). ". . . renewal of the sick soul" (132)	*complexio oppositorum* [dilemma of oppositions]	"Into this world craving for salvation. . . . it [Christianity] surpassed all other religions and cults" (131).
6	**James Denney**	Sin is a sickness, separating man from God.	Salvation as relational and hence spiritual reconciliation with God	Exhort persons to a right relationship through Christ.
7	**Sjogren, Ping, and Pollock***	"Both researchers agree that today's pre-Christian people *are* seeking spiritual answers to life's problems" (45).	"Relationship is the true heart of the matter" (149).	"It takes lots of tiny experiences that build a foundation of trust and inspire people to hope that perhaps there is a God. . . . this natural process" (150).
8	**Mark Mittelberg***	[Some, many, (most) people are genuinely seeking God, answers, community, etc.; Sin includes cultural blindness and secularization.]	"[No joy like seeing a friend] cross the line of faith and begin to follow Christ . . . See how the seeker . . . becomes enfolded into the church fellowship even before receiving Christ?" (80).	People need answers, crave community, and need cultural relevance and time; "A few decades ago, evangelism could be very direct and hard-hitting . . . people in our culture have *moved*" (40).
9	**Augustine**	Sin is the absence of good.	Salvation as the imputation of righteousness	Rightly understanding God's election and Christ's substitution
10	**Charles Hodge**	Sin is total depravity.	Salvation as receiving a new nature	Need: to hear, repent, and believe the gospel

*Please see bibliography for the books from which these quotes are taken.

79. Charting the Doctrine of Sin

System of Thought **Concept**	**TOTAL DEPRAVITY**	**TAINTED REASON—TAINTED WILL**	**UNTAINTED REASON—UNTOUCHED WILL**	**BASICALLY GOOD** (Christianized Stoicism)	**SIN ENVIRONMENTAL** (Behavioral Psychology)	**SIN IS UNREAL** (Buddhism, Christian Science, Existentialism, Scientology)
Sample Scriptural Terms	Depraved, corrupt, crooked, perverse, rebellious, wretched	Falling short, missing the mark, seeking	Separated from God, ignorant, without God, strangers, alien from . . .	Good, good (Gen 1:31), if he does them (Lev 18:5)	Father . . . children (Jer 31:29-30; Ezek 18:2-4)	Calling evil good and good evil (Isa 5:20)
Role of Adam	Adam as federal head	Adam as natural head		Adam example	Adam inconsequential	Adam did not exist
Man's Ability	Total inability	Moral inability		Moral ability		Emphasis on morality shows ignorance
Man's Will	Will is fallen	Will to reject after illumination	Will to receive gift of salvation	Will to obey God's commands	Ability to obey tainted by environment	Ability to follow teachings of Buddha
Man's Volition	Sin as volitional			Sin as volitional but social		Like the animals, instinct and fate guide human volition
Individualistic	Sin as individual		Sin as individual or social		Sin as social	Sin does not exist
Moral Conceptions	Sin as depraved corruption	Sin as degradation; Sin as antithetic		Sin not a part of natural man		Discussing morality is misinformed
Rationality	Sin as irrational	Sin due to tainted reason	Sin likely due to a lack of proper education		Sin due to a lack of proper education	Idea of sin is due to the false notion that right and wrong exist

80. Comparing Issues in Old and New Testament Theology

It is easy to spin off and get embroiled in philosophical theology when discussing the relationship of the Old and New Testaments (OT and NT). One can argue from a system of interpretation (Covenant or Dispensational) rather than from the text, perhaps calling into question biblical authority. In order to avoid (1) question-framing, (2) tangential discussion, (3) incomprehensible complexity, (4) paradox, or (5) a *complexio oppositorum,* I have sought issues that are clearly discussed in the NT (thus the NT is hermeneutically normative), to properly understand the continuity and discontinuity between OT and NT. It must be noted that all of the concepts in the NT are discussed to some degree in the OT, although sometimes hidden or undeveloped.

The philosophical (allegorical) interpretation of the OT goes back to some rabbinic schools, especially Cabbalism and in the church to Origen. Gregory I's lifelong exposition of Job, *Moralia* (moral philosophy), provides an example of early moral philosophy and philosophical theology in the church. Individual evangelism's literalism rarely fares well in the context of philosophical theology. When philosophical theology is applied to the doctrine of the atonement in the OT, outside of a Pauline approach and without a coherent

	Issue		Old Testament	New Testament	General Analysis
NT BIG THREE	Circumcision	1	Necessary circumcision of the flesh [and of the spirit]	Fleshly circumcision unnecessary, Gal 5:11; Acts 15:28-29	Discontinuity
	Food Laws	2	Must not eat forbidden foods	For everything created by God is good, 1 Tim 4:4	Discontinuity
	Association with Gentiles	3	Must not intermarry with Gentiles; NT Jews decried any association	God has granted repentance to Gentiles, Acts 11:18; in Christ no Jew or Greek, Gal 3:28	Discontinuity
GENERAL THEOLOGY	God	4	Trinitarian monotheism (using 4th century terms)	Trinitarian monotheism (using 4th century terms)	Continuity
	Man	5	Man as the highest created being, created in the image of God	Man as the highest created being, created in the image of God	Continuity
	Person of Christ	6	Messiah was prophesied to be the Mighty God and Everlasting Father, Isa 9:6	Christ was God become flesh and dwelt among us, John 1:14; God's exact representation	Continuity
	Biblical Revelation	7	God's written Word (incl prophetic writings) the inerrant record of God's revelation, Ps 119:160	God's Word as fully authoritative and inerrant (John 17:17)	Continuity
		8	Verbal and Plenary Inspiration	Verbal and Plenary Inspiration	Continuity
		9	Progressive Revelation	Completed Revelation	Discontinuity
		10	No adding or subtracting to God's revelation	No adding or subtracting to God's revelation	Continuity
	Revelation of Christ	11	Hidden and mysterious, 1 Pet 1:15-17; revealed by prophets or angels, Heb 1-2	Christ revealed, Mark 12:1-11; Heb 1:1-3; revealed through the Son	Greater Expression
	Moral Code; Definition of Sin	12	Ten Commandments and other moral admonitions, and total depravity	Ten Commandments and other moral admonitions, and total depravity	Continuity
	Intense Individualism	13	If you are wise, you are wise for yourself, Prov 9:12; Ezek 18:4	Each one will be judged for himself, 2 Cor 5:10; Rev 20:12-13; Gal 6:4-5	Continuity

80. Comparing Issues in Old and New Testament Theology (continued)

hermeneutic, numerous views of the atonement emerge. The result is reminiscent of a plural form of views that one scholar has called the "Sea of Midrash."

This chart is an attempt to examine the relationship of select theological and practical issues in the OT as compared with the same issues in the New Testament. This study is of interest as it relates to (1) Paul's teaching of the oldness of the letter and the newness of the Spirit (Rom 7:6), likewise by new covenant, "He has made the first obsolete. But whatever is becoming obsolete and growing old is ready to disappear" (Heb 8:13), (2) Martin Luther's view of the OT,[1] and (3) the Southern Baptist Convention's historic stand on NT evangelism and

EVANGELISM ISSUES[2]

Issue		Old Testament	New Testament	General Analysis
A New Thing	14	Prophecies that God will do a new thing, Isa 43:19; Jer 31:31; Ezek 11:19; 36:26	Old becoming obsolete, Heb 8:13; New Covenant in Christ's blood, 1 Cor 11:25	Continuity/ Discontinuity
Grace Alone	15	Grace is hidden, Gen 6:8; 15:6; Hab 2:4	Grace is revealed, John 1:17	Continuity/ Discontinuity
Justification by Faith	16	By works (impossible, necessitating grace), Lev 18:5; "and he will be forgiven," Lev 4:20, 26, 31, 35	By grace, through faith, Rom 3-4; Gal; Titus	Continuity/ Discontinuity
Imputed Righteousness	17	Earned righteousness, Lev 18:5 (Rom 10:1-4; Gen 15:6; Pss 24:5; 36:10; Isa 53; etc.)	Imputed righteousness (clearly taught), Rom 10:1-4; 2 Cor 5:21	Continuity/ Discontinuity
Message of Salvation	18	Revealed by angels, Heb 2:2-4	Revealed by the Son, 1 Cor 2:2	Discontinuity
	19	Law through Moses, John 1:17	Grace and truth through Christ Jesus, John 1:17	Discontinuity
	20	Preach the law, Luke 16:16	Preach the cross, Luke 16:16; 1 Cor 1:17-18	Discontinuity
	21	Preach Moses, Acts 15:21	Preach Jesus, 1 Cor 2:2	Discontinuity
Spoken Word	22	Emphasis on written Law of God	Emphasis on spoken gospel	Greater Expression
Instantaneous Conversion	23	Seeming gradual ritualistic conversion (contra Gen 15:6; Num 21:9; Hab 2:4)	Clear instantaneous conversion (John 3:3, "you must be born again"; 2 Cor 5:17; Col 1:13-14)	Continuity/ Discontinuity
Voluntary Decision	24	Involuntary, obedience required, disobedience punishable by death	Voluntary, obedience taught, disobedience punished by shunning	Discontinuity
Persecution	25	Christ is stumbling block (Matt 5:11-12; Heb 11:24-26)	Christ is stumbling block (Matt 11:6; 1 Pet 2:7-8), especially to Jews (1 Cor 1:23)	Continuity

[1] "Rather we must be clear and definite in our minds, on one hand, the Old Testament is a volume containing God's laws and commandments. . . On the other hand, the New Testament is a volume containing God's promised evangel, as well as records of those who believed or disbelieved it" (Martin Luther, *Preface [to New Testament]*, 14). "Therefore, beware lest you make Christ into a Moses, and the gospel into a book of law or doctrine, as has been done before now, including some of Jerome's prefaces" (ibid., 17).

[2] A NT emphasis is found going back to the London Confession of 1644, when it discussed the church and its administration, for example, of church leaders "as those which Christ has appointed in his Testament," "That Baptism is an Ordinance of the new Testament, given by Christ," and "The persons designed by Christ" (Lumpkin, *Baptist Confessions of Faith,* 166-67). The NT emphasis continued in the New Hampshire Confession (1833, 1853 addition), which discussed "Of a Gospel Church" (ibid., 365), and continued in the 2000 Baptist Faith and Message's Article 6, The Church: "A New Testament church of the Lord Jesus Christ is . . ."

80. Comparing Issues in Old and New Testament Theology (continued)

the NT church.[3] At issue is the coherence of Scripture. Is the God of the OT different from the God of the NT? Are the revelations of God in both Testaments compatible? My presupposition is that the Holy Spirit speaks with one voice in both Testaments.

	Issue		Old Testament	New Testament	General Analysis
EVANGELISM ISSUES[2]	Assurance	26	Based on grace of God	Based on blood of Christ	Discontinuity
	Eternal Life	27	Duration and quality of life (KJV) = prolonged days (25 times); long life (4 times); versus life for evermore (once)	Eternal life (41 times) versus have life (once)	Discontinuity[5]
	Spirit-Filled	28	Anointing of the Holy Spirit for specific tasks and/or in specific instances	Every Christian receives the Holy Spirit on conversion, Joel 2:28; Acts 2:17-21	Discontinuity
PENTATEUCH'S MAIN THEME[4]	Covenant Relationship	29	Seeming relationship with God through (1) heredity, (2) ritual, or (3) the Law	Relationship with God through faith in Christ's death and resurrection	Continuity/ Discontinuity
		30	Election of Abraham, Isaac, Jacob, and people of Israel (Deut 32:8-9)	Election of true Christians	Continuity
	Land	31	Rulership and/or inheritance of physical land	Church as visible sign of kingdom and Christ as King	Continuity[6]
	Promise and Fulfillment	32	God's presence and blessing in this life here and now	In this life; kingdom of God here and now	Continuity[6]
		33	Emphasis on a long life, "that you may live long in the land"	Emphasis on the life to come	Discontinuity
	Sin and Sacrifice	34	Fall of man and Passover and sin sacrifices as atonement for sin	Sin of man and blood of Christ as fulfillment of OT sacrificial system, hence "Lamb of God"	Continuity
OTHER THEMES[7]	Oppression Deliverance	35	Exodus event as a type of salvation	Deliverance from bondage motifs; demon exorcism	Continuity[6]
	Redemptive Purchase	36	Purchase of a slave; redemption of a kinsman, hence "kinsman redeemer"	Death of Christ as a ransom	Continuity[6]
	Rule of God	37	God's sovereignty over history and society	Kingdom of God motif, especially in Matthew	Continuity[6]
ECCLESIOLOGY	Called People	38	Emphasis on chosen people of Israel to bless the nations, Gen 12:3	Shift to Gentiles grafted in as "New Israel," Gal 6:16	Discontinuity
	Primary Focus	39	Primarily centripetal—Come to Jerusalem	Centrifugal—Go into all the world	Mainly discontinuity
	Mediation	40	Priests as intermediaries	Christ alone as intermediary	Discontinuity

[2]A NT emphasis is found going back to the London Confession of 1644, when it discussed the church and its administration, for example of church leaders "as those which Christ has appointed in his Testament," "That Baptisme is an Ordinance of the new Testament, given by Christ," and "The persons designed by Christ..." (Lumpkin, *Baptist Confessions of Faith,* 166-67). The NT emphasis continued in the New Hampshire Confession (1833, 1853 addition), which discussed "Of a Gospel Church" (ibid., 365), and continued in the 2000 Baptist Faith and Message's Article 6, The Church: "A New Testament church of the Lord Jesus Christ is…."

[3]Disclaimer: All the aspects of the NT salvation are found "hidden," as it were, in the OT but are "revealed" in the NT.

[4]Many additional themes may be considered here, in conjunction with the plethora of views of the atonement. Two themes come from John Driver, *Understanding the Atonement for the Mission of the Church* (F. F. Bruce, *New Testament Development of Old Testament Themes* and John Sailhamer, *Genesis*). This debate shows need for Deuteronomy 32 as the central interpretive motif.

[5]"Without speaking of the new life that has been granted us through the resurrection of Jesus Christ, we have spoken of faith, of which, after a superficial look, one could think that it is no longer ours" (Gerhard von Rad, *God at Work in Israel,* 209).

[6]The continuity of some of these themes or views of the atonement may be due to the presupposition of the authors who use Old Testament images to show that Christ's atonement goes beyond "mere" substitution.

[7]The primary themes of the book of Genesis and of the Pentateuch are much debated between authors, as they frame the question for all of theology and the atonement. I have only included some primary considerations (David J. A. Clines, *The Theme of the Pentateuch).* Again, it seems to this author that Deuteronomy 32, especially in light of 31:16-21, provides a hermeneutical guide.

80. Comparing Issues in Old and New Testament Theology (continued)

	Issue		Old Testament	New Testament	General Analysis
ECCLESIOLOGY	Worship	41	Architecture, vestments, rituals, sacrifices, special days, festivals	Apostle's teaching, fellowship, prayer, and the breaking of bread	Discontinuity
	Worship	42	Sacrifices (Day of Atonement), singing, and reading the Law	Preaching of the Word, singing, and reading the Bible	Continuity/ Discontinuity
	Primary focus of Worship	43	Circumcision as command for entrance into Israel's community	Baptism as first command of Christ for church membership	Continuity/ Discontinuity
	Ordinances	44	Sacrifices	The Lord's Supper	Discontinuity
	Leaders	45	Prophets, priests, and kings	Evangelists, pastors, and teachers	Continuity/ Discontinuity
	Focus of Community	46	Israelite community	Reaching the world with the gospel	Discontinuity
	False Teachers	47	Death by stoning (Deut 13:1-5)	Excommunication (2 John 9-11)	Discontinuity
MINISTRY	Prophet	48	Prophets raised up from among people	All Christians commanded to proclaim the gospel	Discontinuity
	Priest	49	Priests chosen by God and born to minister	Christ is High Priest; priesthood of all believers	Discontinuity
	King	50	Kings chosen from among men	Jesus as King of kings	Discontinuity
	Message	51	Law is wise (Deut 4:6); the nations rage against the Lord, Ps 2:1-3	Gospel is a stumbling block to Jews and foolishness to Gentiles	Continuity/ Discontinuity
	Persecution	52	Persecution due to God's Word	Persecution due to Christ	Continuity
	Demonic Affliction	53	Minor emphasis on demonic	Emphasis on deliverance from demons, especially in narratives	Discontinuity
	General Example	54	OT events provide a divine example to NT Christians, 1 Cor 10:11	OT examples provide instruction to NT Christians, Rom 15:4	Continuity

81. Comparing Old Testament and New Testament Principles for Testifying

This chart introduces select concepts which are too numerous to list in a chart. Daniel 4 was the starting point of this comparison. Isaiah 42:12 and 43:21, quoted in 1 Peter 2:9, make the chief end of the believer proclaiming God's excellencies.

Principle	Old Testament		New Testament Equivalency		Historical/Theological/ Ecclesiological Assessment
	Concept	**Scripture**	**Concept**	**Scripture**	
Messenger	No human listed: Enoch	Gen 5:21-24	God intervenes: Paul; man as spokesperson: Barnabas	Acts 9	The NT requires a human evangelist; this is consistent with the Great Commission, as well as with all other NT teaching about hearing and believing, and NT examples of evangelism.
	No human listed: Noah (who then became a messenger)	Gen 6:8			
	No human listed: Abraham	Gen 15:6	God intervenes: Cornelius; man as spokesperson: Peter	Acts 10	
	No human listed: Moses	Exod 3:1-6			
	No human listed: Job; Elihu listed	Job 1:1; 32:2ff.	Cornelius was similar; however was not saved until he heard gospel from Peter	Acts 10:1-2, 43-44	
	Moses	Exod	Every Christian an evangelist	Mark 16:15; 1 Pet 2:9	
	Spies	Josh 2			
	Jonah	Jon 1, 3			
	Daniel, an exiled Jew	Dan 4			
Recipient	Pharaoh, king of Egypt	Exod	Gentiles are sometimes the recipient of the gospel; universal command—whole world	Acts 14, 17; Rom 1:17; Mark 16:15 et al.	The universal call is made clear in the five Great Commission passages as well as in numerous other Scriptures.
	Rahab, a harlot	Josh 2			
	Nebuchadnezzar, a Gentile king	Dan 4			
	Sailors and all the people of Nineveh	Jon 1, 3			
Initiative	God: calls Jonah to preach	Jon 1	God commissions all his followers to evangelize	1 Pet 2:9	The NT teaches and exemplifies initiative evangelism. Nowhere is stranger-to-stranger evangelism discouraged.
	Messenger: Jonah reluctantly goes to preach	Jon 3			

81. Comparing Old Testament and New Testament Principles for Testifying (continued)

Principle	Old Testament		New Testament Equivalency		Historical/Theological/ Ecclesiological Assessment
	Concept	Scripture	Concept	Scripture	
Initiative (cont.)	Abraham: sends his servant	Gen 24	God gives two commands to Philip	Acts 8:26-29	If the "regulative principle" of hermeneutics is applied to evangelism (as it should be), then the primary means of evangelism is the initiating of conversations about Jesus and His atoning work.
	Messenger: Abraham's servant finds Rebecca	Gen 24:17	Messenger: Philip obeys	Acts 8:30	
	God: tells Elijah to go to Zarephath	1 Kings 17	In NT, usually messenger initiates: Jesus finds woman at the well	John 4	
	Messenger: Elijah finds widow from Zarephath	1 Kings 17:9			
	Third party: servant girl tells of prophet who can heal	2 Kings 5	Third party: friends bring paralytic	Matt 9:1-8; Mark 2:1-12	
	God: God sent a dream	Dan 4	God sends a dream; sent for Peter	Acts 10	
	Contact: Nebuchadnezzar called for Daniel	Dan 4	Sometimes contact initiates: Nicodemus finds Jesus	John 3	
Miracles	Prophet works a miracle	2 Kings 5	Preceded by miracle	Acts 16:31	Miracles do not provide a sure salvific preparation for gospel, Luke 16:30-31; John 6; Acts 14:8-19
			Sometimes no miracle	Acts 16:14	
Analogies	Winner of souls: "He who is wise wins souls"	Prov 11:30	Winning souls (fisher of men, Matt 4:19 et al.)	1 Cor 9:19-23	OT analogies are duplicated and expanded in the NT, as is evident in this section
	Taking men alive	Josh 2:13	Taking men alive	Luke 5:10; 2 Tim 2:26	
	Sowing with tears	Ps 126:5-6	Sower of seed	Parable of the sower, Matt 13; Mark 4; and Luke 8	
	Bearing fruit	Isa 5:1-7 (Ps 1:3; Jer 17:6-8)	Bearing fruit	John 4:35-38; 15:1-16 (Matt 4:10; 7:15-19; 1 Cor 3:6-8)	

81. Comparing Old Testament and New Testament Principles for Testifying (continued)

Principle	Old Testament		New Testament Equivalency		Historical/Theolog-ical/ Ecclesiological Assessment
	Concept	**Scripture**	**Concept**	**Scripture**	
Primary Message	Look at snake to be healed	Num 21:8-9	Look at cross to be saved	John 3	1 Corinthians 1:17-18; 2:2; and 15:1-8 makes the substitutionary atonement the essential message. C. H. Dodd (*The Apostolic Preaching and Its Development,* 1936) framed the question to exclude sin and include more than Christ crucified. He moved the message away from the Five Fundamentals of the 1895 Niagara Bible Conference
	Word of the Lord came to Abraham	Gen 15:4-5	The "word of God" is the primary message in Acts (Luke 8:11)	Acts 4:31; 8:4, 14, 25; 11:1, 19…	
	Story: Nebuchadnezzar shares his story	Dan 4	Sometimes gospel in the form of a testimony	Mark 5:19-20; John 4:40-42	
	Rahab recognized God's deliverance and sovereignty	Josh 2:9-11	God's sovereignty as introduction to the gospel	Acts 14 and 17	
	Daniel interprets the dream	Dan 4	Preceded by miracle	Acts 16:31	
	Faith in God to heal	2 Kings 5	Sometimes no miracle	Acts 16:14	
	Transcendence of God and His earthly rule	Dan 4	God's sovereignty as introduction to gospel	Acts 14 and 17	
	Humility prior to exaltation	Dan 4	Contrite heart justified	Luke 18:13-14	
	God's judgment	Jon 3			
	The just shall live by faith	Hab 2:4	The just shall live by faith	Rom 1:17; Gal 3:11	
Definition of Sin	Pride versus humility	Dan 4:27	Sin in the NT is defined as rebellion against the written laws of God, as in Lev 4:1-3, 27-28	1 John 3:4	Jesus also affirms the Ten Commandments (Matt 5), see expansion in Mark 7:21-23; for substitution as central, Acts 2:38; 5:30-31; 10:43; 13:38; 26:18, 20
	Showing mercy to the poor				
	Wicked way	Jon 3:8			
	Violence				
	Rebellion against the written Word of God	Lev 4	Is sin/substitution the central theme in the NT? Yes!	John 5:14; 8:11; 9:41; 1 Cor 2:2	
	Ten Commandments	Exod 20			
Call for Decision	Repent of his sin and social injustice	Dan 4	Persuaded to become Christian	Acts 26:28	

81. Comparing Old Testament and New Testament Principles for Testifying (continued)

Principle	Old Testament		New Testament Equivalency		Historical/Theological/ Ecclesiological Assessment
	Concept	Scripture	Concept	Scripture	
Call for Decision	Repent: "Turn, turn back from your evil ways!"	Ezek 33:11	Repentance for the forgiveness of sins	Luke 24:47; Acts 3:19	Repentance is a common thread through Ezekiel, and the NT books of Luke and Acts in particular
	"Let My people go"	Exodus	Called to repent and be baptized	Acts 2:38	
	He who believes in it will not be disturbed	Isa 28:16	Repent and believe	Mark 1:15	
			Believe	Acts 16:31	
Response	None: Pharaoh, hardened heart	Exodus	Would not believe	Acts 28:24	The variety of responses to the gospel seem to be similar in every generation and culture
			Belief	John 9:38	
	Naaman pledged to worship God	2 Kings 5	God opened her heart to respond to those things spoken by Paul	Acts 16:14	
	Delay: Nebuchadnezzar, until dream had come true	Dan 4			
	Looked at snake, they "lived"	Num 21:9	The Son of Man will be lifted up	John 3:14-15	
	Abraham believed	Gen 15:6	Justification by faith	Rom 4:3; Gal 3:6	
Point of Decision	Time of humility	Dan 4	Immediate (1) imputed righteousness is a point-in-time occurrence, (2) as is being "born again"	Luke 23:39-43; John 9:35-38; Acts 2:38;	The urgency of conversion and its immediacy are interrelated, 2 Cor 5:20-6:2
	Naaman's conversion was immediate	2 Kings 5			
Affirmation of Decision	Testimony	Job 33:27-28; Dan 4	Told town	John 4:39ff	
			Told hometown	Mark 5:19ff	
Saving Faith?	Nebuchadnezzar: likely no saving faith: (1) no sign of grace (Calvin); (2) from nonnegative (Dan 3:28), to supreme; (3) did he come by obedience of Law (Lev 18:5)?	Dan 4; Jon 3:10	Belief in Christ	John 9:35-38	The NT emphasis is on a verbal confession of Christ, Rom 10:9-10, 13 (Matt 10:32-33)
	Noah found favor in the eyes of the Lord	Gen 6:8			

82. The Reformation Pattern and New Testament Revival

Phases	Compara-tives	Reformation Pattern	Philip in Samaria Acts 8:5-25	Paul in Ephesus Acts 19
Preparation of Leader	Bible	Leader(s) begins to read the Bible (usually in a scholastic language; Latin)	Acts 6:3	Acts 22:3
	Faith	Leader comes to believe in justification by faith (from studying the Bible, the Psalms [Luther and Calvin], Romans, John, or Acts)	Acts 6:3	Galatians and Romans
	Conversion	Conversion of the evangelist-reformer	Acts 6:3	Acts 9:3-19
	NT Evange-lism	Often leader begins NT itinerant evangelism (Balthasar Hubmaier, Guillaume Farel, and F. Lambert d'Avignon)	Begins and ends with itinerant evangelism, Acts 8:4-5, 25, 40	Began and ended with itinerant evangelism ministry, Acts 19:1, 21-22, 20:1
Public Evangelism	Method	More aggressive public preaching; teach and preach, in the church and on the streets (Balthasar Hubmaier, Guillaume Farel, and François Lambert d'Avignon)	(1) Proclaiming, Acts 8:5 (2) Evangelizing, Acts 8:12	(1) Found some disciples, Acts 19:1 (2) Bold speech, reasoning, and persuading, Acts 19:8 (3) Reasoning, Acts 19:9 (4) Declaring and teaching, Acts 20:20 (5) Publicly and house to house, Acts 20:20 (6) Solemnly testifying, Acts 20:21 (7) Preaching, Acts 20:25 (8) Declaring, Acts 20:27 (9) Admonish, Act 20:31 (not ceasing to) (10) Hands ministered . . . working hard, Acts 20:34-35
	Message	Message is justification by faith through the atoning work of Jesus Christ	Included preaching Christ, Acts 8:5-6, 12, 14	(1) To believe in Jesus, Acts 19:4; (2) The kingdom of God, Acts 19:8; (3) Christ was magnified, Acts 19:17; (4) The word of the Lord, Acts 19:20; (5) Repentance toward God and faith in our Lord Jesus Christ, Acts 20:21; (6) The gospel of the grace of God, Acts 20:24; (7) The kingdom, Acts 20:25; (8) The whole purpose of God, Acts 20:27; (9) The words of the Lord Jesus, Acts 20:35
	Miracles	Miracles not an important part of the Protestant Reformation	Included miracles, Acts 8:6-7, 13	Included "extraordinary miracles," Acts 19:11-12
	Audience	Large crowds listened to Luther in Wittenberg, Hubmaier in Waldshut, and Farel in Neuchatel.	Included crowds of people, Acts 8:6	"So that all who lived in Asia heard the word of the Lord, both Jews and Greeks," Acts 19:10
	Approach	Individuals or teams of reformers	Individual, until Peter and John came, Acts 8:12-14	This ministry included a ministry team, Acts 19:22, 29

82. The Reformation Pattern and New Testament Revival (continued)

Phases	Comparatives	Reformation Pattern	Philip in Samaria Acts 8:5-25	Paul in Ephesus Acts 19
Public Evangelism	Time	Sometimes short, sometimes long	Simon had for a long time amazed them, Acts 8:11; in contradistinction, Philip's ministry was short	(1) Three months of preaching in the synagogue, Acts 19:8 (2) Two years of reasoning in the School of Tyrannus, Acts 19:9-10 (3) A total of three years of ministry in Ephesus, Acts 20:31
	Milestone	Removal from Catholic domination a milestone	Baptism of Simon seems like a milestone, Acts 8:13	Included coming, confessing, and disclosing of practices, Acts 19:18, and the burning of books of magic (worth $5 million!), Acts 19:19 The burning of the books seemed to mark that his ministry in Ephesus was finished, and that he should move on, Acts 19:21
Results of Revival	Opposition	Luther hidden; Farel, Lampert, and Calvin fled France	None recorded	Included opposition in the synagogue, Acts 19:9 Included opposition from Demetrius the silversmith and a riot, Acts 19:23-41
	Bible	Translation, publishing, and dissemination of Scriptures (Luther Bible; Olivétan translation and Bible colporteurs)	Word of the Lord received, Acts 8:14 Word of the Lord shared, Acts 8:25	"So the word of the Lord was growing mightily and prevailing," Acts 19:20
	False Teaching	Speaking against evils of hierarchical religion	Spiritual ministry of Philip juxtaposed to carnal ministry of Simon, Acts 8:5-13	Included dealing with false or partial teaching, Acts 19:1-7 Did Paul avoid overt blasphemy of the worship of Diana, Acts 19:37?
	Counterfeit Movements	Counterfeit movements: peasant revolts and Münster	Included antithetical example of a false preacher, Simon the sorcerer, Acts 8:9-11, 13, 18-24	Included imitators, Jewish exorcists, seven sons of Sceva, Acts 19:13-16
	Culture	Renaissance of the culture takes place	Resulted in rejoicing, Acts 8:8	Fear fell upon them all and the name of the Lord Jesus was being magnified, Acts 19:17
	Church Planting	New churches are established	Included baptism, Acts 8:13	Included baptism, Acts 19:5 Including the founding of a church with elders (organized leadership), Acts 20:17
	Government	Friendships are made with rulers (by Luther)		Paul may have become friends with some political leaders, "Asiarchs," Acts 19:31
Post-Revival Patterns	Religious	Lasting reform with persecution (depending on controlling powers)		
	Theological	Theological divisions take place (as theology matures)		The inevitability of false teachers, Acts 20:29-30
	Generational	Second generation leaders begin to take control		Paul's advice to new leaders, Acts 20:18-35
	Church Focus	Scholasticism sets in		
	Revival Needed	Process must repeat itself		

83. Biblical Stages in Theological Drift

This chart seeks to place on a continuum some of the teaching regarding theological drift in the Bible. Jesus said emphatically, "It is impossible that stumbling blocks come not, but woe to him through whom they come!" (Luke 17:1, my trans.).

A place to which false teachers drift is an unwillingness to call sin sin, and an unwillingness to preach repentance from sin. Note the words of Jeremiah, "They keep saying to those who despise Me, 'The Lord has

	THREE STAGES OF DRIFT	ATTITUDE Works/Obligation		
1	**Jude 11**	"Woe to them! For they have gone the way of Cain . . ."		
2	**Passage Referenced**	Genesis 4:1-16		
3	**2 Peter 2:15 (as a parallel passage)**	"Forsaking the right way, they have gone astray . . ."		
4	**Analysis**	Luther called the way of Cain that of a works salvation; going through the motions of repentance (see Cain and Esau on false repentance)		
5	**Issues**	**Scripture**	**Self**	**Ministry**
6	**2 Peter 2:1-22**	But false prophets also arose, just as there will also be false teachers, who will secretly introduce destructive heresies, 2:1 Teach false words, 2:3	And in their greed they will exploit you, 2:3	
7	**Matthew 23:2-32**	They tie up heavy burdens and lay them on men's shoulders, v. 4 Have neglected the weightier provisions of the law, v. 23	They do all their deeds to be noticed by men, v. 5 Self-exaltation, v. 12 On the outside appear beautiful, but inside they are full of dead men's bones, vv. 27-28	Make long prayers, v. 14 Travel . . . to make one proselyte . . . make him twice as much a son of hell as yourselves, v. 15 Clean the outside of the cup . . . but inside, v. 25
8	**Mark 7:6-13**	Teaching doctrines of men, v. 7 Neglecting the command of God, v. 8		
9	**Mark 12:38-40**		Walk around in long robes, respectful greetings, vv. 38-39	For appearance's sake offer long prayers, v. 40
10	**Luke 11:39-52**	Emphasize details and miss the point, v. 42 Legalism, v. 46, placing burdens	Want to be noticed, v. 43	
11	**1 Timothy 4:1-3**	Forbid marriage and advocate abstaining from foods, v. 3		
12	**Luke 20:45-47**		Walk around in long robes, respectful greetings, . . . v. 46	For appearance's sake offer long prayers, v. 47
13	**Correlating Passages and Issues**	"Woe *to you* when all men speak well of you, for their fathers used to treat the false prophets in the same way," Luke 6:26		

83. Biblical Stages in Theological Drift (continued)

said, "You will have peace'"; And as for everyone who walks in the stubbornness of his own heart, They say, 'Calamity will not come upon you'" (Jer 23:17).

	ACTIONS Money/Idolatry and Immorality					**THEOLOGY Basic Goodness of Man**		
1	"...and for pay they have rushed headlong into the error of Balaam..."					"...and perished in the rebellion of Korah" (Jude 1)		
2	Numbers 22-25					Numbers 16:1-40		
3	"...having followed the way of Balaam, the *son* of Beor, who loved the wages of unrighteousness" (2 Pet 6:10)							
4	For pay, Balaam set himself against God's chosen people; partnering with the enemies of God for profit; was this not the sin of Judas? "Prophet for Hire"					"You have gone far enough, for all the congregation are holy, every one of them, and the Lord is in their midst," (Num 16:3).		
5	**Greedy**	**Cunning/ Fetish-ism**	**Immoral**	**Self-justifying**	**Hypo-critical**	**Herme-neutic**	**Man's Nature**	**Conversion/ Christology**
6	And in their greed they will exploit you, 2:3; having hearts trained in greed, 2:14	Enticing unstable souls, 2:14	Many will follow their sensuality, 2:2; 2:13-14, 19			Reveling in their deceptions, 2:13 Reviling where they have no knowledge, 2:12	Promising freedom while they themselves are slaves of corruption, 2:19	Denying the Master who bought them, 2:1
7	Devour widows' houses, 14; Full of robbery, 25	Full of dead men's bones and all uncleanness, 27	Full of... indulgence, 25	Self-justifying hermeneutic, 16-22 Self-justifying appeal to past, 29-32	Full of hypocrisy and lawlessness, 28; kill prophets of God, 34-35	Blind guides, who say ... You fools and blind men... You blind men, which is more important, 16-19	Clean the outside, ignore the inside (their own depravity), 25-28	Shut off the kingdom of heaven from people... 13
8	Steal from father or mother, 11-13				Hypocritical, 6	Set aside command of God for tradition, 9-13		
9	Devour widows' houses, 40							
10	Full of robbery and wickedness, 39		Like concealed tombs, 44		They will kill and crucify true prophets, 47-51	Have taken away the key of knowledge, 52		Hindered those who were entering, 52
11		Seared in conscience as with branding iron, 2				Paying attention to deceitful spirits and doctrines of demons, 1		Fall away from the faith, 1
12	Devour widows' houses, 47							
13	Rev 2:14; 2 Cor 2:17, "we are not like many, peddling the word of God"; "Free from the love of money," 1 Tim 3:3; "not fond of sordid gain," Titus 1:7; 1 Pet 5:2; Acts 19:11-12 (2 Kgs 18:4; Ezek 13:17-23; Hos 5:4; Mic 3:11)					Most theological material on false teachers deals with Christology, 1 Cor 12:2-3; 2 Cor 11:4; 1 John 2:22ff; 4:1-3; 2 Pet 2:1; 2 John 7; Jude 4		

84. Comparing Reformation Churches

	Issue	Roman Catholic	Anglican	Lutheran
1	**Interpretation of the Bible and Tradition**	Traditions of church are equal to and interpret Scripture	Keep all traditions that are not against Scripture	Keep all traditions that are not against Scripture
2	**Deuterocanonical Books**	Keep and defend deuterocanonical books	Separate deuterocanonical books; KJV	Remove and ignore deuterocanonical books
3	**Church-State Relations**	The pope is head over the church and state	Church an arm of the state—king is the guardian of the faith	Churches and states have different realms over which they are administrators; state enforces religious laws
4	**Baptism**	Infant baptism is the first of seven sacraments and communicates grace	Infant baptism is salvific	Infant baptism brings into community of grace
5	**Communion**	Transubstantiation, very body and blood; communicates grace	Include proponents of both transubstantiation and of spiritual presence	Consubstantiation; real presence of Christ in elements
6	**Evangelism**	Evangelism through sacraments	Combine formal evangelism (preaching in church) and/or sacramental views	Emphasize formal evangelism, as well as personal Bible reading
7	**View of New Testament Evangelism**	NT evangelism is method of "heretics"	NT evangelism is method of dissenters	NT evangelism is method of Anabaptists
8	**Persecutors of**	All Protestants	Dissenters; especially during Catholic monarchies	Anabaptists
9	**Persecuted by**	Some Protestant states	Catholic monarchs killed some archbishops	French Catholics and German Catholic rulers

Disclaimer: Some positions are generalizations to show contrasting views; nonhierarchical churches may have greater variety.

84. Comparing Reformation Churches (continued)

	Reformed	Zwinglian	Anabaptist	Radical
1	Keep only traditions that are explicitly taught in Scripture	Organize church as is directly taught in Scripture	Organize church as is directly taught in Scripture	Organize church as is directly taught in Scripture
2	Remove and ignore deuterocanonical books	Remove and ignore deuterocanonical books	Remove and ignore deuterocanonical books	Remove and ignore deuterocanonical books
3	Churches and states have different realms over which they are administrators, state enforces religious laws	Churches and states have different realms over which they are administrators, state enforces religious laws	Churches and states have different realms over which they are administrators, freedom of conscience	Churches and states have different realms over which they are administrators, state enforces religious laws
4	Infant baptism brings into community of grace	Infant baptism brings into community of grace	Infant baptism invalid, believer's baptism only	Infant baptism invalid, believer's baptism only
5	Spiritual presence	Memorial only	Memorial only	Memorial only
6	Emphasize catechetical evangelism	Emphasize personal evangelism	Emphasize personal evangelism	Emphasize personal evangelism
7	NT evangelism allowed if aligned with state church	NT evangelism allowed if aligned with state church	NT evangelism is nonnegotiable, as it is commanded by Christ	NT evangelism emphasized prior to period of social revolution
8	Servetus burned for rebellion against civil law	Anabaptists	No one	Authorities in Münster; peasant revolts
9	French Catholics*	Catholic cantons (counties)	Catholics, some Protestant groups also	German Catholics

*Many French Huguenots were martyred because they did not: (1) take Mass; (2) go to confession; (3) bow to the statue of Mary during a processional; or else because they: (4) evangelized; (5) sold Protestant Bibles; or (6) attended a Reformed church.

85. History of Evangelism Methodologies in U.S. Churches

Solomon was correct when he wrote in Ecclesiastes 1:9, "That which has been is that which will be, and that which has been done is that which will be done. So there is nothing new under the sun." Then he added in verse 11, "There is no remembrance of earlier things." These sayings in the world of thought have no human exceptions and only one divine exception: the revelation of God in Christ and the gospel message. In the

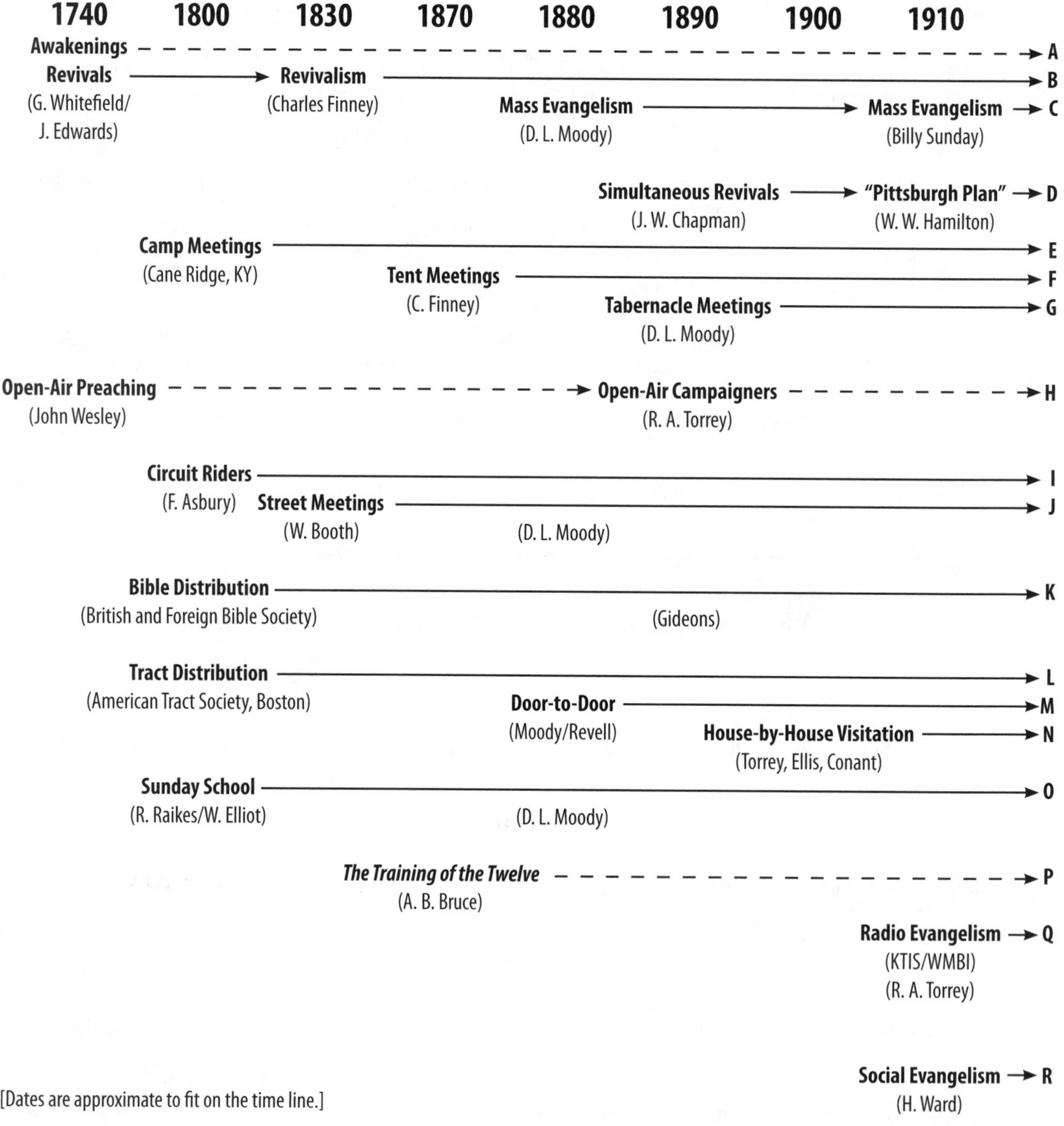

85. History of Evangelism Methodologies in U.S. Churches (continued)

realm of the communication of the gospel, there is nothing new under the sun. Even in the 13th century, the same issues we seek to clarify today were being debated at various levels (e.g. *vita evangelica, vir evangelicus,* and *imitatio Christi*). The following sampling of evangelism methodologies in the history of churches in the United States is not exhaustive or complete.

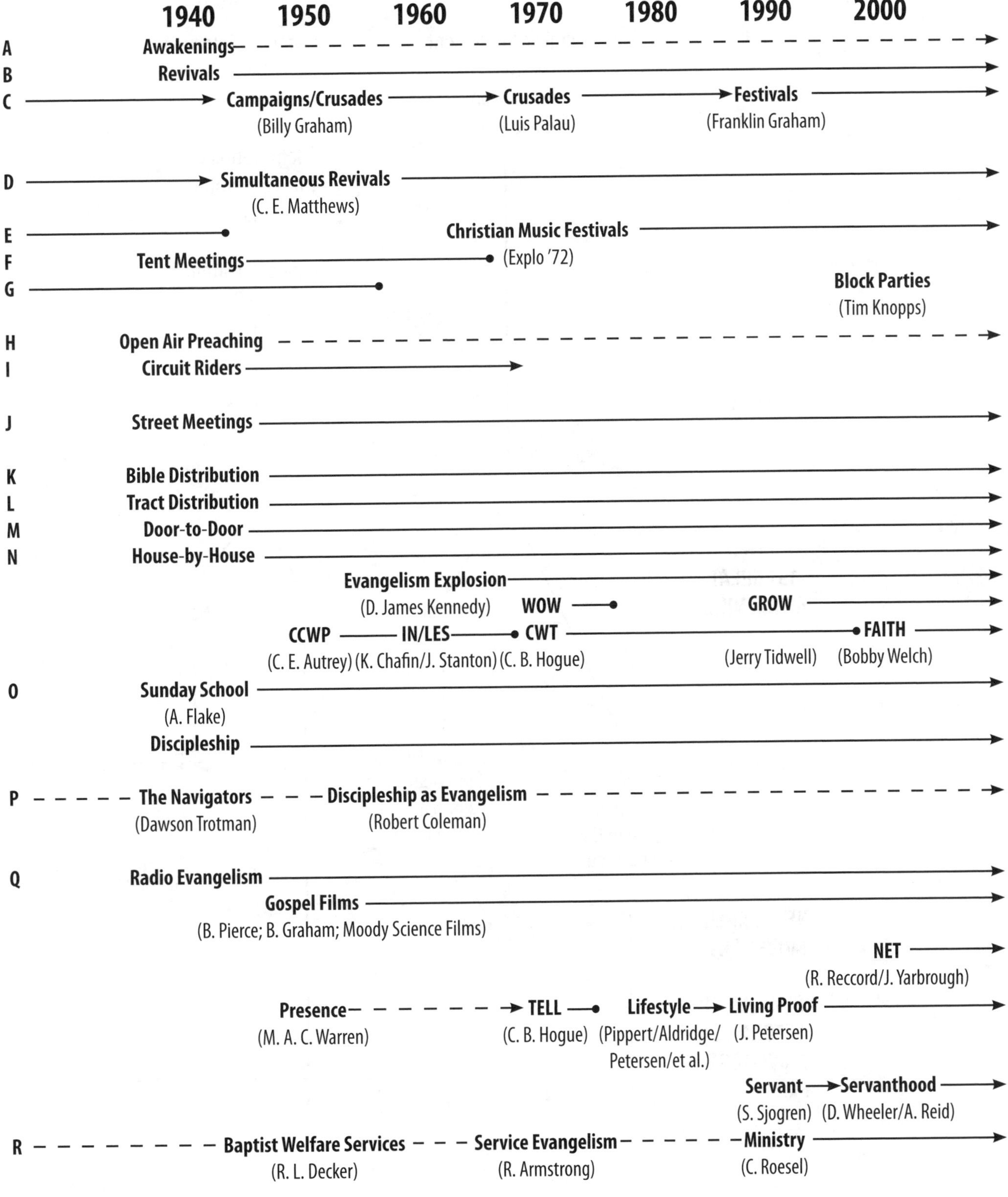

86. The Impact of Revival on U.S. Denominations

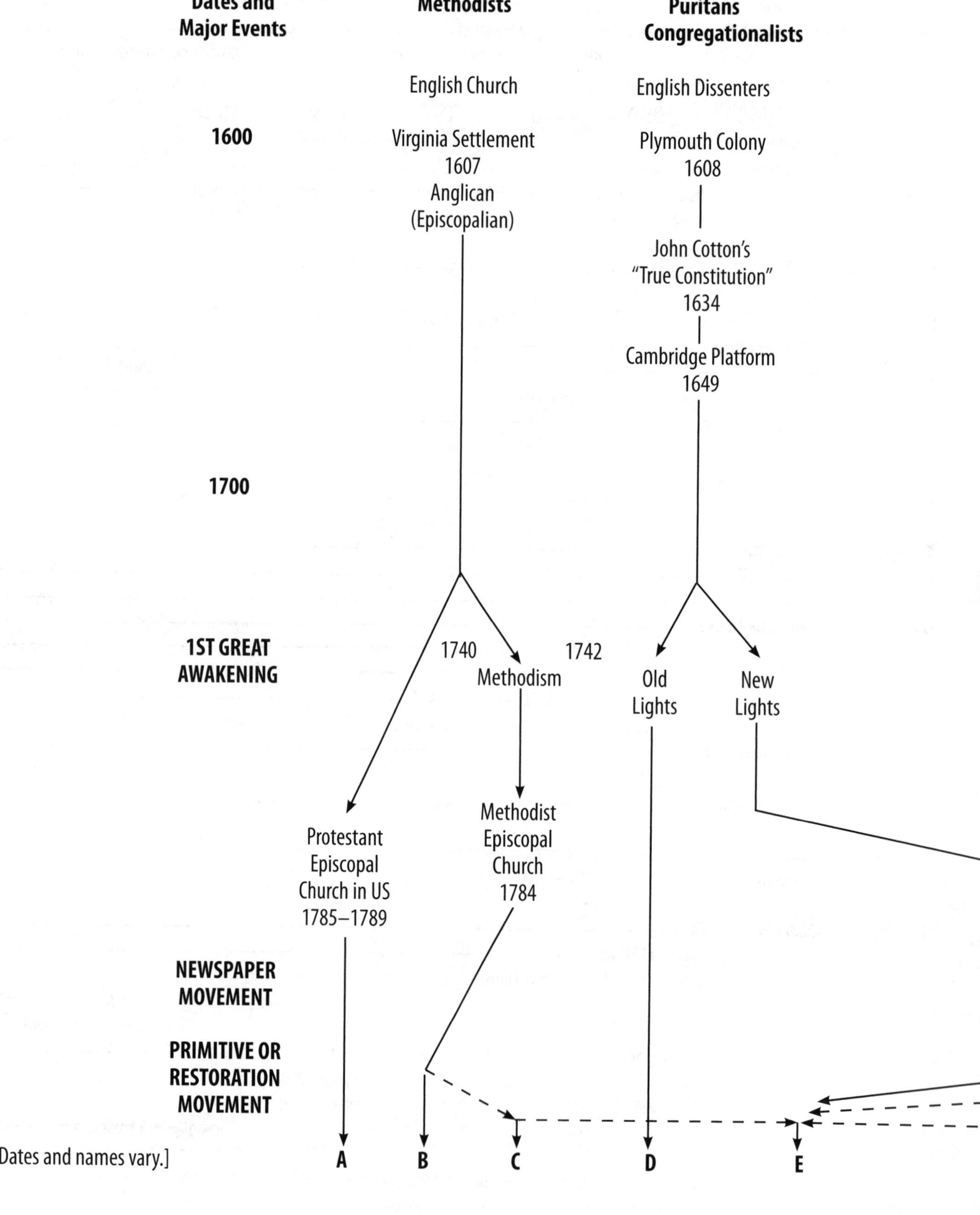
Dates and Major Events
Methodists
Puritans Congregationalists
English Church
English Dissenters
1600
Virginia Settlement 1607 Anglican (Episcopalian)
Plymouth Colony 1608
John Cotton's "True Constitution" 1634
Cambridge Platform 1649
1700
1ST GREAT AWAKENING
1740
1742
Methodism
Old Lights
New Lights
Protestant Episcopal Church in US 1785–1789
Methodist Episcopal Church 1784
NEWSPAPER MOVEMENT
PRIMITIVE OR RESTORATION MOVEMENT
[Dates and names vary.]
A
B
C
D
E

86. The Impact of Revival on U.S. Denominations (continued)

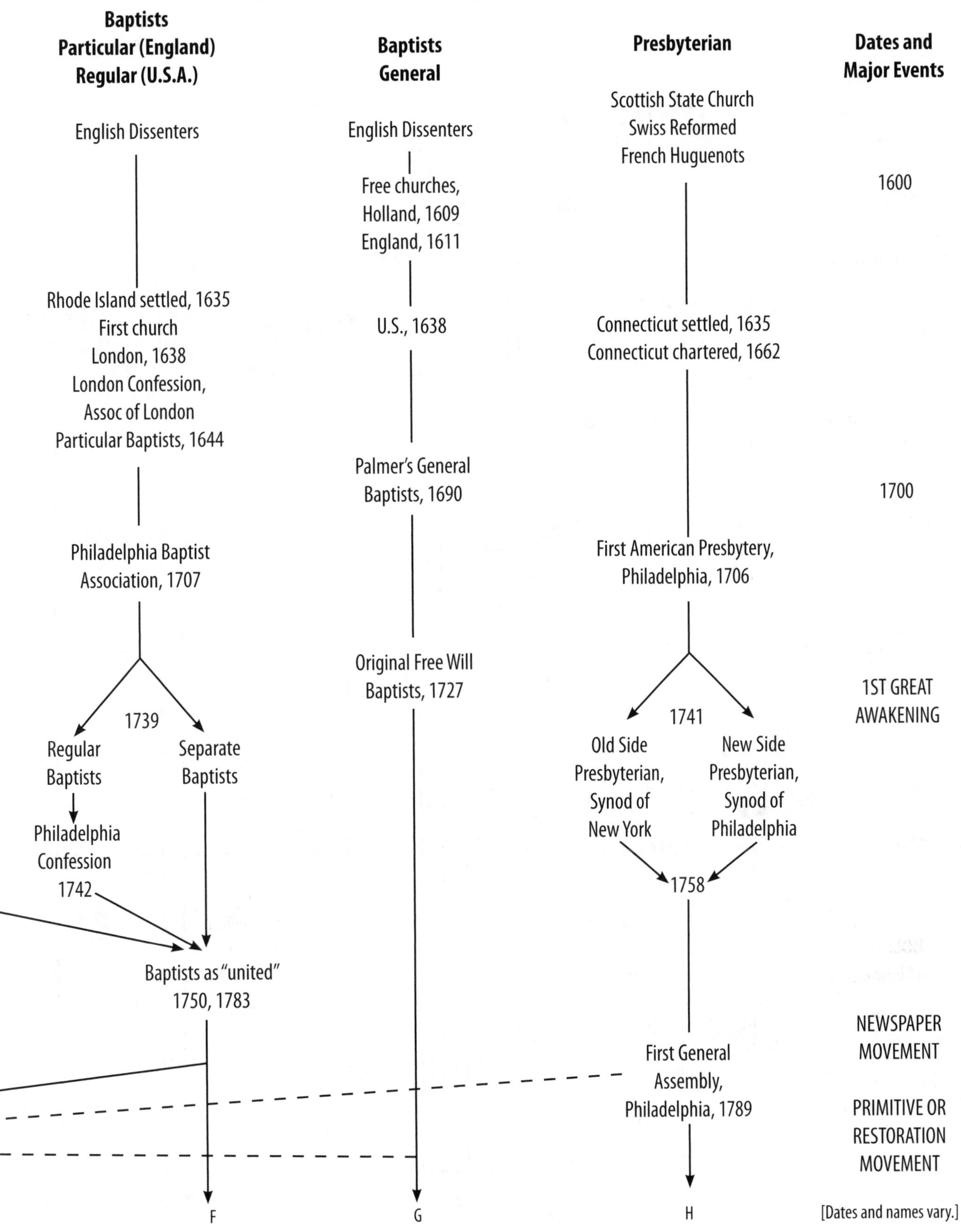
Baptists
Particular (England)
Regular (U.S.A.)
Baptists
General
Presbyterian
Dates and
Major Events
English Dissenters
English Dissenters
Free churches,
Holland, 1609
England, 1611
Scottish State Church
Swiss Reformed
French Huguenots
1600
Rhode Island settled, 1635
First church
London, 1638
London Confession,
Assoc of London
Particular Baptists, 1644
U.S., 1638
Connecticut settled, 1635
Connecticut chartered, 1662
Palmer's General
Baptists, 1690
1700
Philadelphia Baptist
Association, 1707
First American Presbytery,
Philadelphia, 1706
Original Free Will
Baptists, 1727
1739
Regular
Baptists
Separate
Baptists
Philadelphia
Confession
1742
1741
Old Side
Presbyterian,
Synod of
New York
New Side
Presbyterian,
Synod of
Philadelphia
1ST GREAT
AWAKENING
1758
Baptists as "united"
1750, 1783
First General
Assembly,
Philadelphia, 1789
NEWSPAPER
MOVEMENT
PRIMITIVE OR
RESTORATION
MOVEMENT
F
G
H
[Dates and names vary.]

86. The Impact of Revival on U.S. Denominations (continued)

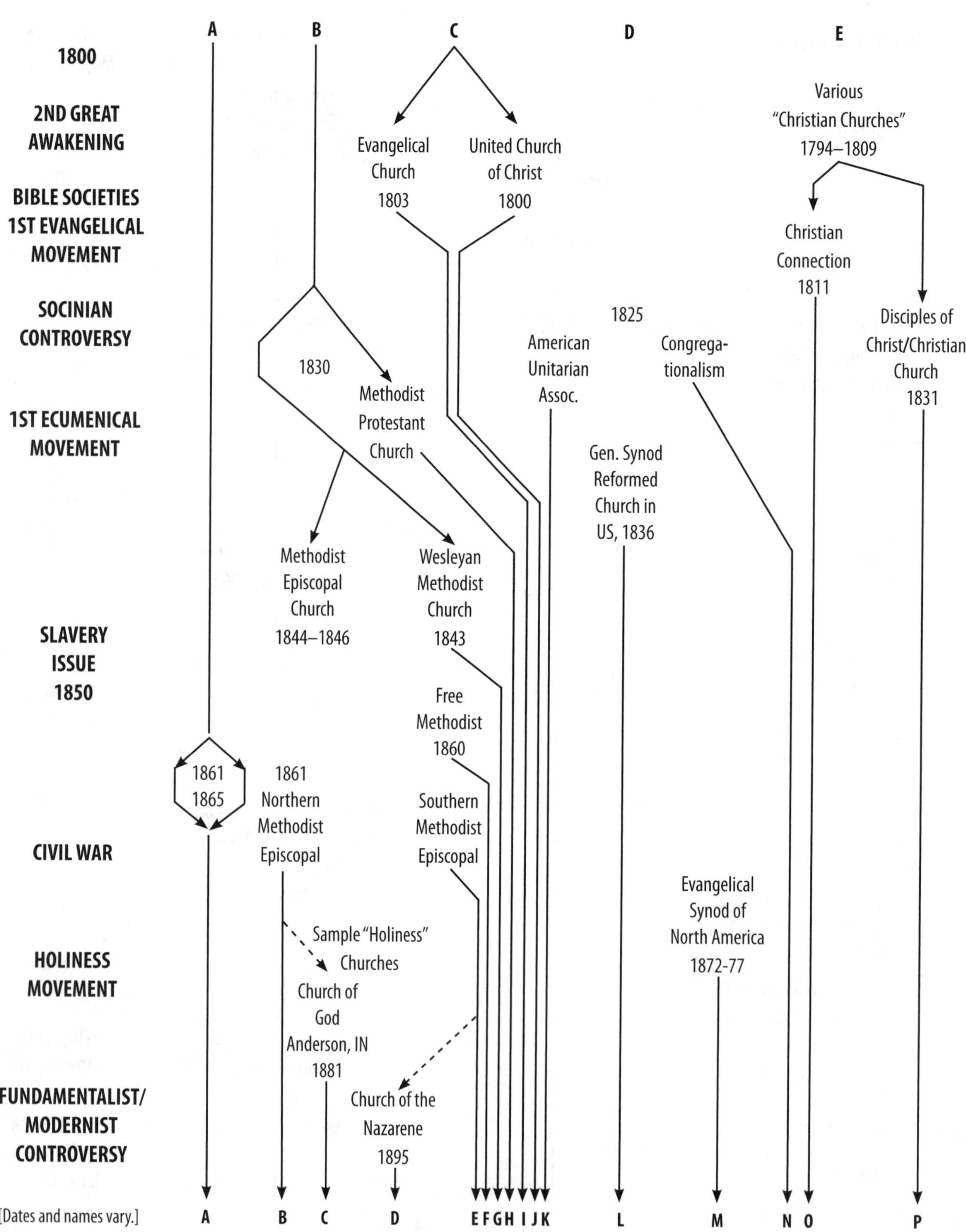

A
B
C
D
E
1800
2ND GREAT AWAKENING
BIBLE SOCIETIES 1ST EVANGELICAL MOVEMENT
SOCINIAN CONTROVERSY
1ST ECUMENICAL MOVEMENT
SLAVERY ISSUE 1850
CIVIL WAR
HOLINESS MOVEMENT
FUNDAMENTALIST/ MODERNIST CONTROVERSY
[Dates and names vary.]
Evangelical Church 1803
United Church of Christ 1800
Various "Christian Churches" 1794–1809
Christian Connection 1811
1825
American Unitarian Assoc.
Congrega- tionalism
Disciples of Christ/Christian Church 1831
1830
Methodist Protestant Church
Gen. Synod Reformed Church in US, 1836
Methodist Episcopal Church 1844–1846
Wesleyan Methodist Church 1843
Free Methodist 1860
1861 1865
1861 Northern Methodist Episcopal
Southern Methodist Episcopal
Evangelical Synod of North America 1872-77
Sample "Holiness" Churches
Church of God Anderson, IN 1881
Church of the Nazarene 1895
A
B
C
D
E F G H I J K
L
M
N O
P

86. The Impact of Revival on U.S. Denominations (continued)

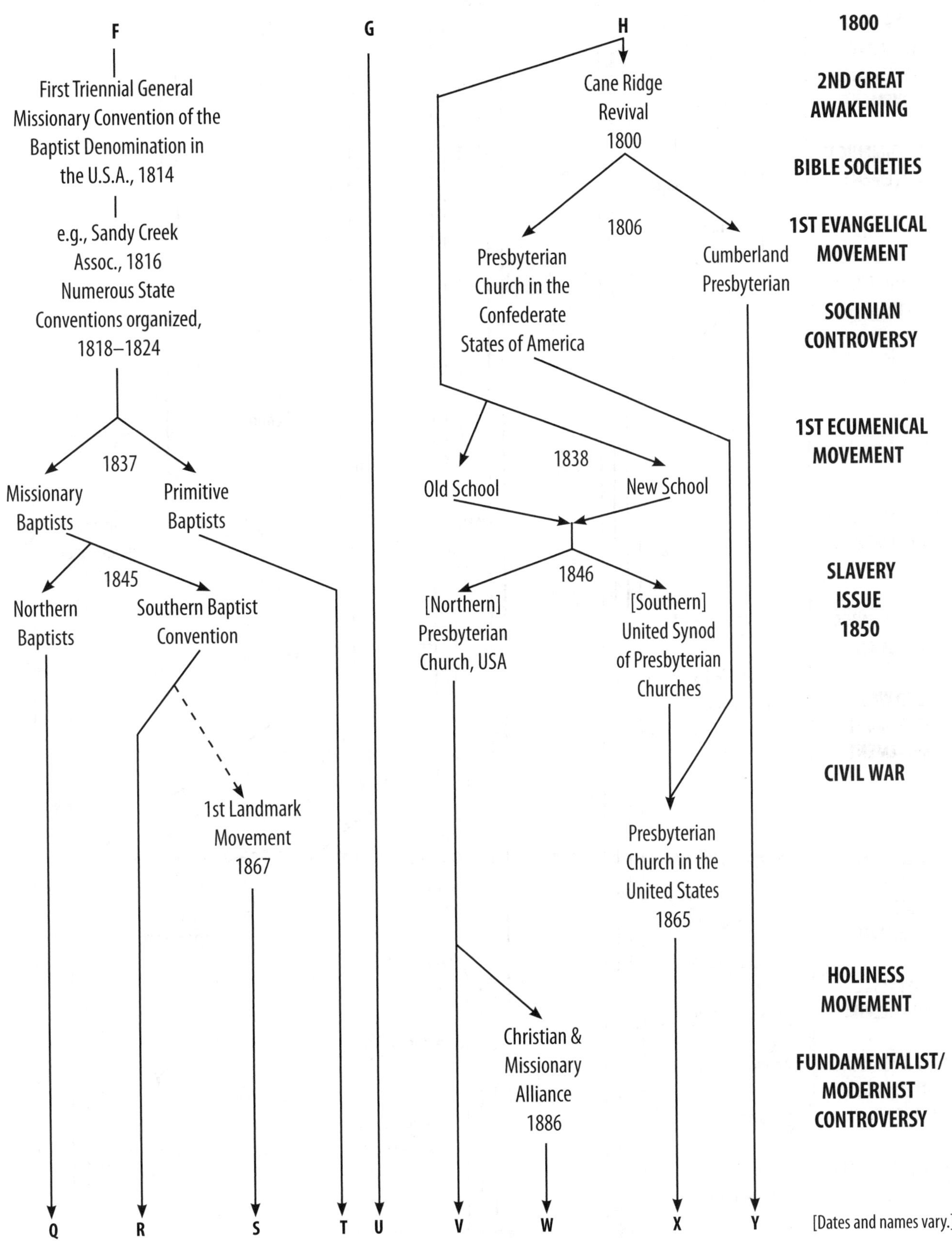
F
G
H
1800
First Triennial General Missionary Convention of the Baptist Denomination in the U.S.A., 1814
e.g., Sandy Creek Assoc., 1816
Numerous State Conventions organized, 1818–1824
Cane Ridge Revival 1800
2ND GREAT AWAKENING
BIBLE SOCIETIES
1806
1ST EVANGELICAL MOVEMENT
Presbyterian Church in the Confederate States of America
Cumberland Presbyterian
SOCINIAN CONTROVERSY
1ST ECUMENICAL MOVEMENT
1837
Missionary Baptists
Primitive Baptists
1838
Old School
New School
1845
Northern Baptists
Southern Baptist Convention
1846
[Northern] Presbyterian Church, USA
[Southern] United Synod of Presbyterian Churches
SLAVERY ISSUE 1850
CIVIL WAR
1st Landmark Movement 1867
Presbyterian Church in the United States 1865
HOLINESS MOVEMENT
Christian & Missionary Alliance 1886
FUNDAMENTALIST/ MODERNIST CONTROVERSY
Q
R
S
T
U
V
W
X
Y
[Dates and names vary.]

86. The Impact of Revival on Select U.S. Denominations (continued)

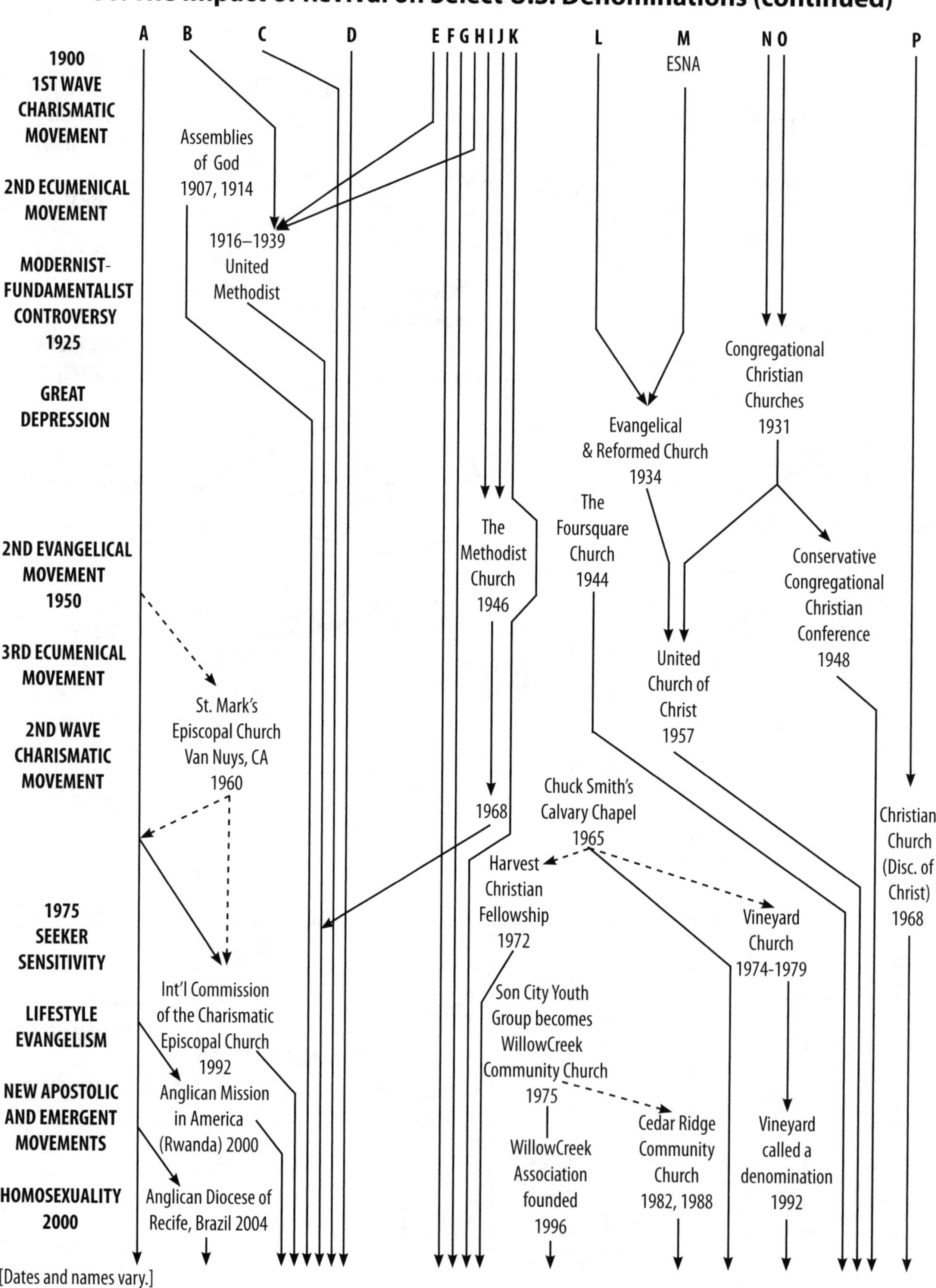
A
B
C
D
E F G H I J K
L
M
N O
P
1900
1ST WAVE
CHARISMATIC
MOVEMENT
2ND ECUMENICAL
MOVEMENT
MODERNIST-
FUNDAMENTALIST
CONTROVERSY
1925
GREAT
DEPRESSION
2ND EVANGELICAL
MOVEMENT
1950
3RD ECUMENICAL
MOVEMENT
2ND WAVE
CHARISMATIC
MOVEMENT
1975
SEEKER
SENSITIVITY
LIFESTYLE
EVANGELISM
NEW APOSTOLIC
AND EMERGENT
MOVEMENTS
HOMOSEXUALITY
2000
ESNA
Assemblies of God 1907, 1914
1916–1939 United Methodist
Congregational Christian Churches 1931
Evangelical & Reformed Church 1934
The Foursquare Church 1944
The Methodist Church 1946
Conservative Congregational Christian Conference 1948
United Church of Christ 1957
St. Mark's Episcopal Church Van Nuys, CA 1960
Chuck Smith's Calvary Chapel 1965
1968
Christian Church (Disc. of Christ) 1968
Harvest Christian Fellowship 1972
Vineyard Church 1974-1979
Son City Youth Group becomes WillowCreek Community Church 1975
Int'l Commission of the Charismatic Episcopal Church 1992
Anglican Mission in America (Rwanda) 2000
Anglican Diocese of Recife, Brazil 2004
WillowCreek Association founded 1996
Cedar Ridge Community Church 1982, 1988
Vineyard called a denomination 1992
[Dates and names vary.]

86. The Impact of Revival on U.S. Denominations (continued)

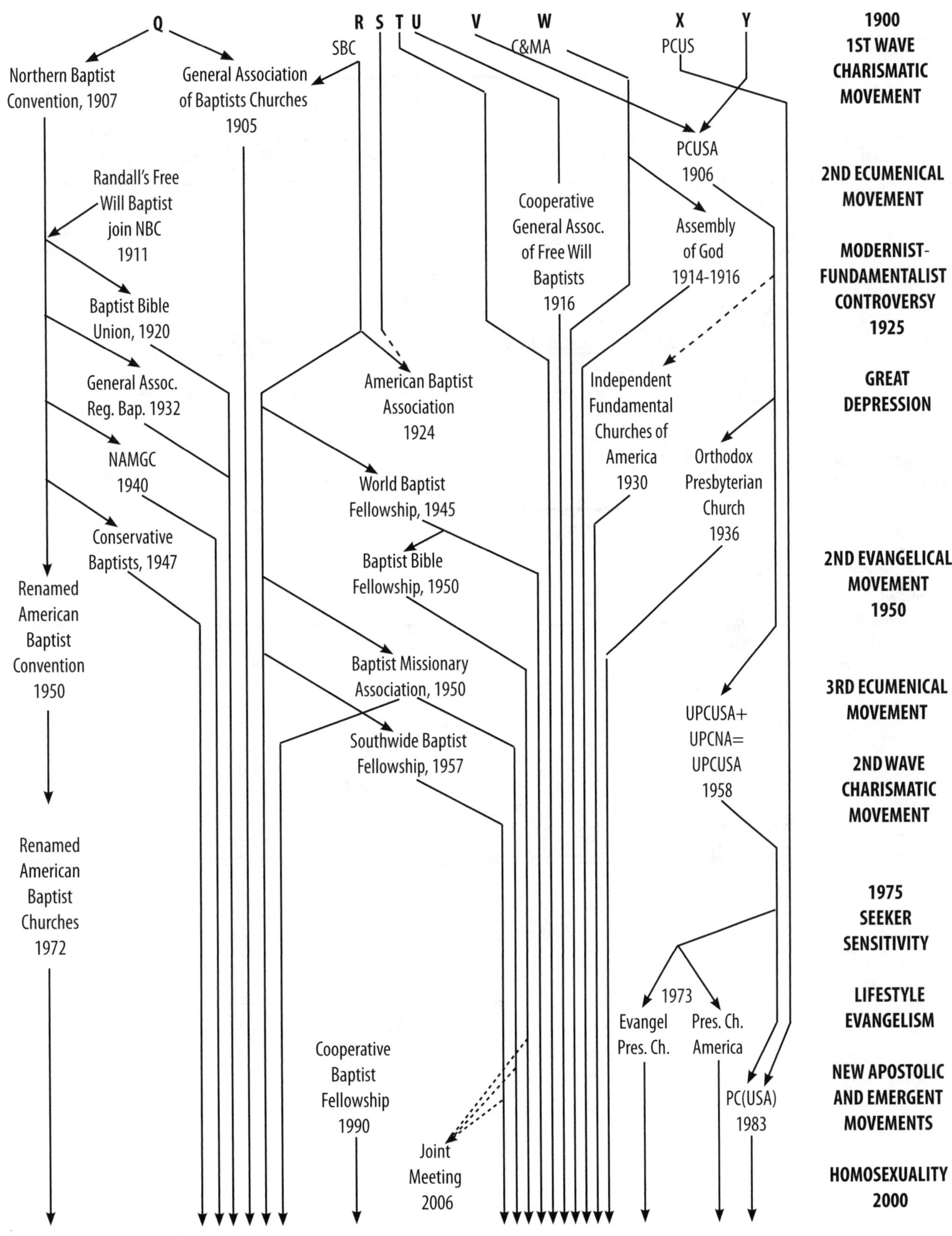
Q
R S T U V W X Y
SBC
C&MA
PCUS
Northern Baptist Convention, 1907
General Association of Baptists Churches 1905
PCUSA 1906
Randall's Free Will Baptist join NBC 1911
Cooperative General Assoc. of Free Will Baptists 1916
Assembly of God 1914-1916
Baptist Bible Union, 1920
American Baptist Association 1924
General Assoc. Reg. Bap. 1932
Independent Fundamental Churches of America 1930
Orthodox Presbyterian Church 1936
NAMGC 1940
World Baptist Fellowship, 1945
Conservative Baptists, 1947
Baptist Bible Fellowship, 1950
Renamed American Baptist Convention 1950
Baptist Missionary Association, 1950
UPCUSA+ UPCNA= UPCUSA 1958
Southwide Baptist Fellowship, 1957
Renamed American Baptist Churches 1972
1973
Evangel Pres. Ch.
Pres. Ch. America
Cooperative Baptist Fellowship 1990
PC(USA) 1983
Joint Meeting 2006
1900 1ST WAVE CHARISMATIC MOVEMENT
2ND ECUMENICAL MOVEMENT
MODERNIST-FUNDAMENTALIST CONTROVERSY 1925
GREAT DEPRESSION
2ND EVANGELICAL MOVEMENT 1950
3RD ECUMENICAL MOVEMENT
2ND WAVE CHARISMATIC MOVEMENT
1975 SEEKER SENSITIVITY
LIFESTYLE EVANGELISM
NEW APOSTOLIC AND EMERGENT MOVEMENTS
HOMOSEXUALITY 2000

[Dates and names vary.]

87. Disunity and Unity in Church History

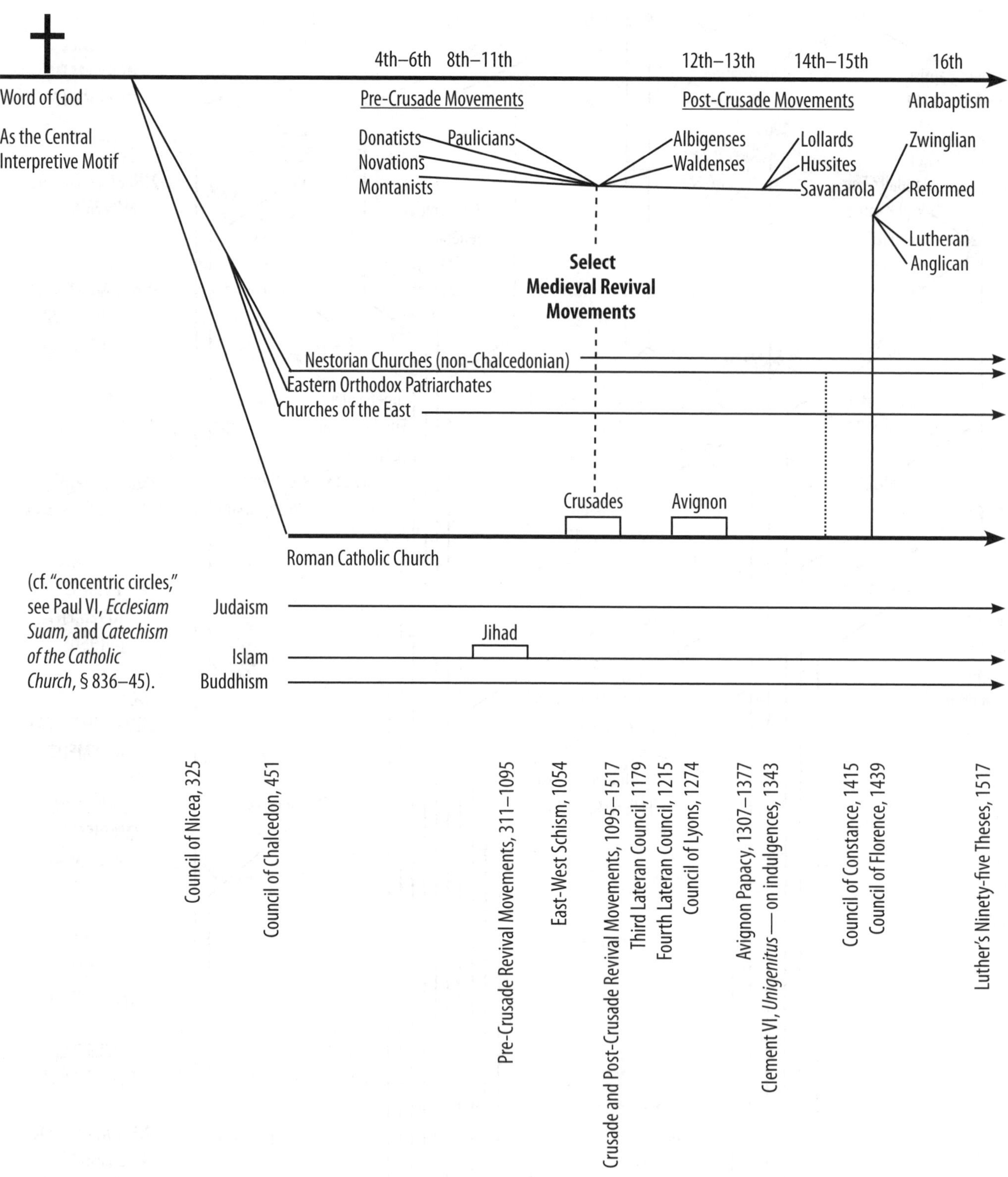

[some dates may vary]

87. Disunity and Unity in Church History (continued)

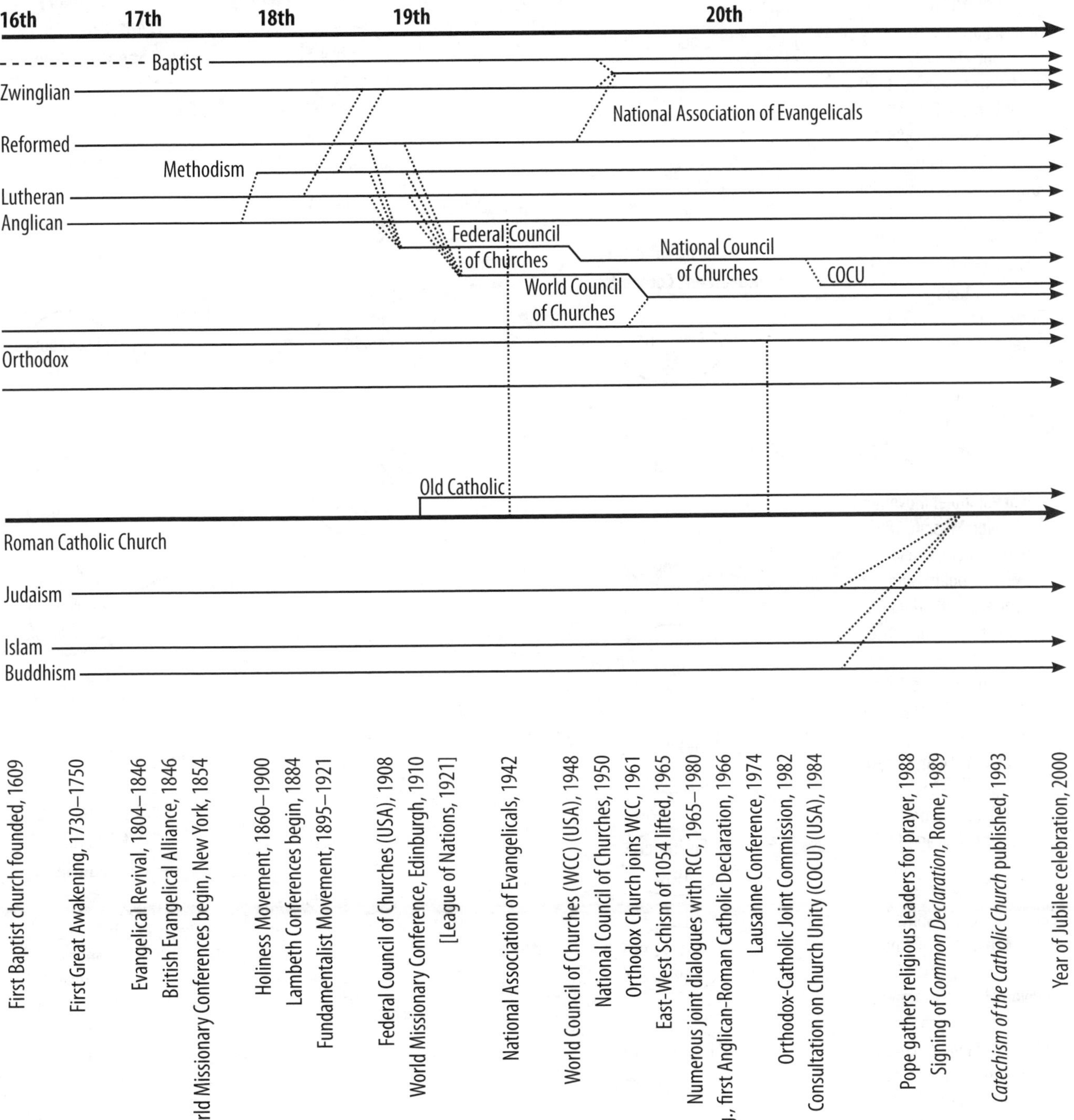

[Some dates may vary.]

88. A Visual History of Cooperation, 1800–1930

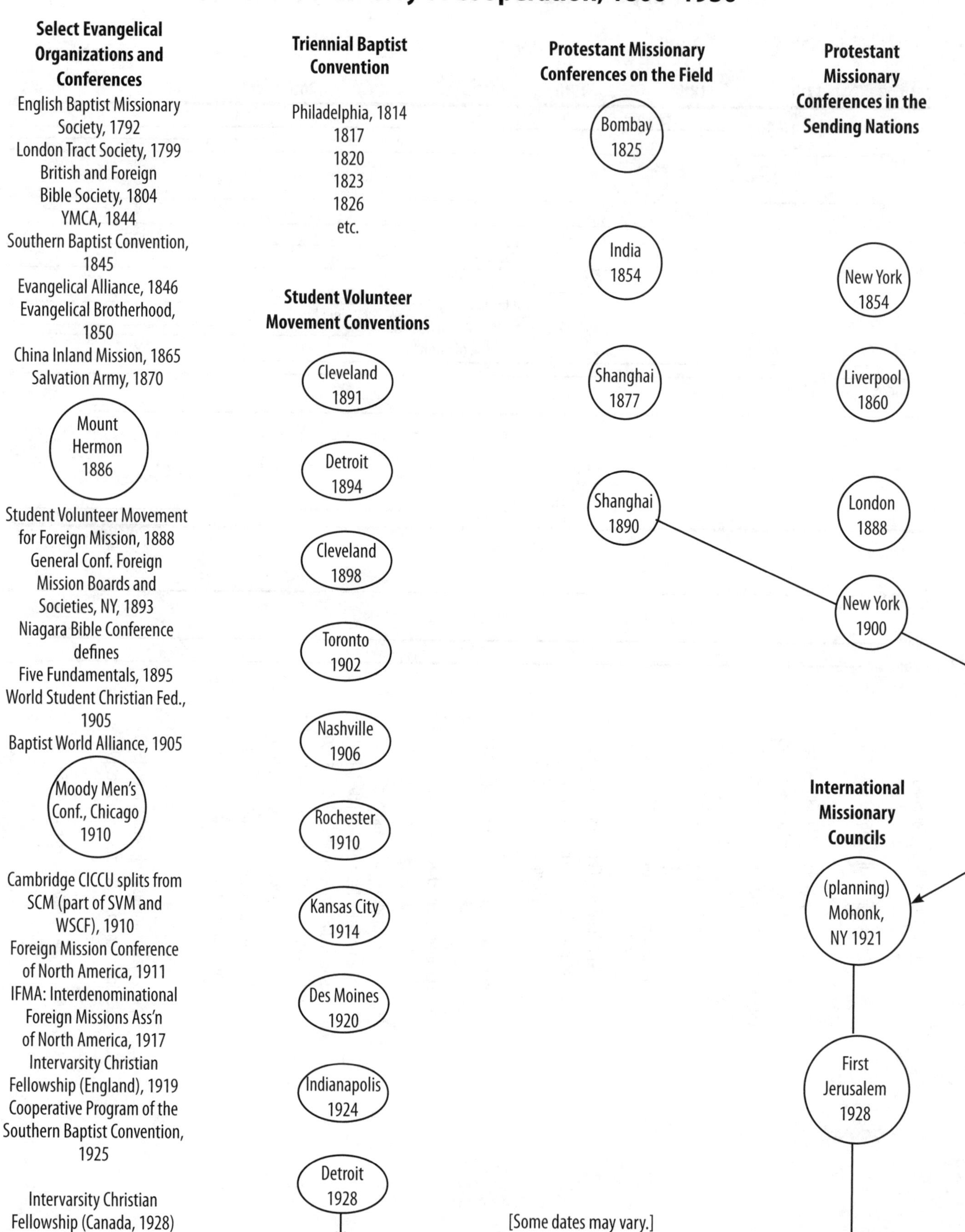

88. A Visual History of Cooperation, 1800–1930 (continued)

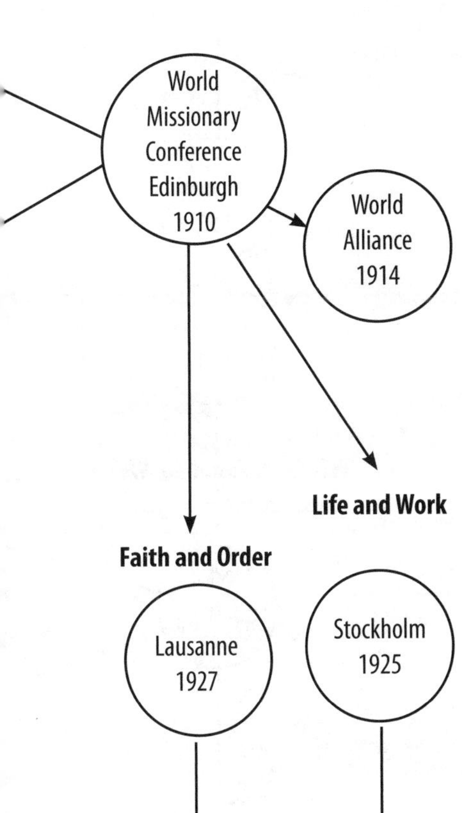

EVANGELICAL COOPERATION—CHRISTIAN COOPERATION—CHRISTIAN PLURALISM—RELIGIOUS PLURALISM?

Anglican, Orthodox, and Old Catholic

Eastern Orthodox and Anglicans hold conferences on unity, 1874–1875

Lambeth 1884

Lambeth Quadrilateral document lays down four points on which unity might be sought

United Church of Canada formed, 1910

Lambeth 1920

Constantinople delegates attend

Anglican orders declared valid by Constantinople "in the case of the union of these two churches," 1922

[Some dates may vary.]

Roman Catholic

Protestants anathematized in Council of Trent, 1563–64

Clement XI, *Unigenitus* (1713), "Outside of the Church, no grace is granted."

Pius IX, *Syllabus of Errors*, 1864

20th Ecumenical Council, Vatican I 1870

Select Encyclicals of Leo XIII:

- *Rerum Novarum*, 1891
- *Providentissimus Deus*, 1893
- *Praeclara Gratulationis Publicae*, 1894
- *Satis Cognitum*, 1896
- *Apostolicae Curae*, 1896, Declared ordinations of Anglican Rite "invalid and void"

Select Encyclicals of Pius X:

- *Lamentabili Sane*, 1907
- *Pascendi Gregis*, 1907
- *Sacrorum Antistitum*, 1910

Pius XI, *Mortalium Animos* (1928), "...nor is it lawful for Catholics either to support or work for such [pan-Christian] enterprises."

88. A Visual History of Cooperation, 1930–1970

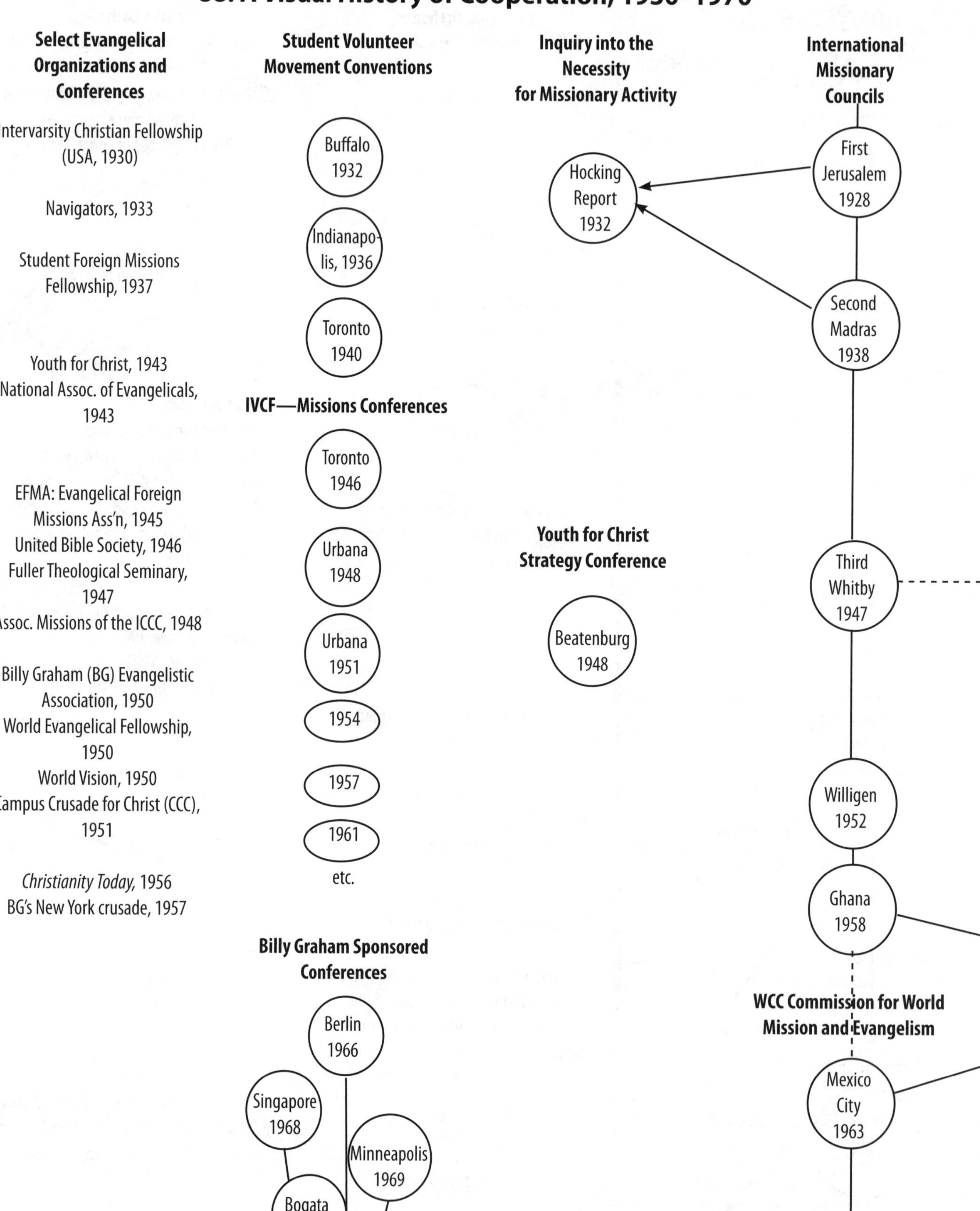

88. A Visual History of Cooperation,1930-1970 (continued)

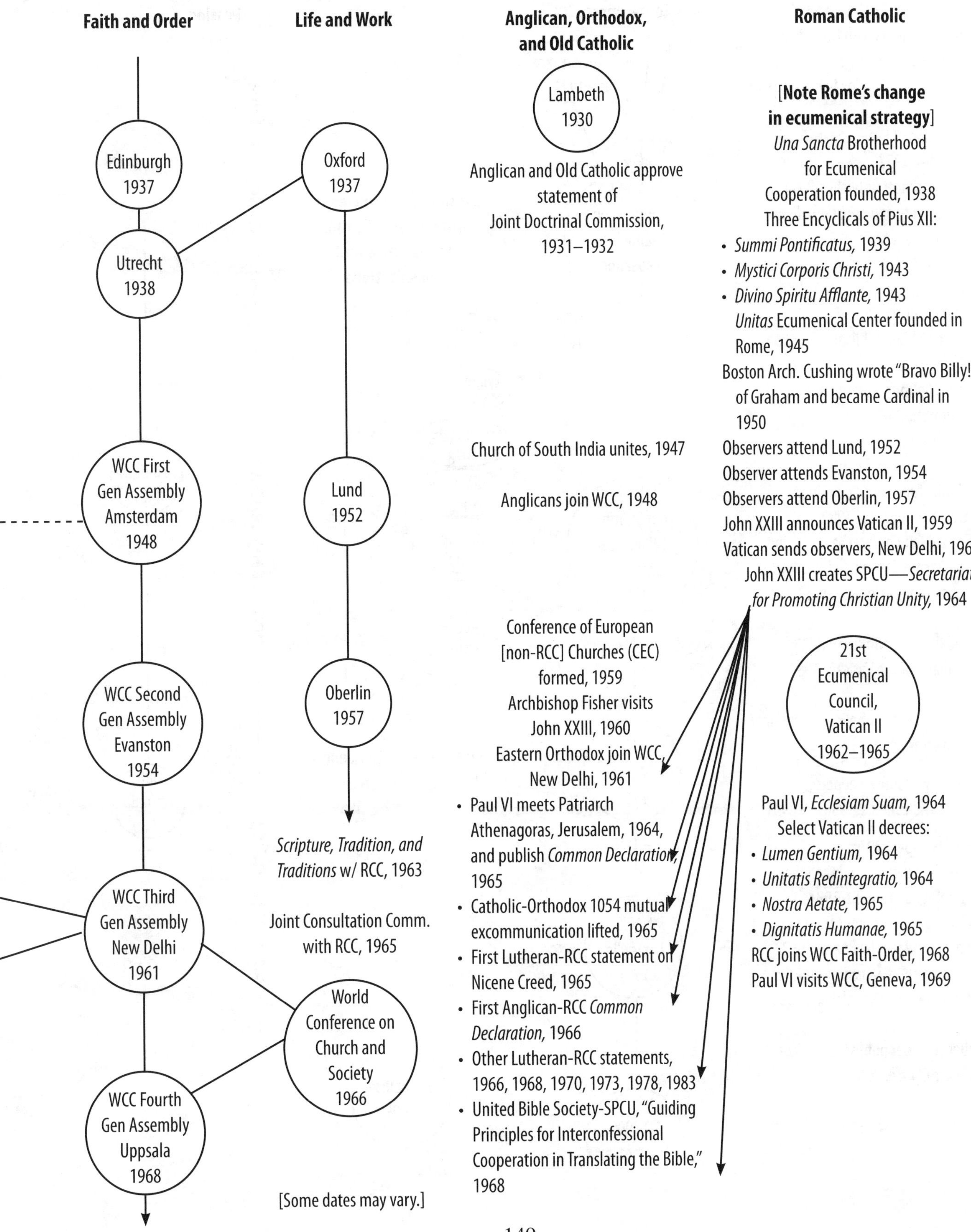
Faith and Order
Life and Work
Anglican, Orthodox, and Old Catholic
Roman Catholic
Lambeth 1930
[Note Rome's change in ecumenical strategy]
Una Sancta Brotherhood for Ecumenical Cooperation founded, 1938
Three Encyclicals of Pius XII:
• Summi Pontificatus, 1939
• Mystici Corporis Christi, 1943
• Divino Spiritu Afflante, 1943
Unitas Ecumenical Center founded in Rome, 1945
Boston Arch. Cushing wrote "Bravo Billy!" of Graham and became Cardinal in 1950
Edinburgh 1937
Oxford 1937
Anglican and Old Catholic approve statement of Joint Doctrinal Commission, 1931–1932
Utrecht 1938
Church of South India unites, 1947
Observers attend Lund, 1952
Observer attends Evanston, 1954
Observers attend Oberlin, 1957
John XXIII announces Vatican II, 1959
Vatican sends observers, New Delhi, 1962
John XXIII creates SPCU—Secretariat for Promoting Christian Unity, 1964
WCC First Gen Assembly Amsterdam 1948
Lund 1952
Anglicans join WCC, 1948
Conference of European [non-RCC] Churches (CEC) formed, 1959
Archbishop Fisher visits John XXIII, 1960
Eastern Orthodox join WCC, New Delhi, 1961
21st Ecumenical Council, Vatican II 1962–1965
WCC Second Gen Assembly Evanston 1954
Oberlin 1957
• Paul VI meets Patriarch Athenagoras, Jerusalem, 1964, and publish Common Declaration, 1965
• Catholic-Orthodox 1054 mutual excommunication lifted, 1965
• First Lutheran-RCC statement on Nicene Creed, 1965
• First Anglican-RCC Common Declaration, 1966
• Other Lutheran-RCC statements, 1966, 1968, 1970, 1973, 1978, 1983
• United Bible Society-SPCU, "Guiding Principles for Interconfessional Cooperation in Translating the Bible," 1968
Paul VI, Ecclesiam Suam, 1964
Select Vatican II decrees:
• Lumen Gentium, 1964
• Unitatis Redintegratio, 1964
• Nostra Aetate, 1965
• Dignitatis Humanae, 1965
RCC joins WCC Faith-Order, 1968
Paul VI visits WCC, Geneva, 1969
Scripture, Tradition, and Traditions w/ RCC, 1963
Joint Consultation Comm. with RCC, 1965
WCC Third Gen Assembly New Delhi 1961
World Conference on Church and Society 1966
WCC Fourth Gen Assembly Uppsala 1968
[Some dates may vary.]

88. A Visual History of Cooperation, 1970–2006

Select Evangelical Organizations and Conferences

B Graham meets with Ghandi and Mother Teresa, 1972
Catholic and Orthodox involved in CCC's Key '73
Declaration of Evangelical Social Concern, 1973
John R. W. Stott publishes *Balanced Christianity* and *Christian Mission,* 1975
Charles Colson publishes *Born Again,* 1976
Chicago Call, 1977
Robert Webber publishes *Common Roots,* 1978
Charles Colson founds Prison Fellowship, 1977
Moral Majority, 1979
BG visits Pope, 1981, 1982
Catholics fully participate in BG crusade, Spokane, 1982
BG speaks at Conference on Saving the Sacred Gift of Life from Nuclear Catastrophe, Moscow, 1982

BG advises Reagan to send U.S. Ambassador to Vatican, 1984

Baptist-Roman Catholic International Conversation, 1988

Promise Keepers Confer's, 1990

BG visits Pope, 1993
ECT—Evangelicals and Catholics Together Statement, 1994
Promise Keepers invites Roman Catholic to join its Board, 1997
The Eastbourne Consultation Joint Statement on Discipleship, 1999

Robert Webber publishes *Ancient-Future Church,* 2003

[Some dates may vary.]

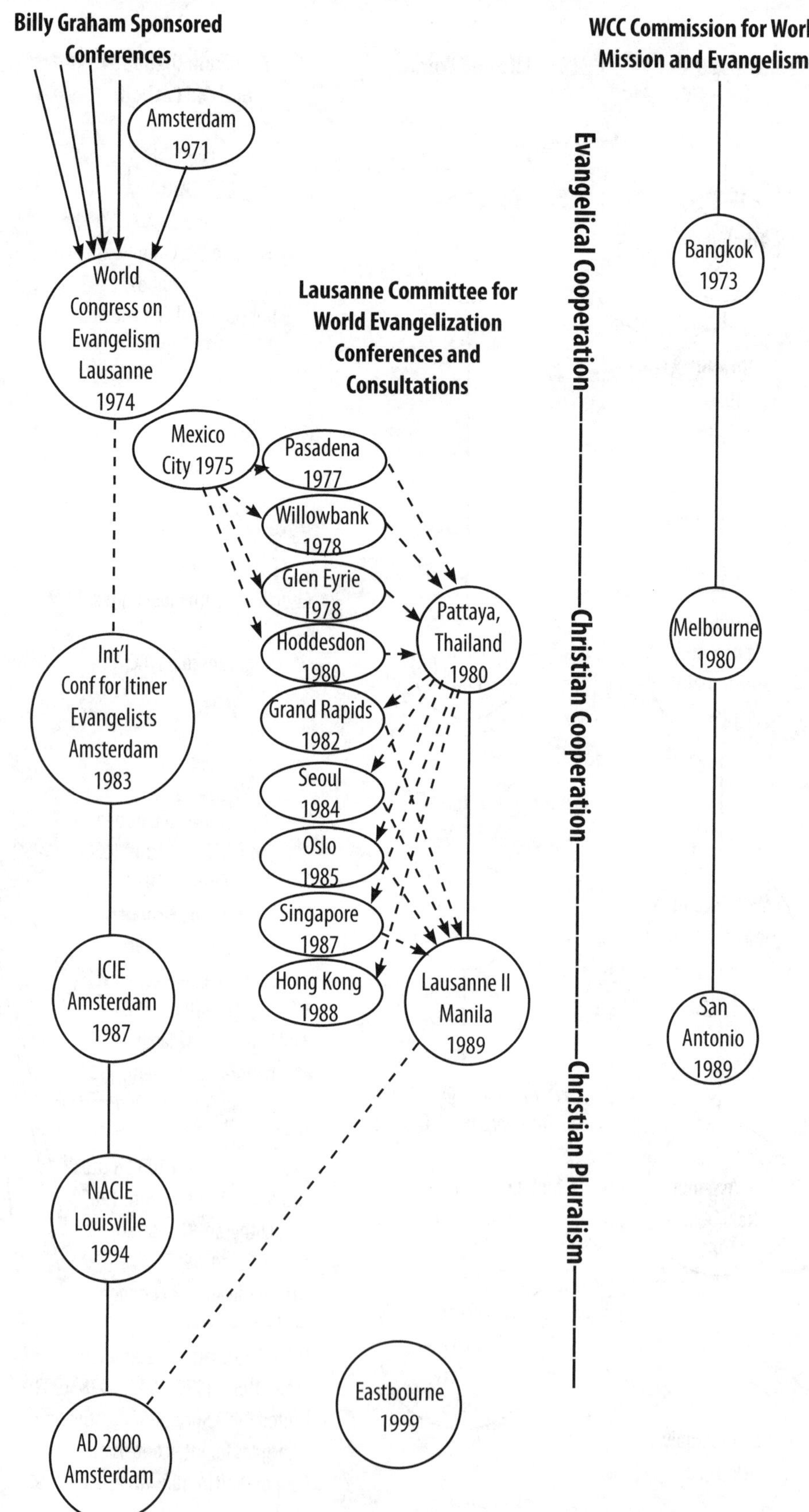

88. A Visual History of Cooperation, 1970–2006 (continued)

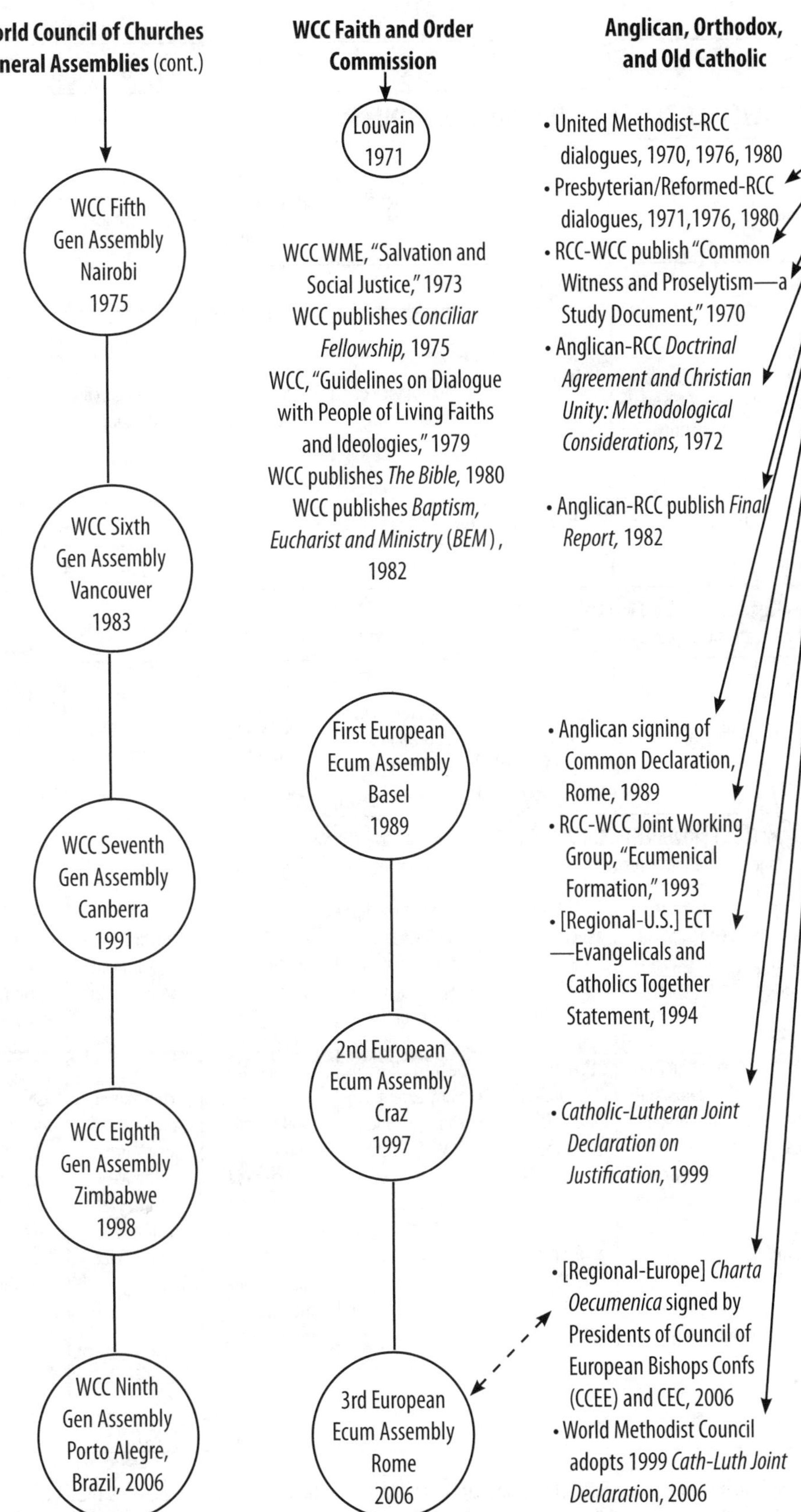
World Council of Churches General Assemblies (cont.)
WCC Fifth Gen Assembly Nairobi 1975
WCC Sixth Gen Assembly Vancouver 1983
WCC Seventh Gen Assembly Canberra 1991
WCC Eighth Gen Assembly Zimbabwe 1998
WCC Ninth Gen Assembly Porto Alegre, Brazil, 2006
WCC Faith and Order Commission
Louvain 1971
WCC WME, "Salvation and Social Justice," 1973
WCC publishes Conciliar Fellowship, 1975
WCC, "Guidelines on Dialogue with People of Living Faiths and Ideologies," 1979
WCC publishes The Bible, 1980
WCC publishes Baptism, Eucharist and Ministry (BEM), 1982
First European Ecum Assembly Basel 1989
2nd European Ecum Assembly Craz 1997
3rd European Ecum Assembly Rome 2006
Anglican, Orthodox, and Old Catholic
• United Methodist-RCC dialogues, 1970, 1976, 1980
• Presbyterian/Reformed-RCC dialogues, 1971,1976, 1980
• RCC-WCC publish "Common Witness and Proselytism—a Study Document," 1970
• Anglican-RCC Doctrinal Agreement and Christian Unity: Methodological Considerations, 1972
• Anglican-RCC publish Final Report, 1982
• Anglican signing of Common Declaration, Rome, 1989
• RCC-WCC Joint Working Group, "Ecumenical Formation," 1993
• [Regional-U.S.] ECT —Evangelicals and Catholics Together Statement, 1994
• Catholic-Lutheran Joint Declaration on Justification, 1999
• [Regional-Europe] Charta Oecumenica signed by Presidents of Council of European Bishops Confs (CCEE) and CEC, 2006
• World Methodist Council adopts 1999 Cath-Luth Joint Declaration, 2006
Roman Catholic
SPCU publishes "Ecumenical Colaboration at the Regional, National and Local Levels," 1975
Paul VI, Evangelii Nuntiandi, defines evangelism, rebukes charismatic movement, advises "popular religiosity," 1975
Paulist publishes Doing the Truth in Charity, Ecumenical Documents 1, 1982
John Paul (J-P) II in 1982:
• Anticipates Year 2000 in his first encyclical
• Visits Canterbury
• Responds to WCC BEM
J-P II proclaims Year of Mary, 1987
J-P II gathers non-Christian religious leaders for prayer, 1988
Vatican publishes Directory [for ecumenism], 1993
Pontifical Commission on Biblical Interpretation, 1993
Catechism of the Catholic Church published, 1993
J-P II proclaims Jubilee, Tertio Millennio Adveniente, 1994
J-P II, Ut Unim Sint, 1995
Ratzinger, Primacy of the Successor of Peter, 1998
Ratzinger, Dominus Iesus, 2000
Year of Jubilee, Rome 2000
J-P II first pope to enter a Mosque, asks forgiveness of Muslims and Orthodox, 2001
Bush first U.S. president to attend funeral of a pope, 2005
Ratzinger voted Benedict XVI

89. Eighteen Models of Unity and Separation

1	2	3	4	5	6	7	8	9
WEISENBECK'S NINE MODELS OF UNITY*								
1. "Return" Model	2. Uniate Model	3. Organic Union Model	[Full *Communio*]	4. Federation Model	5. Spiritual Unity Model	6. Ecclesial Communion Model	7. Ecclesial Types Model	8. Reconciled Diversity Model
EXPLANATION OF CONCEPT								
Reincorporation into RCC	Sharing name, doctrine, and ecclesiology	Sharing identity (name) as step toward unity	Full unity with separate identity	Unity with separate identity	Acceptance of spiritual unity	Mutual recognition	Sister church concept	Unity in diversity
POSSIBLE IMPLICATIONS OF THE MODELS OF UNITY OR SEPARATION								
Some Form of Organizational (hierarchical) Unity				Close Partnership		Mutual Recognition and Verbalized Cooperation		
Unity as a Hierarchical, Theological, Political, or Financial Necessity, and/or for Organizational Improvement						Unity as a Witness to the World		
Submitting to Rome's hierarchy	Sharing name, doctrine, and practice	Sharing name	n/a	Cooperation in church planting	Cooperation in education of ministers	Cooperation in missions	Cooperation in evangelism	Pulpit sharing
HISTORICAL EXAMPLES OF MOVEMENTS, CHURCHES, AND LEADERS AMONG THE VARIOUS LEVELS (There is a wide range of variation as leaders, churches, and movements inter-react to one another)								
This was the model expressed by Leo XIII in his *Satis Cognitum* (29 June 1896) and Pius XI in *Mortalium Animos* (6 Jan 1928); cf. Pius XII, *Summi Pontificatus* (20 Oct 1939).	"The submission of one church to the doctrinal and ecclesiological principles of another, in return for the permission to retain its own liturgical and canonical practices."	"The parts or members of the organism receive their identities from the principal entity, and their identities have no meaning except in reference to the principal."	This seemed to be the goal of John Paul II's *Tertio Millennio Adviente* and for the 2000 Year of Jubilee; the words "full communion" come from John Macquarrie, *Christian Unity* (1975).	"In a federation, the two entities uniting each retains its own identity. . . . their purpose of uniting is to achieve some mutually agreeable common purpose." E. Stanley Jones	"The fellowship of faith is by its very nature spiritual. The unity of the Church cannot be read off from any external characteristics." WCC, Faith and Order Commission, "Concepts of Unity and Models of Union"	Examples of the "Mutual Recognition Model" are Leuenberg Concord between the Lutheran and Reformed churches in Europe, and the Lambeth agreements between the Old Catholic and Anglican Communion.	Used when churches of the East came into communion with the Catholic Church; churches of the East had apostolicity; in the West, churches rely on Rome for apostolicity.	"The aim of this model is to effect church unity while enabling the separate confessions to retain their own identity" (cf. WCC, 1974); used by Lutheran World Federation after 1977.

*"Weisenbeck's Nine Models of Unity" taken from Jude D. Weisenbeck, S.D.S., S.T.L., "Conciliar Fellowship and the Unity of the Church," 62–104. The term "Full *Communio*" taken from Roman Catholic-Orthodox dialogue, "Uniatism . . . the Present Search for Full Communion," 1993.

89. Eighteen Models of Unity and Separation (continued)

10	11	12	13	14	15	16	17	18
UNITY		**JOHNSTON'S SEVEN LEVELS OF SEPARATION**						
9. Conciliar Fellowship Model	[Intercon-fessional Movement Model]	1. Separate but Open	2. Cautious Associa-tionalism	3. Precise Associa-tionalism	4. Local Church Solidarity	5. Moral Disciplinism	6. Theological Disciplinism	7. Third Degree Separation
EXPLANATION OF CONCEPT								
Fellowship in diversity	Fellowship around the nine points of the British Evangelical Alliance	General openness to other Christian denomina-tions	Cautious openness to those with similar theological convictions	Fairly rigorous theological specificity	Strong congrega-tionalism, "closed communion"	Church discipline primarily for moral or ecclesial reasons	2nd Degree Separation: Separating from those who do not separate	Separate from those not practicing 2nd degree separation
POSSIBLE IMPLICATIONS OF THE MODELS OF UNITY OR SEPARATION								
General Openness to Unity			Emphasizing the Need for Theological Clarity				Emphasizing Theological Discipline	
Unity as a Witness	The Gospel as a Witness to the World						Separation as a Witness to the World	
Shared political action	Comity agreements dividing mission fields	Sharing of educational and social resources	Some pulpit sharing outside association	Closed communion within association	Closed communion within local churches	No fellowship with world or excommu-nication	May become defined by what is not believed	Emphasis on what is not believed
HISTORICAL EXAMPLES OF MOVEMENTS, CHURCHES, AND LEADERS AMONG THE VARIOUS LEVELS (There is a wide range of variation as leaders, churches, and movements inter-react to one another)								
The position described by the Faith and Order Commission of the WCC in Salamanca, Spain, 1973.	The evangelical inter-confes-sional ethos of 19th century Protestant missions developed comity agreements based on the nine points of the 1846 British Evangelical Alliance; e.g., H. Taylor's China Inland Mission.	This category could be used of many evangelical or mainline groupings.	Many congre-gational de-nominations fit here: (1) follows NT concept of "priesthood of the believer" and (2) avoids the potentially negative pressure of a bishop; e.g., Baptist Faith and Message, Article 14.	Again, the Southern Baptist's Baptist Faith and Message fits here. The Baptist movement called Landmark-ism may emphasize even more restraint.	Some Plymouth Brethren churches refuse Communion to those outside their fellowship.	For example, some conservative groups regularly practice excommuni-cation to keep their members from becoming worldly, e.g., Church of God in Christ Mennonite.	E.g., John R. Rice reacting to Graham's associations; perhaps in this category could be considered groups such as the Independent Fundamental Churches of America.	E.g., Bob Jones Sr. reacting against Billy Graham's associations; perhaps in this group could be considered the General Association of Regular Baptists.

90. Examining Cooperation

90A. Detailing Three Cooperative Continua

Unity in Missiological Endeavors[1]

- Full Communion—Full *Communio*
- Cooperative church planting
- Some type of conciliar fellowship agreement
- Cooperative discipleship—e.g., follow-up after crusade
- Cooperative evangelism—e.g., crusade evangelism
- Comity agreements—i.e., territorial nonproselytism
- Agreed nonproselytism
- Agreed nonnegativism

Unity in Theological Endeavors[2]

- Sharing resources in Bible publishing
- Sharing resources and personnel in Bible translation
- Combining theological schools
- Curriculum development
- Cooperative publishing of books and commentaries
- Sharing professors in theological education
- Coauthoring commentaries
- Agreed theological minimalism
- Coauthoring theological texts
- Cooperation in academic societies and lectureships

Unity in Social Endeavors[3]

- Merging organizations
- Sharing board members
- Sharing personnel in social causes
- Sharing resources for social causes
- Coauthoring texts on social causes
- Cosponsoring conferences on social causes
- Cooperation in famine and disaster relief
- Cooperation in international AIDS epidemic
- Cooperation in pro-life lobbying

[1]Some contemporary examples of missiological cooperation include the sharing of methods of and resources for evangelism (e.g., lifestyle or servant evangelism), church growth and/or church planting methodologies, inner-city homeless ministry and other social endeavors, evangelistic crusades, workshops on the Holy Spirit, and youth evangelism conferences.

[2]Other ways of leveraging unity in theological endeavors include sharing in worship helps (hymnology, choruses, or creeds), coparticipation in prayer or the Lord's Supper, and an emphasis on "faith." Across religious lines, common ground is sought through prayer to the Supreme Being, faith in faith, human virtues (love, peace, unity), angels, stars, nonverbal music, and family issues.

[3]There seems to be no lack of social issues for cooperative efforts! For example in the U.S. some social issues have been: 1810s keeping the Sabbath; 1840s slavery; 1890s education; 1900s women's suffrage; 1920s temperance; 1950s civil rights; 1960s pacifism; 1970s integration; 1980s adoption, abortion rights, and AIDS; and 1990s homosexual rights and traditional family.

90B. Six Sample Doctrinal Formulations for Ecclesial Cooperation

Theological Formulations	Inerrancy/ Sufficiency of Scriptures	Man's Utter Depravity	Virgin Birth	Deity of Christ	Faith Alone or Substitutionary Atonement	Bodily Resurrection
[Baptist] New Hampshire Confession (1833)	Yes	Yes	n/a	Yes	Yes	Yes
Nine Points of the British Evangelical Alliance (1846)	Yes	Yes	n/a	Yes	Yes	Yes
Five Fundamentals of Niagara Bible Conference (1895)	Yes	n/a	Yes	Yes	Yes	Yes
National Association of Evangelicals—USA (1943)	Unsure	n/a	Yes	Yes	Yes	Yes
Evangelical Theological Society (1949)	Yes	n/a	n/a	Yes	n/a	n/a
Baptist Faith and Message (1963, 2000)	Yes	n/a	Yes	Yes	Yes	Yes

90. Examining Cooperation (continued)

90C. Suggested Guidelines for Ecclesial Cooperation

Unity in Missiological Endeavors ← **Unity in Theological Endeavors** ← **Unity in Social Endeavors** ←

As regards unity in missiological endeavors, given that . . .

- the mission and vision of a church or denomination are extremely important to their state of revival, evangelistic efforts, and spiritual stamina;
- the message of the gospel is both repentance (from sin, falsehood, and deception) and belief (in the gospel); and
- cooperative evangelism is much more than making a show of the gospel (e.g., "presence evangelism") but it also includes discipleship in the local church;

It is recommended that . . .

- preachers of the gospel not be muzzled into preaching an artificially positive gospel due to agreed nonnegativism. Rather they ought to freely preach the Word of God;
- territorial nonproselytism agreements be entered into only with groups that believe in the Five Fundamentals of the faith, and only for a specified time;
- cooperative church planting outside denominational lines is impractical and self-defeating; and
- full Communion can only be entered into when there is almost full theological and missional conformity and a similar ecclesial history.

As regards unity in theological endeavors, given that . . .

- denominational distinctives provide an important hermeneutical grid for the exegesis of the Bible, an understanding of theological issues, and the interpretation of movements in church history and the history of theology;
- aberrant theological views are not easily discerned when dealing with most theological issues, the exegesis of Scriptures, the studying of commentaries, and especially in the translation of Holy Scriptures;
- theological minimalism moves the theologian and exegete to minimalize important and priority foundational doctrines upon which are formed revival movements and their ensuing denominations;
- students of theology need to learn denominational distinctives concurrently with their exposure to varying schools of theology; and
- the Bible is the sole authority of the evangelical Christian;

It is recommended that . . .

- cooperative efforts on theological issues be entered into only with those who hold to the Five Fundamentals of the faith and the priority of apostolic evangelism; and
- because of a fear of doctrinal minimalism, only guarded cooperative efforts may be considered when there is no full theological conformity.

As regards unity in social endeavors, given that . . .

- enticements to dialogue are often started for political and/or social action through a common moral philosophy or a minimal Christian worldview;
- from cooperation on social ventures, united efforts tend to lead over time (subtly or mandated) to further dialogue on cooperation in theological and then missiological endeavors; and
- procedures and priorities in social endeavors are directly related to theological convictions, such as the need for instantaneous conversion;

It is recommended that . . .

- cooperative efforts on social issues only be entered into with those who hold to the Five Fundamentals of the faith, as the priority of apostolic evangelism is often the first thing to be dismissed for the sake of cooperation. Hence, ensues a serious blow to the mission and vision of the conservative counterpart in the cooperative effort.

Works Cited

A Call to Joy: Leader's Guide and *Timothy 1 Packet.* Fort Worth: International Evangelism Association, 1985.
Aldrich, Joseph. *Life-Style Evangelism: Crossing Traditional Boundaries to Reach the Unbelieving World.* Portland: Multnomah, 1981.
_________. *Gentle Persuasion.* Portland: Multnomah Press, 1988.
Aquinas, Thomas. *Summa Theologica.* London: Eyre and Spottiswoode, 1963.
Atkinson, Donald and Charles Roesel. *Meeting Needs, Sharing Christ: Evangelism in Today's New Testament Church.* Nashville: LifeWay, 1995.
Augustine, *The Confessions of Saint Augustine.* Rex Warner, trans. 401; New York: New American Library, 1963.
Aulén, Gustav. *Christus Victor: An Historical Study of the Three Main Types of the Idea of the Atonement.* New York: Macmillan, 1969.
Baptism, Eucharist and Ministry. Geneva: World Council of Churches, 1982.
Barclay, Oliver R. *Whatever Happened to the Jesus Lane Lot?* Leicester: Intervarsity, 1977.
Barth, Karl. *Church Dogmatics,* 4:1, "The Doctrine of Reconciliation." Trans. by G. W. Bromiley. Edinburgh: T & T Clark, 1956.
Bede. *A History of the English Church and People.* Trans. by L. Sherley-Price; rev. by R. E. Latham. 731; Harmondsworth, Middlesex, England: Penguin Books, 1979.
Beginning Steps. Alpharetta, Ga.: North American Mission Board of the Southern Baptist Convention, 1993.
Berkhof, Louis. *Systematic Theology.* 4th ed. 1938; Grand Rapids: Eerdmans, 1982.
The Bible. Geneva: World Council of Churches, 1980.
Blackwood, Andrew W. *Evangelism in the Home Church.* New York: Abingdon-Cokesbury, 1942.
Blanshard, Brand. "Logic." *Collier's Encyclopedia,* 1961 ed.
Blocher, Jacques. *Le Catholicisme à la lumière de l'Écriture Sainte.* Nogent-sur-Marne, France: éditions de l'institut biblique, 1979.
Bonhoeffer, Dietrich. *Life Together.* New York: Harper and Row, 1954.
Bridge to Life. Colorado Springs: NavPress, 1969.
Bright, Bill. *Have You Heard of the Four Spiritual Laws?* San Bernardino, Calif.: New Life, 1965, 1994.
_________. *Witnessing without Fear.* San Bernardino, Calif.: Here's Life, 1987.
Broadbent, Edmund H. *The Pilgrim Church.* 1931; Grand Rapids: Gospel Folio, 1999.
Bruce, F. F. *New Testament Development of Old Testament Themes.* Grand Rapids: Eerdmans, 1969.
Burgess, Joseph and Jeffrey Gros, eds. *Building Unity: Ecumenical Dialogues with Roman Catholic Participation in the United States.* Ecumenical Documents 4. New York: Paulist, 1989.
_________. *Growing Consensus: Church Dialogues in the United States, 1962–1991.* Ecumenical Documents 5. New York: Paulist, 1995.
Bushnell, Horace. *The Vicarious Sacrifice Grounded in Principles of Universal Obligation.* 1866; Hicksville, N.Y.: Regina, 1975.
Calvin, John. *Institutes of the Christian Religion.* Trans. by Henry Beveridge. 2 vols. 1536; London: James Clarke, 1957.
Cameron, Kirk and Ray Comfort. *The School of Biblical Evangelism: 101 Lessons.* Gainesville, Fla.: Bridge-Logos, 2004.
Carroll, J. M. *"The Trail of Blood."* Lexington, Ky.: Ashland Avenue Baptist Church, 1931.
Carson Donald, ed. *Telling the Truth.* Grand Rapids: Zondervan, 2000.
Celek, Tim, and Dieter Zander. *Inside the Soul of a New Generation.* Grand Rapids: Zondervan, 1996.
Chafer, Lewis Sperry. *True Evangelism or Winning Souls by Prayer.* 1st ed. Philadelphia: Sunday School Times, 1911; 2nd ed., Philadelphia: Sunday School Times, 1919.
Chicago Call. Warrenville, Ill., 1977.
Cho, David Yonggi. "Fivefold Gospel." From http://english.fgtv.com/ Gospel/fivefold.asp; accessed 17 Aug 2005; Internet.
Clement VI. *Unigenitus*—on Indulgences. Rome: Vatican, 8 Sept 1713.
Clines, David J. A. *The Theme of the Pentateuch.* Sheffield, England: The University of Shefield, 1978, 1982.
Colson, Charles. *Born Again.* Old Tappan, N.J.: Revell, 1976.
Colson, Charles and Nancy Pearcey. *How Now Shall We Live?* Wheaton, Ill.: Tyndale House, 1999.
Commission Biblique Pontificale. *L'Interprétation de la Bible dans l'Eglise.* Montréal: Fides, 1994.
Conant, J. E. *Every-Member Evangelism.* New York: Harper and Brothers, 1922.
Conciliar Fellowship. Geneva: World Council of Churches, 1975
Council of Constance. Rome: Vatican, 1415.
Council of Florence. Rome: Vatican, 1439.
Council of Trent. Rome: Vatican, 1545-1563.
Criswell, W. A. *Criswell's Guidebook for Pastors.* Nashville: Broadman, 1980.

De Haeretico Comburendo. Rome: Vatican, 1401.
Denney, James. *The Christian Doctrine of Reconciliation.* New York: George H. Doran, 1918.
Do You Know for Certain that You Have Eternal Life and that You Will Go to Heaven when You Die? Alpharetta, Ga.: North American Mission Board, 2000.
Dodd, C. H. *The Apostolic Preaching and Its Development.* London: Hodder and Stoughton, 1936.
Driver, John. *Understanding the Atonement for the Mission of the Church.* Scottdale, Pa.: Herald, 1986.
Drucker, Peter F. "The New Pluralism." *Leader to Leader* (Fall 1999), 19–23.
Drummond, Lewis. *The Word of the Cross.* Nashville: Broadman, 1992.
Duvernoy, Jean. *Le Catharisme: Histoire des Cathares.* Toulouse: Privat, 1979.
Erasmus, Desiderius. *The Enchiridion of Erasmus.* Raymond Himelick, ed. and trans. Gloucester, Mass.: Peter Smith, 1970.
__________. *The Essential Erasmus.* John P. Dolan, ed. and trans. New York: Mentor, 1964.
Erickson, Millard. *Christian Theology.* Grand Rapids: Baker, 1985.
Évangile et évangélisme (XIIe-XIIIe siècles). Cahiers de Fanjeaux 34. Toulouse, France: Éditions Privat, 1999.
Experiencing God's Grace. Louisville: The Billy Graham School of Missions, Evangelism, and Church Growth of the Southern Baptist Theological Seminary, 2003.
FAITH Sunday School Evangelism Strategy. Nashville: LifeWay, 1999.
Fay, Bill. *Share Jesus without Fear.* Nashville: Broadman, 1999.
Finney, Charles. *Systematic Theology.* E. J. Goodrich, 1878; South Gate, Calif.: Porter Kemp, 1944.
Flake, Arthur. *Building a Standard Sunday School.* Nashville: Convention Press, 1934.
Four Spiritual Laws. San Bernardino, Calif.: Campus Crusade for Christ, n.d.
Garda, David J. and Sonlife Ministries. *Foundations for Youth Ministry.* Wheaton, Ill.: Sonlife Ministries, 1990.
Graham, Billy. *Calling Youth to Christ.* Grand Rapids: Zondervan, 1947.
__________. *Just As I Am: The Autobiography of Billy Graham.* Carmel, N.Y.: Guideposts, 1997; New York: HarperCollins, 1997.
__________. *Living in Christ.* Minneapolis: Billy Graham Evangelistic Association, 1980.
__________. *Steps to Peace with God.* Minneapolis: Billy Graham Evangelistic Association, 1980.
Gregory I, Pope, *Epistle LXXVII,* "To All the Bishops of Numidia"; accessed: 8 September 1997; from: www.ccel.wheaton.edu/ Gregory/Register/ E24.htm.
__________. "Letter to the Abbot Mellitus." In Bede, *A History of the English Church and People,* trans. L. Sherley-Price, rev. R. E. Latham (Harmondsworth, Middlesex, England: Penguin Books, 1979), 86–87.
Gros, Jeffrey, Eamon McManus, and Ann Riggs. *Introduction to Ecumenism.* New York: Paulist, 1998.
Harnack, Adolf von, and Wilhelm Herrmann. *Essays on the Social Gospel.* London: Williams & Norgate, 1907.
Hemphill, Ken. *The Antioch Effect: Eight Characteristics of Highly Effective Churches.* Nashville: Broadman, 1994.
Hocking, William Ernest. *Re-Thinking Missions after One Hundred Years [Hocking Report].* New York: Harper, 1932.
Hodge, Charles. *Systematic Theology.* Volume 2. Grand Rapids: Eerdmans, 1993.
House, H. Wayne. *Charts of Christian Theology and Doctrine.* Grand Rapids: Zondervan, 1992.
Hull, Bill. *The Disciple Making Pastor.* Old Tappan, N.J.: Revell, 1988.
Hussey, Joseph. *God's Operations of Grace: but No Offers of His Grace.* 1707.
Jacks, Bob and Betty. *Your Home a Lighthouse.* San Jose, Calif.: Churches Alive, 1986; Colorado Springs: NavPress, 1987, 1990, 1992.
Jensen, Phillip D. and Tony Payne. "Church/Campus Connections." In *Telling the Truth: Evangelizing Postmoderns.* Donald A. Carson, ed. Grand Rapids: Zondervan, 2000.
John Paul II. "Mexico Ever Faithful." *Osservatore Romano* (5 Feb. 1979).
__________. *Tertio Millenio Adveniente.* Rome: Vatican, 10 November 1994.
__________. *Ut Unim Sint.* Rome: Vatican, 25 May 1995.
Johnston, Arthur P. *The Battle for World Evangelism.* Wheaton, Ill.: Tyndale, 1978.
__________. *World Evangelism and the Word of God.* Minneapolis: Bethany Fellowship, 1974.
Johnston, James, ed. *Ecumenical Missionary Conference, New York, 1900: Report of the Ecumenical Conference on Foreign Missions.* New York: American Tract Society, 1900.
__________. *Report of the Centenary Conference of the Protestant Missions of the World, London, 1888.* Vol. 1. New York: Revell, 1888.
Johnston, Thomas P. "Toward a Biblical and Historical Theology of Evangelism." Liberty, Mo.: Evangelism Unlimited, 2007.
__________. *Examining Billy Graham's Theology of Evangelism.* Eugene, Oreg.: Wipf & Stock, 2003.
__________. "There Is Hope." Accessed on 5 May 2005; from www.evangelismunlimited.org/ThereIsHope_LegalSize. pdf; Internet.
Kelley, Charles. *How Did They Do It? The Story of Southern Baptist Evangelism.* New Orleans: Insight, 1993.

Kennedy, D. James. *Evangelism Explosion.* Rev. ed. Wheaton, Ill.: Tyndale House, 1970.
Kierkegaard, Søren. *Concluding Unscientific Postscript.* Princeton: Princeton University Press, 1944.
Kinnamon, Michael and Brian E. Cope, eds. *The Ecumenical Movement: An Anthology of Key Texts and Voices.* Geneva: WCC; Grand Rapids: Eerdmans, 1997.
Lateran Council, Third. Rome: Vatican, 1179.
Lateran Council, Fourth. Rome: Vatican, 1215.
Leavell, Roland Q. *Evangelism: Christ's Imperative Command.* Nashville: Broadman, 1951.
Lelièvre, Matthieu. *De la révocation à la révolution.* Paris: Fischbacher, 1911.
_________. *Portraits et Récits Huguenots.* Toulouse: Société des livres religieux de Toulouse, 1897.
Leo XIII. *Apostolicae Curae.* Rome: Vatican, 13 September 1896.
_________. *Praeclara Gratulationis Publicae.* Rome: Vatican, 20 June 1894.
_________. *Providentissimus Deus.* Rome: Vatican, 18 November 1896.
_________. *Satis Cognitum.* Rome: Vatican, 29 June 1896.
Lessons on Assurance. Colorado Springs: NavPress, 1957, 1980.
Lewis, C. S. *Surprised by Joy.* New York: Harcourt, Brace, 1956.
Lortsch, Daniel. *Histoire de la Bible en France.* Paris: Agence de la Société biblique britannique et étrangère, 1910.
Lumpkin, William L. *Baptist Confessions of Faith.* Rev. ed. Valley Forge: Judson Press, 1969.
Luther, Martin. *A Commentary on St. Paul's Epistle to the Galatians Based on Lectures Delivered at the University of Wittenberg in the Year 1531.* Based on the 'Middleton' edition of the English version of 1575. Westwood, N.J.: Revell, n.d.
_________. "Larger Catechism," from: ttp://www.iclnet.org/pub/ resources/text/wittenberg/ wittenberg-luther.html#sw-lc; accessed 19 Oct 2001; Internet
_________. *Martin Luther.* John Dillenberger, ed. Garden City, N.Y.: Anchor, 1961.
_________. "Of Confession," in Smalcald Articles, Part 3, Section 8 [on-line], accessed 11 October 2001, available from http://www.frii.com/~gosplow/ smalcald.html#smc-03h; Internet.
Macquarrie, John. *Christian Unity.* London: SCM, 1975.
Mandonnet, Pierre, O.P. *St. Dominic and His Work.* Mary Benedicta Larkin, O.P., trans. St. Louis: B. Herder, 1948.
Martyr, Justin. "The First Apology of Justin Martyr [circa 152]." Professor Wills, ed. A Reader for "Introduction to Church History, Part I," The Southern Baptist Theological Seminary, 1999.
Matthews, C. E. *The Southern Baptist Program of Evangelism.* Atlanta: Home Mission Board of the Southern Baptist Convention, 1949.
McCary, Richard. "An Interview with the Prince of Preachers, Dr. Robert G. Lee." Studio Hall, Calif.: World Literature Crusade, n.d.
McGee, Gary B. *This Gospel Shall Be Preached: A History and Theology of Assemblies of God Foreign Missions.* Springfield, Mo.: Gospel, 1986.
McLaren, Brian D. *A Generous Orthodoxy.* Grand Rapids: Zondervan, 2004.
_________. *More Ready Than You Realize: Evangelism as Dance in the Postmodern Matrix.* Grand Rapids: Zondervan, 2002.
McLoughlin, William Gerald, Jr. *Revivals, Awakenings, and Reform: An Essay on Religion and Social Change in America, 1607–1977.* Chicago: University of Chicago Press, 1978.
McRainey, Will. *The Art of Personal Evangelism.* Nashville: Broadman, 2003.
Meyer, Harding and Lukas Vischer, eds. *Growth in Agreement: Reports and Agreed Statements of Ecumenical Conversations on a World Level.* Ecumenical Documents 2. New York: Paulist, 1984.
Mims, Gene. *Kingdom Principles for Church Growth.* Nashville: Broadman, 1994.
Mittelberg, Mark. *Building a Contagious Church.* Grand Rapids: Zondervan, 2000.
Moberg, David O. *The Church as a Social Institution.* Grand Rapids: Baker, 1984.
Moore, Waylon. *New Testament Follow-Up for Pastors and Laymen.* Grand Rapids: Eerdmans, 1963.
More, Thomas. *Utopia.* 1516; Arlington Heights, Ill.: AHM Publishing, 1949.
Morgenthaler, Sally. *Worship Evangelism: Inviting Unbelievers into the Presence of God.* Grand Rapids: Zondervan, 1995.
Muncy, William L., Jr., *Evangelism in the United States.* Kansas City, Kan.: Central Seminary, 1945.
Neighbour, Ralph, Jr. *Survival Kit for New Christians.* Nashville: Convention Press, 1979.
_________. *Where Do We Go from Here?* Houston: Touch Publications, 1987.
Newbigin, Lesslie. *The Gospel in a Pluralistic Society.* Grand Rapids: Eerdmans, 1989.
Nicole, Jules-Marcel. *Précis d'histoire de l'Église.* Nogent-sur-Marne, France: Éditions de l'institut Biblique, 1982.
Niebuhr, H. Richard. *Christ and Culture.* New York: Harper and Row, 1951.
Ogden, Greg. *The New Reformation.* Grand Rapids: Zondervan, 1990.
Pannenberg, Wolfhart. "Christianity and the West: Ambiguous Past, Uncertain Future." *First Things* (Dec. 1994), 18-23.

_________. "The Present and Future Church." *First Things* (Nov. 1991), 47-51.
Pascal, Blaise. *Pascal: Œuvres Complètes.* Louis Lafuma, ed. New York: Macmillan, 1963.
Patterson, George. "The Spontaneous Multiplication of Churches," in *Perspectives on the World Christian Movement.* Ralph D. Winter and Steven C. Hawthorne, eds. Pasadena: William Carey Library, 1983: 601–16.
Patterson, Vernon William. Personal interview by Robert Schuster, March 5, 1985. Wheaton, Ill.: Billy Graham Archives, Collection 5, Tape 4.
Paul VI. *Ecclesiam Suam.* Rome: Vatican, 6 August 1964.
_________. *Evangelii Nuntiandi.* Rome: Vatican, 8 December 1975.
Petersen, Jim. *Living Proof.* Colorado Springs: NavPress, 1985.
Peterson, Susan Lynn. *Timeline Charts of the Western Church.* Grand Rapids: Zondervan, 1999.
Pipes, Jerry. *Building a Successful Family.* Lawrenceville, GA: Completeness Productions, 2002.
Pippert, Rebecca Manley. *Out of the Saltshaker and into the World: Evangelism as a Way of Life.* Downers Grove, Ill.: InterVarsity, 1979.
Pius IX. *Quanta Cura* and *Syllabus of Errors.* Rome, 8 December 1864.
Pius X. *Lamentabili Sane.* Rome: Vatican, 3 July 1907.
_________. *Pascendi Gregis.* Rome: Vatican, 8 September 1907.
_________. *Sacrorum Antistitum.* Rome: Vatican, 1 September 1910.
Pius XI. *Mortalium Animos.* Rome: Vatican, 6 January 1928.
Pius XII. *Divino Afflante Spiritu.* Rome: Vatican, 30 September 1943.
_________. *Mystici Corporis Christi.* Rome: Vatican, 29 June 1943.
_________. *Summi Pontificatus.* Rome: Vatican, 20 October 1939.
Puaux, Franck. *Histoire de la Réformation Française.* 6 vols. Paris: Michel Lévy Frères, 1859.
Rainer, Thom. *The Book of Church Growth.* Nashville: Broadman, 1993.
Ratzinger, Joseph [now Benedict XVI]. *Catechism of the Catholic Church.* Rome: Vatican, 1993.
_________. *Dominus Iesus.* Rome, 16 June 2000; 6 August 2000.
_________. "The Primacy of the Successor of Peter in the Mystery of the Church." Rome: *Osservatore Romano* (18 Nov 1998).
Rauschenbusch, Walter. *A Theology for the Social Gospel.* New York: Macmillan, 1917; Nashville: Abingdon, 1978.
Reid, Alvin. *Introduction to Evangelism.* Nashville: Broadman, 1998.
_________. *Radically Unchurched.* Grand Rapids: Kregel, 2002.
Reid, Alvin, and David Wheeler. "Servanthood Evangelism." Unpublished notes, 1997.
Richardson, Don. *Peace Child.* Ventura, Calif.: Regal, 1975.
Riley, W. B. *The Crisis of the Church.* New York: Charles C. Cook, 1914.
_________. *The Perennial Revival.* Philadelphia: American Baptist Publication Society, 1916.
Ritschl, Albrecht. *The Doctrine of Justification and Reconciliation.* Clifton, N.J.: Reference Book, 1966.
Robinson, Darrell. *People Sharing Jesus.* Nashville: Nelson, 1995.
_________. *Total Church Life.* Nashville: Broadman, 1997.
Sailhamer, John. *Genesis.* Grand Rapids: Zondervan, 1990.
Saillens, Rubens. *The Soul of France.* London: Morgan and Scott, 1917.
Scarborough, L. R. *Recruits for World Conquest.* New York: Revell, 1914.
_________. *With Christ after the Lost.* Nashville: Sunday School Board of the Southern Baptist Convention, 1919; Nashville: Broadman, 1952.
Schaff, Philip. *Theological Propædeutic: A General Introduction to the Study of Theology.* 5th ed. New York: Scribner's, 1902.
Schaller, Lyle. *The Multiple Staff and the Larger Church.* Nashville: Abingdon, 1980.
Scharpff, Paulus. *History of Evangelism: Three Hundred Years of Evangelism in Germany, Great Britain, and the United States of America.* Grand Rapids: Eerdmans, 1966.
Schleiermacher, Friedrich. *Brief Outline on the Study of Theology.* 2nd ed. 1830; Terrence N. Tice, trans. Richmond, Va.: John Knox Press, 1966.
_________. *The Christian Faith.* 2nd ed. Edinburgh: T. & T. Clark, 1960.
Schuller, Robert. *Alphabet for Action! For Possibility Thinkers.* Garden Grove, Calif.: Garden Grove Community Church, 1982.
Schwarz, Christian. *Natural Church Development.* Carol Stream, Ill.: ChurchSmart, 1998.
_________. *Paradigm Shift in the Church.* Carol Stream, Ill.: ChurchSmart, 1999.
Scripture, Tradition, and Traditions. Geneva: World Council of Churches and Roman Catholic Church, 1963.
Simpson, Michael L. *Permission Evangelism—When to Talk, When to Walk.* Colorado Springs: Cook, 2004.
Sjogren, Steve. *Conspiracy of Kindness.* Ann Arbor: Servant, 1993.

Sjogren, Steve, Doug Pollack, and Dave Ping. *Irresistible Evangelism.* Loveland, Colo.: Group, 2004.
Smith, Bailey. *Real Evangelism: Exposing the Subtle Substitutes for That Evangelism.* Nashville: Broadman, 1978.
Spurgeon, Charles H. "Salvation and Safety," *Royal Dainties,* no. 169. Minneapolis: Asher Publishing Co., affiliated with The Union Gospel Mission, n.d. From http//www.wheaton.edu/bgc/ archives/docs/ tract01.html. Internet; accessed 4 January 2001.
__________. *The Soul Winner: or How to Lead Sinners to the Savior.* New York: Revell, 1895; Grand Rapids: Zondervan, 1947; Grand Rapids: Eerdmans, 1963.
Stormon, E. J., ed. *Toward the Healing of a Schism: The Sees of Rome and Constantinople.* Ecumenical Documents 3. New York: Paulist, 1987.
Stott, John R. W. *Balanced Christianity.* Downers Grove, Ill.: InterVarsity, 1975.
__________. *Christian Mission in the Modern World.* Downers Grove, Ill.: InterVarsity, 1975.
Stott, John R. W., ed. *Making Christ Known: Historic Mission Documents from the Lausanne Movement, 1974–1989.* Grand Rapids: Eerdmans, 1996.
Stransky, Thomas F. and John B. Sheerin, eds. *Doing the Truth in Charity.* Ecumenical Documents 1. New York: Paulist, 1982.
Strobel, Lee. *Inside the Mind of the Unchurched Harry & Mary.* Grand Rapids: Zondervan, 1993.
Sweet, Leonard, ed. *The Church in Emerging Culture: Five Perspectives.* Grand Rapids: Zondervan, 2003.
Sweet, William W. *Revivalism in America.* New York: Scribner's, 1944.
Terry, John Mark. *Evangelism: A Concise History.* Nashville: Broadman, 1994.
Thomas, Norman E. *Classic Texts in Mission and World Christianity.* Maryknoll, N.Y.: Orbis, 1995.
Tillapaugh, Frank. *The Church Unleashed.* Ventura, Calif.: Regal, 1982.
Topical Memory System. Guidebook 1. Colorado Springs: NavPress, 1969.
Torrey, Reuben A. *How to Bring Men to Christ.* New York: Revell, 1910.
Troeltsch, Ernst. *Die Soziallehren der christlichen Kirchen und Gruppen.* 1912; *The Social Teaching of the Christian Churches.* Olive Wyon, trans. New York: Macmillan, 1931; Louisville: Westminster/John Knox, 1992.
Truett, George W. *Quest for Souls.* New York: Doran, 1917.
Vatican II. *Dignitatis Humanae.* Rome: Vatican, 7 December 1965.
__________. *Lumen Gentium.* Rome: Vatican, 21 November 1964.
__________. *Nostra Aetate.* Rome: Vatican, 28 October 1965.
__________. *Unitatis Redintegratio.* Rome: Vatican, 21 November 1964.
Von Rad, Gerhard. *God at Work in Israel.* John H. Marks, trans. Nashville: Abingdon, 1980.
Wagner, C. Peter. *Church Planting for a Greater Harvest.* Ventura, Calif.: Regal, 1990.
__________. *The Third Wave of the Holy Spirit.* Ventura, Calif.: Regal, 1988.
__________. *Signs and Wonders Today.* Ventura, Calif.: Regal, 1987.
__________. *Strategies for Church Growth.* Ventura, Calif.: Regal, 1989.
Ward, Harry F. *Social Evangelism.* New York: Missionary Education Movement of the United States and Canada, 1915.
Warfield, Benjamin B. *The Plan of Salvation.* Philadelphia: Presbyterian Board of Publication, 1918.
Warneck, Gustav. *Evangelische Missionslehre: ein missionstheoritischer Versuch.* Gotha: Perthes, 1902; *History of Protestant Missions,* 3rd English edition from 8th German edition. New York: Revell, 1905.
Warren, Rick. *The Purpose Driven Church.* Grand Rapids: Zondervan, 1995.
__________. *The Purpose Driven Life.* Grand Rapids: Zondervan, 2003.
Webber, Robert. *Common Roots: A Call to Evangelical Maturity.* Grand Rapids: Zondervan, 1978.
__________. *Ancient-Future Church: Making Your Church a Faith-Forming Community.* Grand Rapids: Baker, 2003.
Weisenbeck, Jude. "Conciliar Fellowship and the Unity of the Church." Rome: University of St. Thomas, 1986.
White, James E. *Opening the Front Door.* Nashville: Convention Press, 1992.
Willis, Avery T., Jr. *MasterLife Day by Day: Personal Devotional Guide.* Nashville: Sunday School Board of the SBC, 1985.
Wimber, John. *Power Evangelism.* San Francisco: Harper and Row, 1986.
Winter, Ralph D. and Steven C. Hawthorne, eds. *Perspectives on the World Christian Movement: A Reader.* 3rd ed. Pasadena, Calif.: William Carey Library, 1999.
The Wycliffe New Testament: 1388. W. R. Cooper, ed. London: The British Library, 2002.
Yinger, J. Milton. *The Scientific Study of Religion.* London: Macmillan, 1970.
Your Most Important Relationship. San Bernardino, Calif.: Campus Crusade for Christ Int'l; Denver: Youth for Christ/USA., 1985.
Zwemer, Samuel. *Evangelism Today: Message Not Method.* London: Revell, 1944.